ACCLAIM FOR *AMERICAN SOCCER NATION* SPANS THREE DECADES OF PROFESSIONAL COACHES, PLAYERS, EDUCATORS, AND HISTORIANS:

"An essential text for any fan who wants to take a journey into the U.S. game's roots and ambitions. It reads like history but feels like a full-field press into our optimistic soccer future."

— Gregg Berhalter, director of football and head coach, Chicago Fire, MLS; former U.S. Men's National Team head coach

"This book captures the heart, struggle, and progress of the men's game. The chapters offer a sharp, honest look at how elite men's soccer evolved across the nation, and what it will take to impress on the international stage."

— Cobi Jones, 164 U.S. Men's National Team Caps (all-time leader), three World Cups, @cobijones13, @cjfc13

"*American Soccer Nation* tells the full, dramatic story of how the world's most popular sport took root in the U.S., only to be defined by a cycle of struggle, failure, and near-collapse. It traces the journey from immigrant-led leagues and the NASL's high-flying bust to the slow, steady revolution sparked by the 1994 World Cup. Discover the academies and blueprints that are finally producing elite American talent, and why the nation is poised for a spectacular performance at the 2026 World Cup. Mark Franek nails it."

— Mark McKenzie, defender, Toulouse FC, Ligue 1, France

"This book is like a hopeful cross into the hearts of American soccer fans. A well-told history about our gritty past and our potential future."

— John Harkes, 90 Caps, two World Cups, technical director, McLean Youth Soccer; U.S. Youth National Team coach

"This book explores the historical roots of the country's rise, and illuminates the emergence of a new era of power and influence for the sport."

— Brenden Aaronson, midfielder, Leeds United, EPL, England

"A rich and inspiring look at the history of elite American men's soccer. Blending deep historical knowledge with real insight from inside the modern game, *American Soccer Nation* tells our story with honesty, pride, and optimism. Celebrating the sport's roots while spotlighting the progress happening now through MLS and MLS NEXT. Mark Franek's perspective from inside Philadelphia Union and YSC Academy make this book feel genuine, informed, and important. A great read for fans and players who care about the future of the American game."

— Auston Trusty, defender, Celtic FC, Scottish Premiership

"A rare combination of rigorous reporting and compelling storytelling. And, if that's not enough, it's rooted in the DNA of America's up-and-coming soccer stars!"

— Jim Curtin, former head coach, Philadelphia Union, MLS

"*American Soccer Nation* captures something I've always believed: our game in the U.S. has a story worth celebrating. This book showcases the resilience, ambition, and passion that has carried American soccer to this moment—not by accident, but through decades of real investment and belief. Growing up in this system and now living it at the highest level, I know the future isn't just promising—it's already taking shape around us."

— Quinn Sullivan, midfielder, Philadelphia Union, MLS

"Mark Franek's *American Soccer Nation* is an engaging introduction to soccer's long history in the United States. A timely and entertaining starting point for deeper discussion of the myriad topics associated with American soccer's path toward its explosive growth today, this book is sure to become a classroom staple."

— Ed Farnsworth, American soccer historian, writer, and editor, former board member and current communications director at the Society for American Soccer History (SASH)

"A refreshing, in-depth book just in time for the 2026 World Cup, with insights from some top players and thought leaders. A must-read for fans ready to embrace the growing game of American soccer!"

— Jack McGlynn, midfielder, Houston Dynamo FC, MLS

"This book rewrites the way American fans will understand their own soccer story. It's bold, thoughtful, and deeply inspiring."

— Alejandro Bedoya, 66 Caps, one World Cup, current captain of Philadelphia Union, MLS

"This book will be well received by those of us who grew up with the game of soccer in America. Coaches, players, and fans will find that it captures the unique history of our journey to establish the passion, culture, and outcomes needed to compete internationally."

— Michael Curry, veteran American soccer coach, administrator and advocate, including leadership roles with the United Soccer Coaches, YSC Academy, and the United Soccer Coaches Foundation, Inc.

"As a former player and current content creator engaged in growing the sport of soccer in America, this book explores the American soccer development system and our top leagues. It is a reminder of our history, and what's to come."

— Raheem Taylor-Parkes, soccer content creator and media personality, GOAL USA, @Raheemovic

"A beautifully written history of elite men's soccer on American soil. Written from somebody who has a front-row seat, and everyday interaction with some of the upcoming talents and next generation of the U.S. Soccer Federation. I'm recommending it with full confidence to all my teammates, and all soccer fans across the globe!"

— **Paxten Aaronson, midfielder, Colorado Rapids, MLS**

"Mark Franek is a gifted writer and educator who loves soccer! He brings these qualities to bear in *American Soccer Nation*, a beautifully woven story of the evolution of the beautiful game in America. I thoroughly enjoyed it."

— **Eddie Mensah, former CEO, Right To Dream Football Academy, Ghana; former director of programs, Steppingstone Scholars Inc., USA**

"Mark Franek has broken new and fertile ground with *American Soccer Nation*. He goes beyond previous books limited to the failures of the U.S. Men's National Team by providing a detailed—and accurate—history of the sport as well as a thought-provoking and insightful analysis of the growth, development, and present state of elite men's soccer in this country. This is a seminal work and a must-read for players, coaches, fans, and anyone who truly cares about the future of U.S. soccer."

— **William Kashatus, historian, educator, and award-winning author of a dozen books on American sports history**

AMERICAN SOCCER NATION

AMERICAN SOCCER NATION

The Remarkable 150-Year History of Yanks on a Roll, from Mob Football to the Modern Game

MARK C FRANEK

BenBella Books, Inc.
Dallas, TX

BenBella Books, Inc.
8080 N. Central Expressway
Suite 1700
Dallas, TX 75206
benbellabooks.com
Send feedback to feedback@benbellabooks.com

BenBella is a federally registered trademark.

Printed in the United States of America
10 9 8 7 6 5 4 3 2 1

Library of Congress Control Number: 2025046769
ISBN 9781637748640 (trade paperback)
ISBN 9781637748657 (electronic)

Editing by Rick Chillot
Copyediting by Michael Fedison
Proofreading by Jenny Bridges and Rebecca Maines
Text design and composition by Aaron Edmiston
Cartoon on p viii, © Ivan Ehlers / The New Yorker Collection/The Cartoon Bank
Cover design by Morgan Carr
Cover images © Adobe Stock / TWINS DESIGN STUDIO; Augustas Cetkauskas
Printed by Lake Book Manufacturing

For American soccer players, fans, and students everywhere
(to help fill a gap in the syllabus)

"It used to be a lot easier to ignore soccer."

AUTHOR'S NOTE

In this book, the terms "Americans" and "Yanks" refer to all native-born or longtime residents of the U.S.—of any race, background, or original nationality—who support American soccer in what has become a vibrant and rapidly growing soccer nation. The word "Yanks" was coined by British soldiers during the lead-up to the Revolutionary War and used as an insult for American Colonists and their ragtag armies. Over time, the term lost much of its edge and has softened into a mostly playful, ironic label.

I use the words "soccer" and "football" interchangeably in this book. They mean the same thing. The Brits did so, too, for scores of years before boycotting soccer—their own word—when Yanks started using it to differentiate the beautiful game from "gridiron football" (*i.e.*, the American game with helmets, pads, and ads). I omit the periods from frequently used soccer abbreviations—such as FC (football club), SC (soccer club), AC (athletic club), and FA (football association). Foreign words and phrases that are not the names of geographical places and professional sports teams are italicized when used initially. Then they revert to normal text.

My goal in this book is to accurately summarize the major events in the evolution of top-tier men's soccer in the United States. The rich history of women's soccer in America is excluded because of space restrictions. So too are numerous contributions of U.S. college soccer programs, including their role in supporting men's Olympic appearances over the last century. Those stories deserve books of their own.

This book is not an encyclopedia or a compendium of soccer statistics. It's more a collection of chronological stories that move swiftly across the landscape of American soccer history. Yanks have been playing soccer for a long time, almost as long as baseball. Some readers will want more detail in spots, or less coverage in others. Fair enough. A writer is really a coach who builds on the work of others and makes thousands of tactical choices along the way. Any major omissions or mistakes are my own.

Readers seeking a deeper understanding of soccer's evolution in the United States are encouraged to visit the Society for American Soccer History (SASH) at www.ussoccerhistory.org. The SASH website features extensive content authored by prominent American soccer writers, along with links to their published work. For a more interactive and hands-on experience, consider visiting the National Soccer Hall of Fame in Frisco, Texas, located inside the stadium that hosts FC Dallas.

CONTENTS

FOREWORD BY TIM HOWARD

Soccer in America has never known a better time. Soccer fandom, participation, and excitement about its future are the greatest they've ever been in America. And I see this firsthand when talking to constituents all around the country. It's true—soccer isn't part of our collective sports history the way it is in many soccer-loving nations. But that doesn't mean our soccer history is a blank page. It's more like a series of messy pages, as this book lays out. Those gritty stories from our shared soccer past—fun reading for any fan of the game or soccer athlete, from casual to professional—culminate in a final chapter that optimistically lays out a map to a bright future for the game on American soil. And I think Mark Franek mostly gets it right.

We've tried to figure out what the American way is, and the American way has turned out to be a melting pot of different ideas about how the game should be played and how our top league should be structured. And where we've too often failed is in trying to imitate too closely what works in other countries. We tried to do it the English way, and then we ripped that up and started again. We tried to do it the Dutch way, and we ripped that up, too. We jogged along for many decades, experiencing fits and starts and strange pauses, while several other sports in this country made giant strides in terms of popularity.

But lately—especially over the past ten years or so, leading right into the 2026 World Cup—American soccer has been engaged in a high press all across the nation. And we're finally doing a lot of things right, and the sport is gaining significant traction. It will be interesting to see how the landscape evolves over the coming years.

True, I still worry a lot about the grassroots system in the States. No matter how much money we seem to put into the game, we still haven't cracked the code in terms of how to develop elite young talent, nurture it through the teen years, and eventually inspire waves of top-tier players. We have to continue to adjust, experiment, pivot, and get better at every aspect of the game.

As I've laid out in my own book on soccer, *The Keeper: A Life of Saving Goals and Achieving Them*, and in my podcast with Landon Donovan called *Unfiltered Soccer*, coaches are really the foundation of everything. We have to figure out a way to create a better system for the types of coaching our best soccer athletes are getting as they move through our system. America is usually really good at imitating what works, but for some reason, we're not doing that as quickly as we should for young people.

Spain has figured this out. Once you lock in the age groups, and—more importantly—the coordinated coaching system, real development becomes visible and sustainable. In the U.S., too often coaches bounce from one age group to another in our club system. That doesn't help kids unlock their potential and supercharge progression. Twelve-year-olds shouldn't be coached as if they were seventeen-year-olds. It simply doesn't work. In many places in Europe, they understand you can't coach every kid the same way at every age. Training has to be specific and intentional—and players and parents have to be patient. And here's the thing: We actually have enough resources in America to get this right.

As I've said in several contexts over the years, it's really hard to be a great coach—with the hours they put in and the headaches they have to endure. It's incredibly important to give coaches the tools they need to develop young people, which requires space and time where players can learn and gain confidence. It doesn't happen overnight. Good coaches are diligent and set up training progressions that are high-tempo and game-like. At the same time, these coaches gradually teach players how to fully embrace their own experiences and convictions, nudging them to eventually take control of their own preparation cycles and game performances.

I think about the little kid I was, and the coaches I needed. I needed their support, their love, and their drive to push me forward to be better. That's never changed for me. The greatest thing a coach can give a player at any level is self-belief. And that lesson can be applied on and off the pitch forever.

At the other end of the developmental spectrum—for the very best players in America, both young men and women—we need to continue to create and broaden pathways to the pros. And that means more homegrown opportunities and more money in the system to entice our best young athletes—and even better players from abroad—to join our leagues. The owners of professional North American teams rightly want to see a better return on their academy investments. There isn't a tidy solution that will work for all teams. The owners need to keep hammering at it.

Soccer pursuits in America have often been a slow burn because we have had a lot of people singing from different hymn sheets, and not everybody wants to collaborate. But there are at least two constants. The first is that Americans have a way of eventually figuring things out. The second is that our fans are amazing and passionate. And their numbers are growing each year.

Most important, our fans are bringing with them a much better understanding of the game. When I started coming up through the professional ranks, back in the late 1990s and early 2000s, there were very few fans who truly understood the game. Today, that's all changed. The standards are just higher for everybody. This book is one small but important contribution to the rising tide of knowledge about the history of elite soccer in America and our place—and potential future—in the global game. American fans may not out-sing anybody with a clever song at an international match. American players on the immediate horizon may not consistently dictate the tempo of a world-class match. But I'm optimistic that we will eventually find our American rhythm. Through a lot of hard work, tinkering, and patience—we will astonish, both at home and abroad.

FOREWORD BY CAVAN SULLIVAN

I just turned sixteen, so I'm not qualified by age or expertise to give some big soccer history lesson. But I can share what Mark Franek's English class was like, where he shared stories that eventually became chapters in this book. We wrote a lot in his class—mostly a bunch of stories about what we were reading and talking about, and we eventually self-published them in a little book. Mine was titled "Turning the Page," and I finished it about eight months before I turned pro. The name comes from moving on within this sport, season after season, growing older, and facing ups and downs along the way. Perhaps sharing a bit of my origin story will help explain the necessity of Mark's book.

My family's big into soccer—my grandpop played at some successful Philly clubs and coached a Division I university, my uncle was on the USMNT and currently serves as a General Manager for an MLS team, and both my parents played at D1 colleges and beyond. So, I've always been around the game and knew a lot of its history, especially in Philadelphia. But Mark's book takes a national look at the history of elite men's soccer in the U.S. He now teaches a full course on it, helping my friends and peers understand how the sport started and grew, and helping us feel more connected to the game. If you see a footnote, though, just know there's some kind of lesson coming up (and be happy he doesn't quiz you on it). Mark was also good at getting us to tell our own stories in our self-published books, which are full of entries about soccer and what we felt about our student-athlete experiences. Most of what follows comes from things I wrote in his class.

Since I was little, soccer has been my "everything." My dad literally put a ball in my crib to roll around with. After about ten months, I started walking and almost immediately found the ball and started kicking it. I joined my three older brothers in the basement with a mini goal and a bunch of balls flying around. We did that for years. Watching old videos now, I realize how "bad" my dad was as a goalie—constantly faking injuries from our weak shots. Of course, he was just putting on a show. You can see in his smile how much he loved it. That basement was my home within a home. The part of the house where I felt most like myself. When people make you feel good about what you're doing, you fall in love with it. That's pretty much what happened to me with soccer.

I've always been super competitive. The grit I have comes from my family and their urban roots in Northeast Philadelphia. There, I was surrounded by tough kids, including my three older brothers. Kids who could slide tackle, fight, and use curse words properly as toddlers. Kids who could take a hit and get back up every time without complaining. That was how it was; formal or not, we all cared. We would do anything to win. When I moved out of the city, it was not an easy adjustment. I have tons of stories that involve being punished for my competitive behavior on the playground and field. When I moved from Philly I joined a new team, the school I attended changed, I lost my friends, I lost my dad as my coach—I was surrounded by a totally different crowd. These players seemed to want no part of doing what it takes to win. At recess in school, if they were bumped a bit too hard, they stayed on the ground and needed the nurse. With my club team, kids would lie on the ground awaiting treatment, ruining the flow of training.

This is where I first encountered players who'd brag about being able to get 237 juggles and that they could perform a rainbow, yet were invisible in competitive situations. In both environments, whether it was from a coach or a teacher, I was told, "You're playing too rough, it's not the World Cup, just have fun." The answer I gave with a smile on my face every time was, "Winning is fun." As an aside, I really do wish more U.S. soccer players had the privilege to grow in such a place; one where, early on, you learn how to compete, fight, and discover a genuine passion for the game, and a sense of responsibility to your coach and teammates to always try to be your best.

Of course, not every kid will grow up in Northeast Philadelphia, and not every player will have a family who obsesses about the sport like mine did. But clubs can maybe create a simulated version of such an environment to see how that molds players. One of the later chapters in this book will touch upon how the Philadelphia Union is attempting to do this. For me, watching five- and six-year-olds doing ladder drills and trying to juggle tennis balls before they know how to compete hurts my heart. Sure, technique and ball mastery are quintessential, but not at the detriment of determination and competition. The best players fear nothing besides failure. And they always want to win.

Growing up, I always had a ball at my feet. In our basement and backyard, we played all day—balls, makeshift goals, all kinds of athletic games, nonstop. As a toddler at my oldest brother's games, I'd pass the ball with my mom for hours on the sidelines (still today I enjoy stealing the game ball at halftime of my twin older brothers' games and passing with my mother). When I finally got to play on a full field with my U-6 team, I was in heaven. Just being there made me smile. For a few years, my dad was always our coach. I later found out he had handpicked the players—mostly sons of guys he'd grown up playing with. At training, we warmed up as a team with ball work while chatting and joking around. Whenever someone got new cleats, we'd all step on them as a joke. I still don't know why we found that funny.

Training was never boring. My dad crafted games called "Gauntlet" and "Thirty Seconds of Hell," and always added a twist to the drills—some restriction or challenge to keep us on our toes. Sometimes we played two-touch only. If you took a third touch, the ball did not turn over . . . instead you had to take the ball to the house yourself and try to score—and you were guaranteed to get swarmed by defenders. Since no other player was available to receive the ball, you were facing a 7v1. Another way of putting it is, if you wanted to be selfish, you'd better be multiple steps ahead of the opponent's entire team. These were the little things my dad did to create a team that loved what they were doing. Unlike the other teams we played, who had players picking dandelions in their own box. Yeah . . . our fields had those growing, and even sexier, we had broken glass, and occasional needles from junkies here and there. Before games, our parents walked side by side and picked up the debris. Our pitch often had squiggly lines or lines you could barely see. We didn't care what field we were on, who our opponent was, or what time of day it was. We all wanted to get better, have fun, and win in the process, and my dad knew how to get that out of us.

I learned a lot from my dad over the years. He told me things like "be different," "think faster," and "never be satisfied." But maybe the most important lesson was to "Never give up. No matter the circumstances." Even if it wasn't your best day, or if your team was down by three goals, you could always make something happen. In hindsight our conversations about soccer, which started at an early age, definitely challenged me to think more like a pro than a kid.

Every serious soccer player dreams of making his professional debut. But what made mine so special wasn't setting the record for the youngest pro athlete to appear in all four major North American team sports. Sure, that's cool. But in the end, that's just a statistic. What really mattered was getting to share the field with my older brother, Quinn, and seeing my family on the sidelines. Quinn is six years older than me. We never played on the same team growing up—only against each other in the backyard or down the shore. So, stepping onto a professional field with him after he just scored a banger was surreal. Honestly, it felt like he was happier for me than I was for myself.

Soccer has already given so much to my family. My professional journey is just beginning, and I know bigger responsibilities and higher expectations are coming quickly. Thanks to the support of my family and a strong foundation built with the help of incredible coaches and teachers, I feel confident, excited, and ready to go out there and ball. I'm also hopeful and optimistic that my generation—and those that follow—can carry on the American soccer story told in this book, and continue to build on it year after year.

INTRODUCTION

I have one of the greatest jobs in the world. Every day for nine and a half months of the year, I go to work as an English teacher at YSC Academy, a private, accredited high school completely embedded within the youth soccer academy of the Philadelphia Union. The Union is a franchise in Major League Soccer (MLS), which is, as of 2026, three decades old and up to thirty teams. YSC Academy (School) and the Union Academy (the soccer school) have "grown up" with the MLS team, all three working together for over a decade to churn out several pros and about eighteen male college-bound student-athletes per year. More than 15 percent sign professional soccer contracts before graduating from YSC Academy. Several are currently playing in some of the best leagues in the world. Seven graduates have been capped by the senior United States Men's National Team (MNT), collectively earning over a hundred caps in the past five years. These are major accomplishments for a program that didn't even exist a little more than ten years ago.

Of course, most of the School's graduates don't play for the MNT or sign professional contracts. Instead, they graduate from YSC Academy and typically enter U.S. colleges, often on an athletic scholarship—a win-win from the families' perspectives. The student body is about as ethnically and racially diverse as they come: one-third (respectively) White, Black, and Latino. They represent the diversity of America. And they are some very lucky kids. Their academic classes are compressed into the middle of the day within classrooms a stone's throw from beautiful training fields. Most places on campus have a generous sightline to the stadium. The boys get to pursue their dreams within a caring school environment where the students are totally immersed in soccer. The academic school is really the "secret sauce" of the development model.

The Union's model has become very successful and is a template for other MLS academies and has piqued the interest of soccer VIPs. In 2024, I gently scolded a student for being late to my class. I didn't quibble with his excuse, though. He said he lost track of time because he was talking to Ole Gunnar Solskjær in Town Hall. The ex–Manchester United player (and recent Red Devils head coach) was one of many high-profile soccer figures from both sides of the Atlantic to regularly visit the School. After a certain age, if the boys "fail" to impress on the pro path (most will), they don't get kicked off the team or out of school. They graduate, go on to college, earn degrees, and often continue to engage in the sport long after they start leading more sedentary lives.

In this way they are more like the nearly fourteen million other boys and girls each year who attend more traditional schools (or get homeschooled!) and play for all kinds of youth soccer teams, from recreation to elite. Despite the flawed pay-to-play model (discussed later in this book), Americans continue playing through college—both varsity and club—and into adulthood, joining thousands of amateur leagues across the country. Today's American soccer players and fans are connected globally to the soccer world and can join many vibrant soccer communities at a rate that rivals or exceeds most of their international peers. When you look at the big picture and think optimistically, America might just be the land of soccer opportunity. The lead-up, communal game experiences, and residual glow of the 2026 World Cup will bear this out.

But the unfortunate truth is that most players, parents, fans, and even coaches, from the recreational to the professional level, don't understand or appreciate our country's soccer heritage. This collective ignorance of the historical roots and evolution of soccer in America weakens our ability to advocate for our kids, teams, and programs. It also makes us sound uninformed anytime a soccer issue appears. When the Head of School asked me to design a course on the "history of American soccer," I leaped at the chance. I played varsity soccer for a time as an undergraduate at Duke

University before beginning my teaching career. Each summer during my first six years of teaching, I took off for Iceland to play semiprofessional soccer in a tiny town on the north coast. Then, in the early fall, it was back to the U.S. to teach English and coach varsity soccer. I coached youth teams in a variety of contexts, in the U.S. and Iceland, but not particularly well. My mantra to the boys was to just "play harder and pass the ball to the next guy." I also booted up every week for the Philadelphia Ukrainian Nationals, one of America's oldest soccer clubs.

During my twenties and thirties, I wrote and published about fifty opinion-editorials on a wide range of educational and sports-related topics, often with a human interest theme—including a grumpy soccer piece about why a group of investors in my neck of the woods would name a team the Philadelphia Union and bring it to Chester, Pennsylvania, a small, economically challenged city about twelve miles southwest of Philadelphia, which wouldn't know a soccer ball if it washed ashore from the Delaware River. I juggled these teaching, coaching, and playing gigs for about two decades. Today, my classroom window overlooks the Delaware River and I can see the Philadelphia Union's training fields and stadium in the distance. When I explain the concept of *irony* to my students, I pull out my published soccer diatribe, mentioned above, which they find amusing.

In my early forties, I stepped out of the classroom, earned a law degree, then entered a big law firm where I drafted legal arguments in civil matters (*i.e.*, non-criminal proceedings) for senior attorneys and partners. The disputes were almost always about money. I continued to play soccer in adult leagues a couple of nights a week. But only after getting permission from my girlfriend, then wife. When my son was born and "took" to soccer (as if he had a choice!), my love affair with the game began anew. I started looking at the game—its bonds and evolving relationships, on and off the pitch—through his eyes. Though personally and continuously devoted to soccer for almost half a century, I was, until very recently, oblivious to about 90 percent of the soccer history presented in this book. I bet many readers are on a similar journey.

One of the best places to start in designing a history of soccer course for students, so I was told, was with the magnificent opus penned by the Englishman David Goldblatt, called *The Ball Is Round: A Global History of Soccer*. The paperback comes in around 1,100 pages and weighs about a pound—not the sort of thing you want to bring into a modern high school classroom or recommend to a friend. Goldblatt covers more ground in his book than a bevy of students playing *EA Sports FC* after school. Yet he gives American soccer the short shrift. At times, he is dismissive of the Yankee experience.

Another book, more compact, is the Uruguayan Eduardo Galeano's *Soccer in Sun and Shadow*, which covers a lot of global soccer history, but from a Latino perspective, using informative vignettes. But Galeano is downright hostile to the U.S. and to American soccer (he says so right in his book). Even many American soccer writers are blasé about the history and status of American soccer. I don't blame them, entirely. As you'll read in these pages, our soccer pioneers and ambassadors, from our past and present, have too often shot each other in the foot, slowing our progress. That part of the story must be told. But too many powerful stories of American grit and perseverance have been overlooked or minimized.

The titles of many recent American soccer books—even if most writers don't get to choose the final title of their books—introduce topics and themes that march down the page in the same stubborn formation, attacking our sport with one condemnation and complaint after another. Imagine aspiring young soccer stars and American fans (from curious to serious) confronting the following books, which are most of the major publications about American soccer over the past twenty-five years: *Offside: Soccer and American Exceptionalism* (2001); *Soccer in a Football World: The Story of America's Forgotten Game* (2006); *Distant Corners: American Soccer's History of Missed Opportunities and Lost Causes* (2011); *Why American Soccer Isn't There Yet* (2014); *What's Wrong with US?: A Coach's Blunt Take on the State of American Soccer After a Lifetime on the Touchline* (2018); *Encyclopedia Blazertannica: A Suboptimal Guide to Soccer, America's "Sport of the Future" Since 1972* (2018); *Why the US Men Will Never Win the World Cup: A Historical and Cultural Reality Check* (2019); *What Happened to the USMNT: The Ugly Truth About the Beautiful Game* (2021); and *Switching Fields: Inside the Fight to Remake Men's Soccer in the United States* (2022). If I didn't know any better, I'd think many American soccer writers and book publishers are playing on the wrong team. Or suffering from a chronic concussion. Why are so many people confused and utterly pessimistic about American soccer's possibilities for success?

When I tried piecing together chapters and stories from the books on this list (some are very good, despite the titles) and shared them in my classroom, my students complained. They asked: Why so fragmented, boring, negative? (OK, they didn't use the word *fragmented*. But they did say why so *boring* and *negative*.) At any given time, about a score of them represent U.S. Youth National Teams from Under-15 (U-15) to U-19 (those age-restricted categories requiring participants to be younger than the stated age at the start of the competition year). A handful of students in my classes are already signed to professional contracts. But they stay in school to finish their high school degrees even while their soccer commitments ramp way up. Most of the boys and young men on campus, regardless of where they are on their student-athlete journeys, are frequently ambivalent, even hostile, to things that don't help them improve on and off the field. It's part of their DNA.

Instead of tales of woe about why the U.S. will never succeed on the international soccer stage—which make them want to stab their eyes out with the nearest corner flag—they want vibrant content with hopeful messages. They want a book that focuses on the peculiar and powerful legs of the American journey. And they want it delivered like an exceptional, hopeful cross into the box, without downplaying the historical context of the global game or sugarcoating the facts. They also want to see themselves represented in pages that are easy and fun to read, like a game of rondo.

The best rondo (*i.e.*, a brisk small-sided keep-away game) requires skill and elements of style. But what kind of style for a book on American soccer for our athletes, parents, and fans? Once again, I looked to students for inspiration. During my first year back in the classroom, after a ten-year absence when I was in the legal field, I was asked to help students revise our school's core values (what many schools call an honor code). After reviewing codes published by some of the best European soccer academies and exceptional American high schools, both public and private, the boys whittled down a list of about fifty words to a final five values. Those values are now prominently displayed on banners outside the School and on every classroom wall: Respect, Honesty, Commitment, Inspiration, and *Confidence*. The latter value was a bit of a surprise to the teachers and coaches. But maybe it shouldn't have been. Confidence—a curious mix of courage, naivete, and brazenness—has always been an important part of the American soccer soul. We Yanks embrace our underdog status and exude a can-do attitude, qualities forged from our complex and intertwined national character.

So, let's get some style points out of the way before we start our journey in earnest, looking back on 150 years of soccer on American soil. The English created and codified the game in 1863 and did more to spread the game around the world in the latter half of the 1800s than any other country. The English (and Scottish, to be honest) gave soccer to us Yanks, and for many decades they helped us as we tried to advance the sport in our country. But very often we mucked it up. Meanwhile, English football steadily evolved, though its evolution wasn't all in a straight line, either. But as I'm writing this, the top-tier English Premier League (EPL) is the most economically successful, watched, and competitive league in the world. Major League Soccer, a toddler by comparison, is gaining adherents but it still falls a few prodigious steps below the EPL in nearly every metric. The countries are at different points on their soccer journeys, and will face different prospects moving forward.

Nobody has a monopoly on soccer success—including the English, who have won exactly one World Cup and zero European championships, and have never beaten the MNT at a World Cup tournament. Still, over the past century, the English, and more broadly the Brits, have never missed an opportunity to criticize just about everything having to do with soccer coming out of the U.S. Likewise, the international soccer community loves watching the Yanks get beat, probably because of long-standing resentments and jealousies regarding the USA's geopolitical power. Lately, the level of animosity has increased considerably, especially in England, most likely due to a slew of American owners who have made their way (really, just their money) across the pond to take over football clubs that have been under local ownership and control, some for over a century.

But the millions of Yanks who play or support soccer in this country don't care about foreign ownership issues or judgments by our international peers. We believe in our soccer future. So, too, do a growing number of foreign scouts at shrewd football clubs who are signing young American players who have tremendous upsides. So, too, do a growing number of savvy investors. In June 2022, Apple signed an agreement with MLS for an exclusive media contract worth $2.5 billion over ten years. Less than a year later, the MLS added its thirtieth team (San Diego FC), whose ownership group forked over a record $500 million expansion franchise fee. Numbers this large are based on intelligent sustainability and profitability models. Anyone with even a basic understanding of soccer knows the beautiful game is here to stay in North America, and will surely continue to grow.

The final chapter of this book connects American soccer's past to its present and provides a quick look ahead at what it will take to move from good to great on the international stage. This chapter grew out of a score of interviews with current and retired professional players, MLS academy and first team coaches, sporting directors, and owners across a half-dozen professional clubs. These conversations outline the essential elements needed to move the soccer needle at its highest level. A rising tide of professionalism, knowledge, and coordination will lift all boats in the vast U.S. soccer ecosystem.

So, to the English, who introduced us to soccer, and to everyone else—home or abroad—who doubts us, let's begin with some pithy words from Ted Lasso, the coach from that delightfully eccentric American TV series of the same name that no one should ever confuse for a serious exposé on coaching or football. Responding to his mother, whom he loves, but who has been arrogantly aloof and dour for decades, Ted says, "Thank you and fuck you."

Let's move on. We Yanks are on a roll.

1

★★★★★

PRE-FOOTBALL IN AMERICA

Toward organized games (1600–1875)

"There was nothing but land: not a country at all, but the material out of which countries are made."

— Willa Cather, *My Ántonia*

Balls have been used in sport for thousands of years. We just don't know how far back the games go, especially for kicking games. Bits of evidence start to appear in the record about 4,500 years ago. Egyptian tombs contain balls made from linen, papyrus, leather strips, and wood. The living prepared the dead for their journey to the underworld and the possibility of eternal life—packed with their favorite ball. Murals in Egyptian tombs show a pharaoh holding a ball and a bat, men playing field hockey, and girls juggling balls with their hands. None of the murals, however, display kicking activity. Evidence of team-related kicking activities starts to show up in China and in Mesoamerica about 3,500 years ago. The Greeks and Romans kicked the ball, too. Kicking games were ubiquitous in ancient civilizations, though most were not direct ancestors of modern football. Readers interested in learning more about ancient (thousands of years ago) pre-football activities should consult the Appendix.

As Europeans (explorers, then settlers) and enslaved Africans started trickling into North America in the early 1600s, the land was not a blank slate when it came to pre-football activities. The earliest account of indigenous pre-football activity in the New World comes from a journal entry made by Englishman John Davis regarding an expedition arriving on the southwestern tip of Greenland in 1586. After setting anchor, the English had a series of interactions with the native Greenlanders that included gift-swapping and athletic competitions. Apparently, the English were "waved" ashore to "play with them at the foot-ball" wherein Davis's entry boasted that his sailors "cast them down as soon as they did come to strike the ball." Nothing more is said about the game, leaving us to wonder if the Greenlanders' game was tamer than the English version.

Expeditions paved the way to colonization. According to several accounts from Colonists and Pilgrims in the New World—arriving in the first few decades of the 1600s and spreading out from Jamestown, Virginia, and Plymouth, Massachusetts—indigenous North Americans were already kicking balls and playing games akin to the mob football activity in the British Isles. An Englishman named Henry Spelman, who lived among the Powhatan in what is now the Commonwealth of Virginia, observed boys and women in about 1610 playing a ball game with kicking activity and goals, "yet they never fight nor pull one another down." Another Englishman, William Wood, living in the Massachusetts Bay Colony from 1629 to 1633, described peaceful gatherings within clearings or along sandy beaches, "flat as a board," where as many as one hundred Narragansett people assembled to "play ball with the feet." Tribesmen appeared along the ocean shoreline, hung their weapons on trees, painted their faces, and drew a line in the sand "over which they sh[ook] loving hands, and [then] with laughing hearts scuffle[d] for victorie." The daylong game involved "swift footsmanship," gambling, and ended with a feast. The painted faces, according to Wood's account, were clever disguises that eased post-game tensions during mealtime—since the orchestrator of a painful in-game kick, punch, or knock was difficult to determine once the face paint was removed with ocean water.

Farther north, in 1721 and back in Greenland again, Norwegian missionary Hans Egede described a match between two teams on a giant open field. A ball was tossed into the center of the crowd, and each team endeavored to kick the ball toward one of two objects positioned at opposite ends of the improvised field. The Greenlanders, according to Egede, believed that the dead also played football and that such play manifested itself as the Northern Lights.

In the late 1700s, in northwestern Ohio, the American Jacob Brunet observed a ball-playing competition "in the true aboriginal style" between two teams of Lenape Native Americans. An elderly chief called Buckongahelas (written as "Bu-kon-ge-ha-las" in Brunet's account) invited his white American guests to a field outside of town where two pairs of stakes, six feet apart, were positioned at opposite ends and served as goals. The game involved about one hundred men on one team, and one hundred women on the other. The men could only kick and dribble the ball with their feet, while the women could throw and run with the ball in their hands. During gameplay, men grabbed and tackled the women, twirling them to the ground, playfully. But women had the last laugh in Brunet's account. To end the game, a dexterous woman avoided tackles and ran through the goalposts for a score—all this at least a half-century before the creation of the English FA and Rugby Football Union.

Except for these accounts and a few other stray remarks in journals and books, explorers, arriving Colonists, and African slaves (the horrifying trade in the U.S. began in earnest in 1619) took no interest in the pre-soccer activities of the indigenous people of North America. The new arrivals had more pressing concerns, like how to survive the next winter. And they went about their business* and whatever pleasures the "fresh, green breast

* The business of Colonists and then American citizens, it must be acknowledged, would eventually include forced removal of Native Americans from their homelands, theft of resources, and assault and murder—actions similar to those discussed in Appendix A regarding Spanish and Portuguese conquistadors in Mesoamerica, and British colonizers in Australia.

of the new world" had to offer with a temperament not particularly receptive to football.

The Puritans—those devout Christians who believed the Church of England wasn't sufficiently reformed—stepped off the *Mayflower* with hard attitudes about fun and sport. Dancing between men and women was discouraged. Unsurprisingly, Puritans condemned mob football (whether native or imported) as the devil's work: "Now who is so grosly blinde that seeth not that these [football] exercises not only withdraw us from godliness and virtue, but also haile and allure us to wickednesse and sin? For as concerning football playing I protest unto you that it may rather be called a friendlie kinde of fyghte than a play or recreation—a bloody and murthering practice than a felowly sport or pastime." The Quakers, too, led by William Penn, also disapproved. Penn's "Holy Experiment" in Pennsylvania banned "Riotous Sports," including pre-football games. Such activities could tempt Colonists into immoral or licentious behavior. Whatever kind of football was being pursued in Colonial America was probably being played by boys who spent most of their time trying to avoid church officials and constables.

Pre-football activities in the New World faced numerous other headwinds—chiefly, rapidly expanding population (in geographically scattered cities), persistent inter-city travel logistics, and low-population densities when viewing the nation as a whole. The population of the Thirteen Colonies grew exponentially, fueled by religious and economic opportunity for white Europeans, the odious slave trade, and high birth rates. After U.S. independence, the population grew by nearly a third each decade between 1790 and 1860. However, even by the mid-1800s, East Coast towns and cities remained small, spread out, and difficult to navigate by train compared to urban areas in England, which had a centuries-long head start. Rural America, meanwhile, was vast, largely unexplored, and growing. The 1803 Louisiana Purchase doubled the young nation's size, the French virtually giving the U.S. everything west of the Mississippi and east of the Rockies. Westward expansion soon followed, with explorers, settlers, and railroads pushing across the land. By 1865, the Mountain States, American

Southwest (including Texas and California), and Pacific Northwest were under U.S. control. The country was massive. Today, all the countries of modern Europe (excluding the part of Russia within Asia) fit comfortably within the land area of the contiguous U.S.

Between the run-up and conclusion of two major wars—the Revolutionary War (1775–1783) and the Civil War (1861–1865)—Americans were concerned with matters far greater than ball-playing activities. To offer a one-hundred-year generalization worthy of a yellow card: The Yanks fought a war to get rid of British rule; spread westward, thousands of miles; pushed Native Americans off their lands; put an end to Britain's maritime restrictions and anti-American influence on Native Americans and Canadian militias (which led to the War of 1812); entered the industrial revolution (particularly within the port cities of the East Coast); expanded and then rescinded slavery; and fought and concluded the Civil War. This was a lot for a new nation to tackle in a single century.

Outside of a few cricket matches that were quickly eclipsed (after the Civil War) by baseball games, team contests involving balls were rare. Pre-football activities during the first three-quarters of the 1800s were local affairs involving mostly children and young people kicking and throwing balls, and running around. These games—which probably existed in every town and city—were celebratory (often related to holiday gatherings and festivals) and transient, and thus inconsequential for the vast majority of Americans.

Pre-football in North America, like in England (as we'll see in the next chapter), found a fragile "home" in the only place where large numbers of young men could gather without the direct oversight of adults: private high schools and elite colleges, mainly in the Northeast, when their tedious classes (no less tedious than their English analogues) weren't in session. On fields of grass and mud around campus, mob football reigned. The games probably took their cue from the ball-playing habits of their English peers. The oldest university in the nation, Harvard (est. 1636), unofficially began hosting a one-day activity on the first Monday of each school year that pitted freshmen against sophomores. The violent kicking melee probably began in the late 1700s and eventually earned the name "Bloody Monday." From a student's 1827 mock-heroic poem:

> The Freshmen's wrath, to Sophs the direful spring
> Of shins unnumbered bruised, great goddess sing;
> Let fire and music in my song be mated,
> Pure fire and music unsophisticated . . .
> Through warlike crowds a devious way it wins,
> And advancing shins meet advancing shins;
> Across the rampart many a hero bounds;
> But sing Apollo! I can sing no more,
> For Mars advancing threw the dust before.

Smaller, less-violent versions of Bloody Monday continued throughout the academic year.

As early as 1820, students at Princeton (called the College of New Jersey prior to 1896) played a ball game called "Ballown" that involved kicking and batting the ball with hands and fists. Dartmouth students played something called "Old Division Football." Yale, Columbia, Cornell, and Rutgers hosted their own versions. Not much is known about any of these games other than that they involved many students, a ball, and very little or no adult supervision. It's likely that the games evolved, as in England, according to campus geography and rules handed down from older students. A Princeton student from the class of 1845 recalled boys collecting money to buy a football (an inflated animal bladder covered in leather). A goal was scored by kicking it into the wall between East and West Campus. Unlike earlier Ballown games, the 1845 version had only one inflexible rule: "You must not touch the ball with your hands—you must only kick."

Indeed, Harvard students kicked the ball (and each other) right on up to the eve of the Civil War. In 1860, campus authorities finally stepped in and banned the games altogether because they were causing too much commotion and too many injuries. Harvardians responded with a mock funeral for a figure called "Foot-ball Fightum"—which consisted of a round leather ball made from a pig's bladder and a sheet, both of which were placed in a full-sized coffin, carried across the quad, and then laid to rest under the crust of the Delta (now Memorial Hall). A bevy of students appeared at the gravesite for the mock eulogy:

> Exult ye Freshmen, and clap your hands! The wise men who make big laws around a little table, have stretched out their arms to encircle you, and for this once at least, your eyes and noses are protected, you are shielded behind by the aegis of Minerva. [No more] eyes 'bunged up,' of noses wonderfully distended, of battered shins, the many chance blows anteriorly and posteriorly received and delivered, the rush, the struggle, the victory! On the football that is soon to be buried. We'll bury him sadly, at dim twilight.

Foot-ball Fightum would not rise to be kicked again (in earnest) until a decade after the Civil War. Yalies, too, around the same time as Harvard's football funeral, and under pressure from the city of New Haven, were forced to shutter their mob football games.

Many colleges closed or significantly struggled during the Civil War, as most young men left the classroom for the battle or to help at home. Letters, diaries, and newspaper articles provide glimpses into the pre-football activity of soldiers. In a November 27, 1862, letter to his parents, titled "Thanksgiving Day," George Patch describes "a dinner of pork and potatoes [and] turkey and plum pudding [noting] I have been kicking football today and it made me think of home." "I have plenty of time to read and nothing to read," laments Elmar Messinger. "[But] Thanksgiving Day we expect to have a Regimental game of foot-ball. The boys all say I am growing fat [but] I don't see what upon—hard tack and coffee would not fat a hog." A soldier named Nathan Hale showed "agility [that] was remarkable. I have seen him follow a football and kick it over the tops of the trees in the Bowery at New York." In Camp Jackson, Louisiana, a newspaper writer "witnessed the most animated game of foot-ball I ever beheld" with Captain Gunnels "way back in the rear, dignified, grand, gloomy, and peculiar," like a modern-day Virgil van Dijk. "It was a magnificent sight. Louisianians playing football."

Harper's Weekly became popular during the Civil War for its battle reports and detailed illustrations—which included two woodcut prints of soldiers playing pre-football. One, in 1861, shows Confederate troops from the First Maryland Regiment, divided into two groups, charging a single round ball. The other, in 1865, depicts a close-up of Union soldiers from the Army of the Potomac, attacking a round ball and each other. In both prints, army tents appear in the background. A third image, a remarkably clear 1865 (probably) photograph (negative), shows a man from New York's Thirteenth Heavy Artillery Regiment leaning in to kick a round ball toward another man, about five yards away, whose arms are outstretched, like a modern goalie. A semicircle of uniformed men watches the kick. These prints and the photo are among the earliest images of Americans—indeed, of anyone in the world—playing pre-football.

As the war wound down, Union forces, preparing an assault on Port Royal Sound, South Carolina, packed "several hundred foot-balls for the amusement of the troops." After General Robert E. Lee surrendered at the Appomattox Court House, in Virginia, in April 1865 (and after a few more wayward armies, especially west of the Mississippi River, finally gave up), soldiers on both sides—having witnessed the horrors of war and casualties according to recent historians in the 750,000 range (more than *all* other American wars)—returned home by rail, horseback, or on foot, to restart their lives. Many returned to farms or local concerns. Others returned to cities, which, especially in the Northeast, were beginning to burst at their population seams. Some enterprising veterans poured their energies into baseball, which had taken root in American culture before the war. A surge in press coverage during and after the war helped turn baseball into a profession, with leagues spreading coast to coast by the turn of the century. Other veterans became private school and college teachers, and heads of school. Like their English counterparts a generation earlier (more about the Brits in the next chapter), these American educators began shifting campus attitudes about team sports, which, when organized, could build teamwork, discipline, and morale. By the late 1860s, ambitious students with pre-football ideas of their own began organizing competitions and pushing for intercollegiate games. Academic classes were still painfully dull—but extracurricular team activities started to muscle their way into school life.

And it was there, on campus, that American soccer was born. A cluster of schools in the Northeast looked across the pond to the English and the Laws of the Game as their kickoff point.* The beautiful game was born in London, but its gestation period in the British Isles lasted nearly a century. During this long stretch of time—covered in the next chapter—mob football for the masses (pre-football for the historians) rattled on and survived countless fights, broken bones, death, mud, mayhem, and serious prohibitions from church officials, constables, and a long line of kings.

---

* Some soccer historians will debate these claims—and will spiritedly assert that these campus activities fall under a hopelessly generic term called "football," or could more accurately be called American proto-soccer. My rationale for the inspirational British aspects of soccer in America is framed in chapter two. The American birth of soccer on campus, followed quickly by its near extirpation there, and then its undebatable manifestation and spread within working-class immigrant communities are examined in chapters three and four.

2

★★★★★

PRE-FOOTBALL GESTATION, BRITISH BIRTH, AND SPREAD

From mob football to codification to ships bringing rulebooks to faraway coasts (circa 1000–1900)

"The ancients knew the ball, but football is born of modernity."

— David Goldblatt, *The Ball Is Round*

The English created the game, as they often like to remind the world. But football did not spring from the minds of English private school graduates in a London pub in 1863 like Athena springing from the head of Zeus, fully grown and clad in her soccer cleats. Instead, pre-football in England—and later in Scotland, Wales, and Ireland—had been kicking and mauling along for hundreds of years, perhaps over a thousand, all the way back to the Celtic Britons. In this chapter we'll jump back in time, switch continents, and learn about the history of pre-football in the British Isles. Understanding football's origins deepens respect for the game and helps the Yanks appreciate their role in establishing and growing the game in America.

The game took many forms and was called many names over the

centuries: mob football, folk football, knappen, caid, the ol' ba' game, ba', or just foot-ball (signifying games on foot as opposed to activities on horseback). Many of these activities included movements on offense such as kicking, dribbling, throwing, catching, running with the ball, and passing the ball in any permutation (hand or foot). Defensive tactics included deliberately kicking opponents' legs, shins, ankles, and heels (all brutish efforts to cause pain to dislodge the ball), tripping, grabbing, pushing, hand-and-arm tackling, punching at the ball, and maybe even punching each other. Dribbling and kicking the ball—like the moves of a modern soccer player—were probably minority activities. We just don't have an accurate picture. Nobody was tracking activities or keeping score until the mid-1800s. Once soccer was codified in 1863, the British* were uniquely positioned to spread the game around the globe (by the turn of the century, the British Empire was ruling a quarter of the world). Within a century after codification, football, with all its attendant warts and growing pains still to come, had become the most popular sport on the planet, just about everywhere. But we are getting way ahead of ourselves.

The basic idea of mob football was for two sides to meet at a starting point—the center of a field or town, or down by the water—and wait for a single ball to be thrown or dropped into a throng of anxious players, ranging from a few dozen to a few hundred. The objective and literal goal was to gain control of the ball and move it—using any body part—to a team's designated immobile object (a tree, rock, body of water, or building wall). There were no boundaries (those came later, perhaps in the Renaissance) and almost no rules (those came much later, during the Victorian era) about how to move the ball—or stop an opposing player, or a phalanx of players, with possession. The first team to touch the ball to its landmark

* British (or Brits, informal) refers to anyone from the United Kingdom (U.K.), a sovereign country, which includes England, Scotland, Wales (these three, together, Great Britain), and, if they so choose, Northern Ireland. Sports people in the U.K. often refer to these four geographic entities as the "Home Nations." FIFA permits each Home Nation to compete as a separate country in FIFA soccer events due to each country's status as an originator of the beautiful game and long-established independence of its football association. Ireland is a separate country. There will not be a quiz on this.

won. Sometimes landmarks were in adjacent towns, turning the game into a chaotic inter-town melee. Or, as we say today, a derby.

Such loosely structured, ball-centered activity likely predates recorded history. Some historians believe the ball symbolized the sun or an animal's head (and sometimes *was* a head), and that moving it across the ground related to harvest or fertility rites. Others argue ancient people played ball mainly for fun. In any case, ball games appear to be intrinsic to many agrarian societies worldwide. Perhaps they simply followed people into town. This may explain how the people of ancient England, Greece, France, Italy, and other regions developed ball games independently (as far as historians can tell).

Despite this, legend claims England was an empty football canvas until Roman legionaries introduced a pre-football game called *harpastum* (Latin/Greek for "snatched away"—see the Appendix) to the island. But that story is likely apocryphal—or a joke. A fake scholarly article, written by a German professor, somehow slipped past an editor and claimed that in 200 CE, on a field outside Londinium, a rugged squad of Britons lost to a band of Romans, citing two hoary academics: A. Pila (Latin for "ball") and B. Pedes ("feet"). In all probability, the ancient Britons were playing their own version of ba' before and after the invaders.

Pre-football activities across the British Isles get a bad rap in most of the surviving written accounts, which were most often proclamations and edicts from government and church officials who tried to stamp it out wherever the damage to life, limb, and property became intolerable. But for centuries, the people played on, ignoring the various bans. Or perhaps they just moved the playing venue to another street or farther into the countryside to duck the authorities. One of the earliest confirmed accounts is an 1175 Latin description of an already "famous game of ball" penned by a London monk, William Fitzstephen. His brief journal entry described students from different fields and workers from different trades assembling on a plot of earth, each with their own ball, while elders watched the contest on horseback, the latter "aroused by the joys of unrestrained youth."

Twenty-five years later, in 1200, another reference to a ball game appears, this time involving several of King Arthur's knights who were "driving a ball far over the fields" during coronation festivities. The knights surely removed their armor before moving the ball. Some eight hundred years ago, then, we have references to several walks of life—students, tradespeople, and knights—already playing ball games that surely involved the feet.

It's not hard to imagine the property damage that might result from scores of people assembling (especially in town) to maneuver a ball from one place to another, with no rules. Not to mention the inevitable serious injury, or even death. On September 1, 1280, a police report, of sorts, reads: "Henry, son of William de Ellington, while playing at ball on Trinity Sunday with David le Keu and many others . . . received an accidental wound from David's knife. They were both running to the ball, and ran against each other, and the knife hanging from David's belt stuck out so that the point through the sheath struck against Henry's belly . . . and [he] died of misadventure." Henry's fatal misadventure (perhaps in pursuit of a fifty-fifty ball) was not unique. Other accidental ball-playing deaths crop up in notices of the time. Playing ball was certainly violent, noisy, widespread, and becoming more disruptive to the social order. So much so that the mayor of London, in 1314, issued a proclamation titled "Preservation of the Peace": "Concerning malefactors and night-prowlers: whereas there is a great uproar in [London] through certain tumults arising from the striking of great foot-balls in the fields of the public, from which many evils perchance may arise, we do command, on the King's behalf, upon pain of imprisonment, that such game shall not be practiced henceforth within the City."

The people of London did not swiftly comply. In fact, it's possible the mayor's command had little effect. Westminster, central London, issued additional anti-football proclamations in 1331–1332. The church, too, got into the anti-football act. In 1364, fed up with the evils of the game and attendant malefactors, the clergy banned their sect from participating in ball games altogether. Around the same time, a sermon by John Wycliffe warned Christians not to be tricked by hypocrites and "antiChrists" who cause unwitting people to "cobble their shoes with censures, as who should chulle [bandy about] a football." Henry Stubbes, a Puritan of the purest cloth, later penned a similar denunciation of the evil pastime: "Sometimes their necks are broken, sometimes their backs . . . Football encourages envy and hatred, murder and a great loss of blood." To boot, it was often played on Sunday.

By 1365, pre-football found itself the target of King Edward III of England, who issued a total ban across the land (coincidentally, his ban occurred at about the same time in history that the first ruler in the Ming Dynasty in China outlawed a kicking game called *cuju*). King Edward III's edict, directed to the sheriffs of all English counties, called football "vain games of no value" and ordered his subjects to focus on archery and the national defense. This directive heralded a score of similar pronouncements by succeeding rulers (Richard II; Henry IV, V, VII, and VIII; and Elizabeth I) and lesser magistrates, spreading to Scotland, all outlawing mob football games—whether to promote patriotism and strengthen the national defense, to halt property damage, to prevent injury or death, or to appease concerns of the church.

References to balls being specifically kicked by the feet show up in a nursery rhyme and literature of the time. An antisemitic Scottish ballad, probably originating sometime in the 1300s (there are several iterations of the same ditty), tells of "24 bonny boys . . . playing at the ba'" where "sweet Hugh kicked the ball with his right foot, and caught it with his knee" before kicking it through "a Jew's window." The ball finds its way to the Jew's daughter who uses it to lure Hugh to a dressing room in her father's castle where she stabs Hugh to death. Chaucer's Knight's Tale, in his famed *Canterbury Tales*, written between 1389 and 1400, describes a rider and a horse both tumbling to the ground where the unfortunate rider "rolleth under foot as dooth a ball." So, the obvious is confirmed: Balls were being kicked.

They were also being dribbled within boundaries. Sometime between 1480 and 1500, a remarkable Latin description of pre-football gameplay appears, though the author abhorred the activity he chronicled:

> The game at which they had met for common recreation is called by some the foot-ball game. It is one in which young men, in country sport, propel a huge ball not by throwing it into the air but by striking and rolling it along the ground, and that not with their hands but with their feet. A game, I say, abominable enough, and, in my judgment at least, more common, undignified, and worthless than any other kind of game, rarely ending but with some loss, accident, or disadvantage to the players themselves. What then? The boundaries had been marked and the game had started; and, when they were striving manfully, kicking in opposite directions, and our hero had thrown himself into the midst of the fray, one of his fellows, whose name I know not, came up against him from in front and kicked him by misadventure, missing his aim at the ball.

Ouch! Despite the injuries—and the bans, which kept coming—the abominable, undignified, worthless game was just too much fun. The elites still engaged in their hunting and field sports, while gamblers and spectators of all social classes looked forward to horse races, rowing competitions, and boxing matches. But for the masses, in their free time, the ball rolled on.*

With centuries of accumulated pre-football activity behind them, it appeared that the pre-football gangs were on an indomitable march to general acceptance and uniform rules—except that they weren't. In the early decades of the 1800s, English authorities struck back and pre-football activities seemed to be in decline, at least in larger towns and cities. The 1835 Highways Act gave tremendous power over the country's network of roads to local parish boards, which rushed to explicitly ban ball activity: "[I]f any person . . . shall play at Foot-ball or any other Game on any Part

---

* The British were not the only pre-football crews in Europe during the Middle Ages. The French had their *la soule* or *choule*, dating as far back as the late 1300s. And the Italians had their *calcio*, a stylized brawl over a ball, with goals on either side, which appeared in Florence at least as early as 1530.

of the said Highways, to the Annoyance of any Passenger or Passengers, [that person shall] pay any Sum not exceeding Forty Shillings." Forty shillings, the max, was a phenomenally hefty fine in the 1830s. One shilling was roughly a day's wage. Simultaneously, the mob-type urban games were being shut down or moved to the countryside. Public authorities, merchants, and factory owners—the latter pumping and thumping amid the world's first industrial revolution—flexed their collective muscles. Protecting public and private infrastructure, now intrinsically linked to commerce, had finally become a priority. By the mid-1800s, ba' games were being "pushed to the fringes of the kingdom." Everywhere, perhaps, but in elite English private schools.

It is hard for American readers to imagine what life was like at an elite English private school in the early- to mid-1800s. The English have always called these places of learning "public schools," which is a misnomer. They were public only in the sense that anyone from the public could apply. For many years, only the ruling elite matriculated, making them essentially private schools. At about age eight or nine, several years before puberty, rich white boys (virtually all of them were rich white boys) were sent to elite single-sex schools, often as boarders. Upon arriving on campus, their trunks were carried from carriages past grass fields or dirt plots of various sizes (relevance later) to sleeping quarters that were overcrowded and cramped. And often overseen not by adults but by prefects (older boys, nearing graduation), whose first priority was to dominate younger students the way their prefects had dominated them: imperfectly, often cruelly. Today, the names of these schools carry great academic weight and potential—Rugby, Eton, Harrow, Winchester, Westminster, Shrewsbury, Charterhouse. But back then, these places were bubbling cauldrons of belligerence and bullying, Draco Malfoys through and through.

Disruptions to both the school environment and local community had been going on for over a century. Students at Manchester Grammar School, around 1700, took over part of campus and held off teachers with guns and food smuggled in by locals. The argument was supposedly over the length of the Christmas holiday. In 1710, at Winchester, a reduction in beer rations led to a mutiny. In 1797, Eton students took a staff member hostage (at sword-point) over an ambiguous ignominy that precipitated a response from constables and local militia. At Harrow, in 1808, prefects rebelled to protect their right to flog younger students. The army, with fixed bayonets, arrived at Winchester in 1818, its sixth appearance on campus in fifty years.

Writing of his time at Westminster in the 1810s, a graduate reflected: "The boys fought one another, they fought the masters, the masters fought them, they fought outsiders; in fact, we were ready to fight everybody." Schoolmasters did not stand idly by. They fought back with a steady diet of beatings and suspensions. Remarked Lytton Strachey, a vocal private school critic: "It was a system of anarchy [students] tempered by despotism [masters]." In this way, school life chugged along for scores of years, perhaps centuries.

If that were not bad enough, school days were long, regimented, and boring. Classroom instruction was rote and consisted almost entirely of boys copying text from a board or listening to a teacher drone on for hours from a book in (or about) Latin and ancient Greek. The moment a boy stepped outside of a classroom, there was almost no adult supervision. Extracurriculars, like sporting activities, were not very well organized, if they existed at all. Occasionally there might be a rowing activity (if there was suitable water nearby), an impromptu sprinting or cross-country race, or a cricket match (if enough space existed and if the weather complied). While these activities may have required cardiovascular efforts, they lacked what hundreds of unsupervised boys truly craved each day: physical contact. For that, the boys got their kicks, quite literally, from engaging in mob football wherever they could find enough space on campus.

Mob football would have remained just that if not for some enterprising teachers and determined students. Loosely organized pre-football activities had been going on at English private schools for many years, maybe hundreds, as explained by British soccer historian David Goldblatt.

The school you went to determined which version of the game you played. Each school had its own set of traditions and oral "rules" handed down by older students and alumni. Gameplay was also influenced by the configuration of field space on campus.

By the mid-1800s, two general types of pre-football activities existed on campus: (1) a predominantly handling and running-with-the-ball game that included what we now call English rugby or American gridiron football tackling (accomplished with the hands, arms, and upper body) as well as "hacking" (*i.e.*, trying to deliberately kick a player in the legs, shins, ankles, and heels to dislodge the ball); and (2) a predominantly kicking and dribbling game with different forms of tackling techniques that included (i) holding, shoving, tripping, and hacking, or (ii) something less violent and more akin to the modern game, albeit with defensive tactics that would still result in a spate of cards and ejections today. Today, thankfully, hacking is no longer permitted in any organized ball-based sports, from amateur to professional.

Virtually all variations of pre-football, at mid-century, permitted catching the ball with the hands. The overarching goal of both games was to move the ball to an object or across a line. As to campus grounds, some schools, like Rugby and Marlborough, had expansive fields that promoted the handling game; other schools, like London-based Charterhouse and Westminster, had cloisters with tighter boundaries that fostered the kicking game. You'd think it would've been the other way around. But the English have their own way of doing things, and no amount of research on this issue leads to a clear explanation.

The ball games—organic, widespread, and valuable from the students' perspectives—"were a big problem . . . [t]he boys were greatly addicted, and the masters greatly opposed." A game "more fit for farm boys and labourours than for young gentlemen," derided the Headmaster of Shrewsbury School around 1815. But if the games were a big problem, they also presented a big opportunity for enterprising faculty. David Goldblatt describes: "The central dilemma . . . was not initially how to create a different kind of student but simply how to take control. Engaging with team games, especially football, allowed staff to insert themselves into the pre-existing hierarchy of power with themselves at the top, senior boys below, and new arrivals at the bottom."

Modern readers, especially Americans, may assume that the integration of sports into school life was inevitable. Historians, however, point to the mid-nineteenth century as the true beginning of this shift. Educational pioneer Dr. Thomas Arnold, Headmaster at Rugby School from 1828 to 1842, was perhaps the first school leader to recognize and skillfully build on students' existing playing habits. He brought "order and hierarchy" to games without co-opting them. It helped that some of Arnold's teachers (called "masters," even today) actively joined in, and even more when Rugby staff moved to other schools, some becoming heads themselves. Increased faculty involvement in the 1840s and 1850s began to shift attitudes, leading to more school-specific rules and organized sporting activities. Similar developments occurred in elite American schools and colleges, though the U.S. lagged by about fifteen years—slowed by the Atlantic divide and the Civil War (1861–1865).

Britain's pre-football pioneers weren't working in a vacuum—their efforts aligned with broader social shifts. The church and a rising bourgeoisie from the industrial revolution supported expanding school life to include organized athletics. By the mid-1800s, Victorians embraced "muscular Christianity," promoting health, manners, and patriotism to reinforce Britain's global identity. Games served as an ideal way to unite the old aristocracy and the rising bourgeoisie through shared experiences in the school environment. Pre-football activities finally had an official toehold on the ruling class's very stepping stone to power and influence.

History would demonstrate that harnessing and directing adolescent energy in one's own "schoolhouse" was an intrinsically valuable enterprise for establishing order and an esprit de corps. This endeavor, repeated across public (private!) high schools, still left considerable challenges for inter-school competition and for the inevitable scenario arising when students graduated and matriculated to Cambridge, Oxford, etc., or to the military, and later to social clubs, with their own pre-football rules in tow.

The English, to borrow a Latin phrase with deep historical meaning for us Yanks, had an *E Pluribus Unum* ("out of many, one") problem. No two schools were playing precisely the same game.

Most historians agree that the first set of complete rules for any kind of proto-football game was established at Rugby School in 1845 by a trio of students led by William Arnold, seventeen at the time, the son of former head of school Thomas Arnold. The thirty-seven rules read like a pre-rugby manual. They included rules giving deference to the head of school ("That whenever a match is going to be played, the School shall be informed of it"); rules banning objectively dangerous habits ("No player may wear projecting nails or iron plates on the heels or soles of his shoes or boots"); and rules underscoring that Rugby was firmly in the rugby camp ("No player may be held, unless he is himself holding the ball" and "No player but the first on his side, may be hacked, except in a scrummage"). The word "kick" was used twelve times but mostly concerned "place-kicks." The rules were not soccer friendly.

The precise details of what happened next is subject to controversy (there being no video assistant referee, or VAR, for the historical record). Many football historians assert that a group of college students assembled at Cambridge University in about 1848 to pin down a set of rules for an activity that had been kicking around in club form for nearly a decade on Parker's Piece, a pumpkin-shaped commons at Trinity College, Cambridge. Henry Charles Malden reflected in an 1897 letter about his Trinity days, a half-century earlier: "An attempt was made to get up some football . . . [b]ut the result was dire confusion, as every man played the rules he was accustomed to at his public school. I remember how the Eton man howled at the Rugby man for handling the ball." So, each school put forward its own representatives. The result was a set of compromise rules called the Cambridge Rules, which unfortunately have not survived. These rules, to the degree they were written down, were not steadfastly followed, even at Cambridge. Various versions appeared between 1848 and 1862.

Other schools and clubs got into the rule-making act. In 1858, the Sheffield Football Club penned their noble Sheffield Rules, which were more soccer friendly than the rules crafted a decade earlier by William Arnold at Rugby School. Pre-soccer received more help from J. C. Thring (former Cambridge student who had a hand in hammering out the 1848 Cambridge Rules), Head of Uppingham School. In an 1862 pamphlet called "The Rules of Foot-Ball: The Winter Game," Headmaster Thring proposed a short list of soccer-friendly rules that eradicated hacking and carrying the ball with hands. Thring called it "the simplest game." Curiously, at schools all around England, the "game" before the game often entailed negotiating which rules would govern. Sometimes the first half followed one team's rules, and the second half the other team's code. Out of this milieu, and by 1860, pre-football vanguards at schools and independent clubs (mostly cricket clubs with ample grounds and downtime during the winter months) started sharing rules and talking about codification, conversations that piqued the interest of readers of London newspapers.

The climax of all this pre-football talk occurred at the Freemasons' Tavern, Great Queen Street, West End London, in the late fall of 1863. Starting on October 26 and concluding forty-four days later, on December 8, representatives from eleven London clubs met six times around a table (where nary a pint of beer was served), debating various rules and regulations. Coming to a consensus, at first, seemed impossible. A vocal camp insisted on a code that permitted catching and running with the ball, and hacking. Another camp wanted to outlaw both actions and instead focus gameplay on kicking the ball and dribbling. Another group, perhaps a combination of the two camps at loggerheads, wanted to hear from university, cricket, and social club representatives before deciding on a final set of rules.

Negotiations were contentious. In a now notorious and amusing quip, Francis Campbell from Blackheath Club remarked that doing away with hacking would remove "courage and pluck of the game, and I will be bound to bring over a lot of Frenchmen who would beat you with a week's practice." Fortunately, for soccer's sake, other voices prevailed. "If we have hacking, no one who has arrived at the age of discretion will play football and it will be entirely left to schoolboys," stated Ebenezer Morley, honorary secretary and skillful leader of the newly formed group, now calling itself the "Football Association" (FA). Headmaster Thring corroborated in the press at the time: "To kick a player on the shins purposefully is neither fair play nor manly; nay, I do not hesitate to call it thoroughly un-English and barbarous." From the ease of hindsight and simplification, it was essentially a rugby versus soccer debate—with the soccer contingent present during all the meetings and presiding over the all-important final vote. On December 8, 1863, the FA adopted a set of unified rules (thirteen in all) called "The Laws of the Game." One rule near the front clarified that goals could not be scored with the aid of hands. And four rules near the end banned running with the ball and throwing it, and outlawed hacking, tripping, holding, and pushing an opponent. These rules cleared the way, quite literally, for using the feet to dribble and pass the ball—the very heart and soul of the beautiful game to come.

From our modern vantage point, these particular rules seem absolutely obvious and necessary. But that they survived the vocal pre-rugby contingent and arrived, on December 8, unscathed, explicit, and easily understandable, is a minor miracle. The adoption of the Laws of the Game, however, and publication days later by John Lillywhite of Seymour Street, London (publisher of cricket sports books)—and the first official match played under the new rules, on December 19, 1863 (Barnes versus Richmond)—did not settle the matter. Dissemination of the Laws of the Game and consistent compliance still had many obstacles to clear. But soccer finally had a tentative grip on earthly terrain.

General adoption of the FA's Laws—to say nothing of universal compliance across the kingdom and elsewhere—was not a foregone conclusion. For the first decade or so after publication, teams continued to argue about which rules would be followed, and some clubs, according to Goldblatt, "retain[ed] the hacking and carrying practices that the FA had sought to abolish." Further, the Rugby Football Union, formed in 1871, provided a first-rate rival activity. "In the early 1870s, football remained a minor recreational pastime for a very narrow stratum of Victorian society." As to the name of the new game, the English FA originally chose "association football" or "football." By the 1880s, "soccer" was added (a creative abbreviation for "asSOCiation"—with the "-er" appended according to the "suffix" fad at the time among OxfordERs and LondonERs). For about a century, the Brits used all three terms interchangeably—until the Yanks established their first genuine coast-to-coast professional North American Soccer League (NASL), from 1968 to 1984, which attracted high-profile international players during its later years. With the rise of the NASL, Brits nixed "soccer" from their active vocabulary and have been mischaracterizing the word as an Americanism ever since.

Despite the impediments to quick universal adoption of the Laws of the Game, soccer steadily spread around the British Isles—before finally taking off. Historians claim that England, and to some extent Scotland, were aided by the confluence of man-made and geographic factors. By 1865, England had a century of industrialization under its belt, the fruits of which had created a little extra income for the working class, some leisure time on the weekends, and a fairly comprehensive rail system connecting the country's large towns and cities. England's total land area is roughly the size of Alabama. All of the countries in the U.K., combined, equal only the size of Colorado. (Brits detest these helpful comparisons for us Yanks.) By 1875, a steam engine could take players and fans to the grounds of most of the nascent clubs in a few hours' time. Though gaining momentum, the young sport was still subject to the whims of rules and public appeal, and sometimes prohibitive travel costs, particularly for teams of workingmen. Football needed one more spark to set the game on fire.

According to many, that spark came in the form of the "Football Association Challenge Cup," conceived and begun in 1871–1872. The FA Cup, for short, was the world's first annual national knockout competition. As any ambitious player, coach, and fan in any sport will acknowledge: Bracket play is pure genius for reinforcing uniform rules, generating competition, and spreading enthusiasm. The inaugural year of the FA Cup—incidentally the year after the FA banned all non-goalies from catching the ball in any context—about fifty clubs were eligible for the FA Cup and fifteen amateur sides entered, composed almost entirely of graduates of elite high schools and universities. The final, won by Wanderers, was attended by about two thousand fans. Twenty-five years later, in the 1896–1897 FA Cup, 244 clubs entered, with scores of teams fielding professional players from the working class, including bands of Scotsmen who had been making their way south for decades. The final between Aston Villa and Everton, won by Villa, was witnessed by nearly 66,000 fans.

By the turn of the century, gameplay looked very much like a modern game of football. Goals had crossbars, players had opposing kits, restarts had goal kicks and corner kicks, fouls in the box had penalty kicks, and the entire event had a neutral referee to oversee it all. Nearly every weekend, there was a train and a football match on many an Englishman's horizon. On just about everyone else's horizon was a British ship bringing rulebooks and balls to shore. According to the Uruguayan journalist and novelist Eduardo Galeano, the balls were carried up from the bowels of ships and down planks to new lands. There, the balls "no longer confounded customs officers, who at first had not known how to classify the species."

Out of a muddy pot of mob football games, simmering for centuries, the graduates of England's elite schools had codified and served up a new game. After a few decades of marination in the British Isles, it did not take long for the joyous contagion to spread. Nearly all around the globe, football games started in port cities and followed rail lines and roads inland. Soon, along that growing grid of commerce, native people took to the sport and began their own journey and love affair with the ball. "Tell me how you play," suggests Galeano, "and I will tell you who you are and where you are from." But the game did not take hold everywhere, and it did not grow evenly. In the United States, soccer progressed unsteadily through 150 years of missed opportunities, self-inflicted wounds, and hard-won victories, a curious mix of ineptitude and fortitude. We return now to the American journey—not as a referee, to judge every misstep. But as a fan, to discover and to celebrate.

3

★★★★★

AMERICAN BIRTH AND SPREAD

Vast territory and scattered football footings (1869–1900)

Long have you timidly waded holding a plank by the shore,
Now I will you to be a bold swimmer,
To jump off in the midst of the sea, rise again, nod to me, shout,
and laughingly dash with your hair.

— Walt Whitman, "Song of Myself"

American soccer communities, from the start, have always been simultaneously timid waders and bold swimmers. Only now, in the modern era, have elite-level soccer players in America truly found their sea legs. It was a shaky start. The earliest officially documented intercollegiate soccer game in North America was a contest played on November 6, 1869, in New Brunswick, New Jersey, between Rutgers and Princeton. Rutgers won 6–4. Gridiron football folk, including many worthy historians who should know better, unabashedly point to this event as the first gridiron football game. But gridiron football did not exist in 1869.

Gridiron evolved from English rugby, slowly, over many decades. The line of scrimmage and the system of downs were added in the mid-1880s, while the forward pass made its first sanctioned appearance in 1906. After a serious national debate in the early 1900s concerning injuries and campus deaths, gridiron changed some rules and added equipment. It continued to grow in college and finally entered the professional ranks in the early 1920s. Gridiron football did not overtake baseball as America's most popular sport until the early 1970s.

The 1869 Rutgers–Princeton contest was certainly a soccer-esque game. While there is no direct evidence that the young men from both schools patterned their 1869 encounter specifically on the Laws of the Game (adopted in London in 1863, and reprinted by Beadle and Co., in New York City, in 1866), the activity was much closer to soccer than to rugby. The ball was round; the rules were agreed upon by the captains; the teams consisted of twenty-five players each; and the points were awarded *only* if the ball was kicked (not run while in-hand) over the other team's goal line. "Headlong running, wild shouting, and frantic kicking," noted a writer from a Rutgers newspaper. "Keep your kicks short and low," exhorted the Rutgers captain. A week later, the schools met again, this time in Princeton, where Princeton won 8–0, under slightly different rules that were still more akin to soccer than to rugby. A third match to decide the affair was proposed but never played.

A few days later, in mid-November 1869, and about fifty miles south, another game took place, between two Germantown (Philadelphia) cricket clubs: the Young America Cricket Club versus the Germantown Cricket Club. The contest occurred at the latter's grounds (which still exist today) on November 18, 1869—the official Thanksgiving Day, *i.e.*, the new national holiday President Lincoln had assigned six years earlier and the specific day of November President Ulysses S. Grant had designated for 1869. Cricket clubs in Philly, at the time, dabbled in association football (and perhaps included Rutgers and Princeton players from Philadelphia's elite). Historians, however, often refer to this cricket-club event as the very genesis of the gridiron, turkey, and gravy combo served up every Thanksgiving for over 150 years. But this is just gridiron football folk, after a full-course meal, stretching the truth. The first official Thanksgiving holiday ritual of food and sport started as a rugby-style game played according to the then-rules of the Rugby School of England—where goals could be scored only with the feet and dribbling rushes were common.* The activity afoot at the Philly cricket ground in November 1869 was more akin to soccer than it was to gridiron football, which, as a Thanksgiving treat, was still decades away.

By 1870, most major American educational institutions that had recovered from the Civil War—as well as various cricket clubs and social groups—were playing some form of soccer-rugby. Just like in 1850s England, some places were fond of the kicking game. Others preferred the handling game. Many were probably playing a hybrid game. As to the kicking game, Americans were reluctant to adopt the English FA's Laws of the Game lock, stock, and barrel. By 1870, the U.S. and the U.K. (with the Revolutionary War and War of 1812 distant memories) were *literally* on speaking terms—the two countries became the first transatlantic nations to be connected by a telegraph cable in 1865, which cut down communication time from two weeks (by ship) to two minutes. But post–Civil War communications between the Yanks and the Brits vacillated from cold to bitter. Though officially neutral, the U.K. supplied the Confederacy with at least five gunships and a plethora of blockade runners (small, fast boats), indirectly prolonging the Civil War and causing more deaths in the internal conflict, estimated to be well over one hundred thousand Americans. In 1871, the Treaty of Washington resolved disputes, with Britain paying $15.5 million, which warmed relations and ushered in a long period of accord between the two nations.

In the decades after the Civil War, with Reconstruction underway, the North attempted to remake the nation in its own image. Americans, especially Southerners, experienced profound changes in labor, land, and social

* A *dribbling rush* was a classic early-rugby tactic—prominent in the mid- to late-1800s—used by forwards to advance the ball by repeatedly kicking it while running together in a tight pack.

matters too numerous and complex to recount here. What most Americans agree on, though, is that post–Civil War America did not want to adopt foreign games *wholesale* for its leisure activities. Instead, Americans wanted to carve out their own sporting space—much like baseball, which was, at the time, already calling itself "the national pastime." This much is incontrovertible. But the story is more complex as to what happened next. Teasing out soccer and rugby, which had both arrived in rulebook form from across the pond and in the minds and legs of immigrants (and their leisure activities), and fabricating gridiron football out of the material of the two, did not happen overnight.

In 1873, Princeton, Rutgers, and Yale (all fond of the kicking game) attempted to found America's first "intercollegiate football association" (which was really a soccer association) during a meetup in New York City. But Harvard refused to attend, so the association never got off the ground. Harvard, early on, experimented with the kicking game but soon gravitated to the handling game. In 1874, Harvard looked north, to Montreal, Canada, and to McGill University, which enjoyed rough and tumble activities akin to rugby. Two games were played, away and home, each under a slightly different code, whereupon Harvard and McGill kicked, tackled, and scrummed their way to a near-even point record.

But history would witness the ball squirting out of the melee in favor of rugby. Thereafter, Harvard—the bellwether and beacon of all things academic and "scientific" (a popular and elitist term at the time used to describe a variety of human activities)—leaned on its American college peers for more rugged handling competition. In 1875, Harvard coaxed Yale into a contest resembling rugby. Harvard won. Yale apparently enjoyed the turbulent game and pivoted to rugby. "From that moment on, [gridiron] football never looked back," opines the American historian David Wangerin. If a birth certificate were to be assigned to gridiron football (albeit still in its fetal stage), the 1875 Harvard–Yale rugby encounter would be it.

Princeton students, seeing the number of schools on their short list of viable soccer opponents rapidly dwindling, met in November 1876, in Geological Hall (now Stanhope Hall), to figure out what to do. Princeton's

Nassau Literary Magazine, one of the nation's oldest, campaigned for soccer: "We confess ourselves utterly unable to account for the taste which prefers Harvard's rough and tumble scrimmages to the uncomparably [sic] more genteel game under the rules of 1873." A writer for the school's newspaper, *The Daily Princetonian*, called for a compromise—just keep playing away games according to the hosts' rules and hope that soccer would eventually win out. But Princetonians, perhaps sensing themselves in an inferior tactical position, voted in favor of the oval ball and joined the advantage pressed by Harvard and Yale.

Three weeks later, on November 26, 1876, delegates from Princeton, Harvard, Yale, and Columbia met in Springfield, Massachusetts (about thirty miles over the Connecticut border), and hammered out "a uniform system of rules" at the Massasoit House hotel (where nary a pint of beer was ingested). The result was the first legitimate "Intercollegiate Football Association" (IFA), which settled on rugby as its blueprint. A house divided could not stand. Soccer was cast aside. The IFA's rugby decision and subsequent rulebook immediately provided a powerful imprimatur. Virtually all colleges and universities in America quickly followed suit. Over the coming decades, and under the auspices of the IFA, colleges modified rugby and melded it gradually into gridiron football. Twenty-eight years passed before another intercollegiate soccer match took place.

Soccer writers, even the fantastic ones—like David Wangerin, perhaps America's greatest soccer historian—apply a fatalistic, almost defeatist view to this most inauspicious moment. They argue that soccer would not have flourished in college, let alone on American soil, even if the vote had gone in favor of soccer. Wangerin concedes, almost apologetically: "America's strong desire to assert its cultural independence by developing games of its own would almost certainly have prevented" soccer from rising "to heights similar to those it had attained elsewhere." "Soccer would have become unrecognizable," opines the British-American writer Paul Gardner. "It would have been subjected to countless modifications," just like what the Yanks did "to dear old rugby." But the young men who assembled in 1876 to form a new association, while eager to establish an American-style sport, were not choosing between an American game and a foreign game; they were choosing between two foreign games (soccer and rugby) that already had their own associations, their own published codes, and their own distinctly shaped balls.

That the Yanks would reconfigure rugby over the next few decades and create gridiron—an entirely new sport—could not have been predicted in 1876. Nor should it be assumed that soccer, had it won the vote, would have withered on the college vine. Less than a week after Princeton capitulated and the IFA was born, about one thousand spectators (a decent crowd for the time) watched Princeton lose at home to Yale, where several student-athletes suffered serious injuries. A writer in the *Nassau Literary Magazine* cynically noted the rugby-esque contest "resulted in giving [Princeton] the appearance of a hospital for disabled veterans." What if this had been a soccer game? What if the IFA had chosen soccer as its archetype? Perhaps it would have gained a regional foothold in colleges and spread more quickly across the U.S. In any case, when Harvard convinced the other schools to link up, soccer lost its most logical path to wider, faster acceptance. It has been playing catch-up ever since.

Pre-gridiron football spread quickly among the colleges. Annual photographs of Princeton's "soccer" team during the 1860s and early 1870s, pre-IFA, display round balls front-row center—then, post-IFA birth (fall of 1876), an irreversible switch to oval balls for the rest of the 1800s. Indeed, right after the IFA was formed, Princeton ordered new balls from Canada. When round balls were sent by mistake, Princeton asked Harvard for an oval ball, which was soon provided. Princeton students, having a new ball but no idea how to use it, watched their opponents warming up and tried to imitate their technique. They learned fast.

From 1876 to the close of the century, American soccer was gasping for air—completely unlike soccer in much of Great Britain, which was expanding with help from the FA Cup (the oldest national knockout tournament in the world). American cities were spread out and separated by vast distances, which made even pseudo-regional competitions difficult for any American citizens or arriving immigrants willing to devise a coherent soccer league. Yanks at the time had no overarching soccer association, no national soccer cup (yet), no material foothold in the colleges, and virtually no athletic or social clubs completely devoted to soccer.

A possible exception was the Oneida Football Club, composed of young men from elite high schools and Harvard alumni who played a hybrid soccer-rugby activity called the "Boston Game" on the fifty-acre Boston Common, the oldest city park in the U.S. Not much is known about the Boston Game, except that the Oneidas and other student-led groups competed on the Common as early as 1862, and that the ball was round. The Oneidas were dominant for about a decade—historians claim virtually no team scored on them. Whatever the original rules were, they soon evolved into proto-gridiron rules once nearby Harvard and the IFA got into the rule-making act.

Today, Bostonians and tourists play all kinds of games on Boston Common. Behind the scenes, and for the past one hundred years or so, an odd competition has simmered. Ardent supporters of American soccer and gridiron football have engaged in post hoc "commemorative endeavors" (fueled by the press) to pinpoint their sport's origin to a specific spot within Boston Common. Zealots have even defaced each other's plaques. Such endeavors are pointless. Neither fans nor historians will ever agree on an undisputed geographic origin for either sport. To quote the Harvard-educated American novelist Gertrude Stein, which won't appease either group: "There's no there there."

Throughout the rest of the 1800s, soccer was dead on arrival and virtually ignored by most colleges and universities, who were busy chasing gridiron. American soccer, after a few tentative breaths on college campuses, survived with the help and support of people far from the madding crowd of school and elite social clubs—people living in working-class communities scattered mostly throughout the East Coast. Places like (1) Philadelphia/Trenton areas; (2) West Hudson/Kearny, New Jersey, areas (about a score of miles from Ellis Island and the Statue of Liberty); (3) Manhattan/Brooklyn areas; and (4) Fall River/Pawtucket/Boston areas. I call these contiguous areas (which encouraged inter-city team competition) the original

Four Corridors of American soccer. Teams were also kicking the ball in Baltimore, Washington, Pittsburgh, St. Louis, Chicago, Cincinnati, Cleveland, Detroit, New Orleans, Los Angeles, and in working-class pockets of other cities and towns across the United States. Soccer historians might argue that the geographic "arc" linking St. Louis, Chicago, and Detroit represents another original corridor.

In any event, the Four Corridors, and many of the other places, had one key attribute in common: They were absorbing waves of newly arriving immigrants, many from Scotland and England, and to a lesser extent Ireland, Wales, Germany, and Scandinavia. Many were lured to the U.S. by the prospect of steady work and more opportunity. Between 1860 and 1914, around fifty-two million Europeans left the continent. The majority settled in North America. Their employers were primarily textile mills and related factories, and shipyards, which were spurring America's continued industrial revolution. Many who immigrated to the U.S. became Americans through a relatively easy (compared to today's standards) naturalization process. They mixed with Americans who were already there, some with family histories as old as the nation's founding. They were all Americans, or rapidly becoming Americans, despite being labeled "immigrants," "ethnic Americans," "foreigners," and "hyphenated Americans"—unfortunate names that would prove hard to slough off, even to this day.

Many of these Americans and soon-to-be Americans joined the baseball bandwagon (stealing bases and hearts of Americans in all social classes) and eventually teamed up with the gridiron football folk (crushing bones in college and gaining momentum). But a decent number of arriving immigrants and Americans ignored the buzz and ruckus of those sports and instead established teams and leagues in their own rugged communities and played association football. For fifty years, maybe longer, they kept the unassuming embers of soccer alive in this country.

4

★★★★★

PLANTING SEEDS OF HOPE IN THE FOUR CORRIDORS

Amateur, semiprofessional, and proto-professional soccer leagues (1884–1900)

"Do what you can, with what you've got, where you are."

— Theodore Roosevelt, quoting Bill Widener

Having been excluded from the college ranks and lacking strong economic support in working-class communities, soccer smoldered in the Four Corridors and the USA's aforementioned cities and regions. There, it might have died out completely. But arriving immigrants fanned the embers and occasionally sparked regional interest. In May 1884, two British expatriates helped form the American Football Association (AFA) at the Caledonian Hall in NYC (where not a single beer was ingested), making the U.S. the second country—after Canada—outside the U.K. to follow England's FA.

According to a newspaper writer from New Jersey, the rookie AFA adopted "the rules of the English association, subject to alteration from time to time." By 1882, the Laws of the Game had been harmonized by the FAs of England, Scotland, Wales, and Ireland. So, there was consensus on gameplay, despite how umpires (soon to be called referees) officiated particular matches. A lingering dispute, however, remained over whether to legalize professionalism. The English sanctioned professionals in 1885; the Scottish followed in 1893.

The AFA originally adopted a no-professionals rule and tried to remain amateur through the late 1800s and into the early 1900s. The AFA's position, however, was problematic from the start. Many American teams were created and being maintained by textile mills, shipyards, and factories. And the owners of the biggest and most active clubs were clearly paying players in some fashion. The professionalism issue would remain a sticky wicket for about twenty-five years, similar to the time it took the British FAs to resolve it.

America finally had a football association based on the English model, but the American version was flimsy from the start. The AFA was regional in scope (nothing west of Philadelphia) and spanned disparate soccer communities along the Four Corridors (Philadelphia to Boston)—270 miles straight as a crow flies—in an era when traveling 100 miles was more unusual than 1,000 miles today. Also, the AFA was insular and poorly managed—it did not include top teams from Philadelphia and New York City, neglected amateur and recreational games, and lacked the essentials needed to build strong leagues and a truly representative governing body.

Starting in 1885, the humble AFA did succeed for a time (1885–1898) in overseeing an annual AFA Cup, a nominal "national" championship. The first three titles went to a team sponsored by the Scottish-owned Clark Thread Mill called ONT Kearny, from Kearny, New Jersey. ONT stood for Our New Thread, the mill's marketing campaign, which helped reinforce its reputation for the next forty years as the world's leading manufacturer of high-quality sewing thread. The next seven AFA Cup titles went to teams from Fall River, Massachusetts, a burgeoning textile town fifty miles south of Boston, affectionately known as Spindle City, named after the slender rods used to twist and store thread and yarn.

Rounding the new century, and for about twenty more years, Fall River soccer squads were primarily supported by textile mills and related factories dotting the horizon, pumping out enough thread and yarn to become the "Textile Capital of America," edging out Lowell, Massachusetts. This pattern repeated for decades. Successful early-twentieth-century soccer teams usually arose from blue-collar communities where immigrants mixed with hardscrabble Americans and gained sustainability with financial support from local textile companies (and, by the 1920s, all kinds of companies). Or, as in St. Louis, steady growth and success came through strong support from churches and local parishes.

From the beginning, team names changed mercilessly every few years. Owners and organizers were being pulled in multiple directions. Names referenced American towns and regions, honored sponsors, or paid homage to foreign clubs: Fall River Rovers, Fall River Olympics, Fall River East Ends, Pawtucket Free Wanderers, New York Thistle, Brooklyn Longfellows, British Hosiery, Paterson True Blues, Paterson Crescent, Kearny Rangers, Kearny Arlington, Newark Almas, Newark Caledonian, Philadelphia Crescent, Philadelphia North End, Philadelphia Manz. The names were well-intentioned but failed to excite many fans—including the hearts of some players on the rosters.

In what has been billed as the first international game played outside the Home Nations of the U.K., squads from the U.S. (though none were U.S. born) and Canada played one-off games in 1885 and 1886 in front of about two thousand fans at the same pitch in East Newark, New Jersey. The Canadians won the first meeting 1–0 in what an American writer called "a hard fight" and "one of the best contested games ever seen in this neighborhood." A year later, the Yanks (still a team of pseudo internationals) won 3–2. It would be another thirty years before the nascent U.S. Men's National Team* legitimately cobbled an elite team together for a 1916 summer trip to Sweden (more about this team in the next chapter).

* The United States Men's National Team (USMNT, MNT) will always be capitalized in this book when referring to the senior team (*i.e.*, the elite of the elite) and all the age-restricted Youth National Teams operating beneath the MNT. As of 2026, there are eight distinct teams: USMNT, U-23 (Olympic Team), U-20, U-19, U-18, U-17, U-16, and U-15. The women have the same number of teams.

During the last decade of the 1800s, the rickety soccer train—weighed down by local whims and encumbered by the vast American landscape—chugged erratically through the Panic of 1893 and lingering depression. There were a few bright spots, but soccer had little chance of gaining enough steam to enter the mainstream, and instead rounded the century in a moribund state.

Meanwhile, by the 1890s, baseball had spread coast to coast. The National Association of Baseball Clubs (one of two major leagues surviving today), operating since 1876, increasingly delighted fans despite team turnover and rival leagues. Jockeying for fans and market share led to bidding wars, contract disputes, legal battles, and frictions between major and minor leagues. It was a mess, but with increasingly more money at stake (if only the AFA had such problems). In hindsight, baseball's growing pains were rites of passage on its journey to the top of the American sports heap for about seventy more years.

Gridiron football also started grabbing a national audience, stemming from New York newspapers involved in a circulation war. In 1893, Joseph Pulitzer (a first-generation immigrant and then an American!) created the first genuine sports section overseen by a full-time sports editor. Pulitzer's ploy was soon imitated nationwide. Endless columns adorned with black-and-white sketches—and later photos—of young men in primitive gridiron uniforms started marching down pages of the nation's papers.

What reader wouldn't want stories offering glimpses into an elite world, punctuated by violence, injuries, and high-scoring games? In 1883, a touchdown was worth two points. By 1900, a touchdown and a field goal were each worth five points—and gridiron started pumping out high-scoring games. Soccer scores, since the beginning, rarely escaped low-single digits, including many inconclusive ties. Nobody minded much in the nineteenth century. But soccer's low-scoring albatross, way off in the distance, was already circling the American sporting landscape.

Gridiron college games rapidly gained significance beyond their campus gates, and started attracting fans eager to follow the social elite of top colleges. Fascination and readership also grew as gridiron's rules evolved. By the early twentieth century, the sport began to resemble the modern game: Interference (blocking), the series of downs, and the forward pass had finally been formalized. This trio irrevocably separated gridiron from rugby. Pigskin had become an authentic American sport. But whether it would become professional and a cultural pastime was unclear. It still had several hurdles to overcome. In the early 1900s, campus games resulted in serious injuries and increasingly more fatalities—inching into the high teens annually. The culprits were dangerous tactics like "the flying wedge" and "v-trick formations"—with players locking arms and moving quickly in tight formations—leading to funerals and negative press, threatening the sport's future.

Political pressure from Congress in 1905–1906 spurred reforms. An athletic association was formed, which banned the most dangerous plays, mandated equipment (pads, but not helmets yet), and legalized the forward pass to break up the mass of bodies at the line of scrimmage. Unfortunately, teams avoided passing for years, since an untouched forward pass (in the air) automatically resulted in a turnover. In 1910, the association became the National Collegiate Athletic Association (NCAA), aiming to regulate college sports and protect athletes. In 1939, the NCAA finally mandated helmets—a sluggish response to a serious issue, reflecting its modus operandi over the last century. During the 1920s and 1930s, gridiron's injuries persisted, rules multiplied, and interest soared. Fanfare grew with college bowl games, new stadiums, a pro league, and the spread of sports coverage in print, radio, and, in 1939, TV. Soccer, of course, charted a different course.

During the 1890s, hardly anyone with a lot of money was paying attention to association football. But that changed when six National Baseball

League owners, aiming to use their idle stadiums during the long winter offseason, formed the American League of Professional Football (ALPF), with soccer teams from Washington, D.C.; Baltimore; Philadelphia; Manhattan; Brooklyn; and Boston (essentially, the Four Corridors). This 1894 venture was a comedy of errors from the start. David Wangerin notes that "the owners insisted each club take the name of its baseball counterpart, and many hired their baseball managers as 'coaches.' Some even promised their favorite baseball players would feature in matches (which in Philadelphia [and Washington] they actually did)."

Games were scheduled for late fall and early winter (on predictably frigid fields, adjacent to even colder stands), often at midweek, which virtually guaranteed low turnouts from soccer's mostly working-class audiences, who were already burdened by grueling work schedules and meager incomes. Matches took place within the outfields of baseball parks—which sometimes had goals without nets, scoreboards without numbers, and players and fans without refs.

The ALPF aimed to involve local and regional talent but abandoned that goal almost immediately. A Baltimore Orioles FC manager recruited at least five English pros, which boosted excitement and increased home fans into the thousands. Baltimore's recruitment efforts irritated the other team owners and managers, whose home games drew hundreds, or (in one case) only eighteen paying fans. The AFA, angered by the ALPF's challenge to its authority, barred any player who signed with an ALPF team from future AFA events like its AFA Cup. Immigration officials from Washington, D.C., were alerted to the "foreign" menace, and sent agents up the road to Baltimore. Orioles reps reportedly claimed their players with the weird accents were from Detroit. With AFA anger, federal pressure, soaring costs, and news of a rival second national baseball league, the six baseball owners pulled the plug on their soccer experiment on October 18, 1894—after just twelve days of league play.

News of the closure didn't reach all teams by the second weekend's fixtures*—or some managers ignored it. Some teams played on. Days later, after the league unraveled, an official tally showed the Brooklyn Bridegrooms† had amassed a 5–1 record. But Baltimore, late to start, had played only three games and won all of them (a perfect winning percentage). In the ensuing months, Brooklyn, Baltimore, Philadelphia, and Boston played more games against each other and local sides, fueled by their managers' desire to settle scores, and the players' efforts to recoup lost wages from (any) gate receipts. But by spring 1895, these efforts fully expired. Brooklyn had played and won the most games in this unofficial record of America's first formal (though abandoned) professional soccer league.

The ex-ALPF players—mostly first-generation Americans and immigrants from England and Scotland—returned to their old teams under the auspices of the AFA, which soon forgave their foray into professional soccer. The English pros in Baltimore, who had arrived on American soil via second-class steamship tickets, were sent home in steerage class. Years later, a group of baseball men from the Midwest proposed another soccer league, but it folded before the league's opening whistle.

Incredibly, the ALPF wasn't the only professional soccer league trying to take root in 1894. Unbeknownst to the ALPF until weeks before its first game, a rival group called the American Association of Professional Football (AAPF) had organized a league with teams from Pennsylvania (Philadelphia), New Jersey (Trenton, Newark/Kearny, and Paterson), and New

* In *football* and *soccer* parlance, a *fixture* refers to a scheduled *match* (*game*) between two teams that occurs on a *pitch* (*field*) where players often wear *boots* (*cleats*). If a player commits a *direct-free-kick offense* (*foul*) inside his own *penalty area* (*eighteen-yard box*, *box*), a *penalty kick* (*penalty*, *pen*, *PK*) is awarded at the *penalty spot* (*spot*). Americans should use all these italicized words interchangeably—unless coaching football in the U.K. The Brits snobbishly don't use the term PK—as the American coach Jesse Marsch discovered while coaching Leeds United in the English Premier League from 2022 to early 2023. He was hounded by football writers and fans who viewed his use of "PK" during press conferences as an "Americanism" and out of step with traditional English football lingo. Silly Limeys.

† The Brooklyn Bridegrooms was indeed the name of an actual professional baseball team in 1894.

York (Manhattan and Brooklyn), though the teams from NYC never joined. The AAPF scheduled its games on Saturdays and holidays to allow players to keep their day jobs. It was likely a semiprofessional endeavor. When it launched on September 29, a week before the other league, Philadelphia crushed Trenton 11–1 before around one thousand fans. Two weeks later, Trenton, with three losses and a goal differential of -18, quit, leaving just three teams.

Incredibly, an October 13, 1894, *Philadelphia Inquirer* advertisement lists two professional soccer games, in separate leagues, starting simultaneously at 3:30 PM, each costing twenty-five cents, at venues about three miles apart. In the AAPF, it was Philadelphia vs. Trenton at Stenton Grounds at Wayne Junction. In the ALPF, it was Philadelphia vs. Washington at the baseball park at North Broad Street and West Huntingdon Street. Both matches were abandoned due to bad weather. When the baseball owners killed the ALPF days later, a New York paper mistakenly stated the AAPF had folded, which it hadn't, yet. The AAPF limped along for several more months before succumbing to high costs, bad weather, and low attendance. It was all very confusing and made no economic sense.

That the AAPF and the ALPF soccer-baseball endeavor struck out in short succession delighted the AFA, a decidedly amateur organization that apparently deplored ventures into full professionalism—or at least despised having its authority benched. The AFA was never in full control of leagues in its own region. Instead, it focused most of its time and energy on its AFA Cup, which produced a steady stream of revenue for nearly three decades.

After the demise of the professional soccer experiments, and in December 1894, a new league formed—the National Association Football League (NAFBL)—made up of mostly amateur teams from NYC and nearby New Jersey towns. It wasn't national or even regional in scope. Over time, the NAFBL expanded slightly (geographically), running from 1894–1899 and 1906–1921. But it never ventured west of Philadelphia or north of Boston. Meanwhile, northern teams formed a circuit called the New England League. Thus, soccer teams in the Four Corridors stumbled along with no powerful umbrella group capable of uniting factions and promoting growth, especially westward. The AFA was not up to the task. This unfortunate scenario plagued American soccer for decades.

A litmus test for the health of American soccer, at least in the 1890s, was the AFA Cup, which peaked at twenty entrants in 1892. But the Panic of 1893 festered for years and led to labor unrest, mill closings, and layoffs by century's end. The 1898 AFA Cup was contested by only two teams—that's right, two—playing a home and an away match that concluded on April 30. Kearny Athletic Club beat crosstown rival Arlington Athletic Association at the Cosmopolitan Park in Newark, New Jersey. Nobody knows how many fans watched the deciding match. Earlier that month, in south London, at the grounds of Crystal Palace, over 62,000 fans witnessed Nottingham Forest defeat Derby 3–1 in the FA Cup final. The following year, the AFA Cup was suspended, and attendant leagues went dormant.

American soccer limped into the twentieth century.

5

★★★★★

PROGRESS IN THE FOUR CORRIDORS

Feuding continues, but soccer spreads (1900–1920)

"Reserving judgments is a matter of infinite hope."

— F. Scott Fitzgerald, *The Great Gatsby*

As far as historians can tell, soccer reemerged from its slumber in about 1905, boosted by better economics, the return of soccer to some college ranks, and the success of several English touring teams in North America. The AFA and the NAFBL got back on their feet and focused on clubs from West Hudson, New York City, and Boston. Philadelphia was thriving soccer-wise but insular. In 1906, the AFA Cup was relaunched but attracted only thirteen teams, all from New Jersey. An attempt to include teams from or near Fall River, Massachusetts, failed, as the AFA insisted on eight teams from New England. When the Yanks from New England could only muster five, the AFA Cup went ahead without them.

The New England teams formed a new competition, the New England Cup Tie Series, and began their own league and tournament. Thus, the soccer splintering continued. There was too much geography, too few dollars, and not enough prudent leadership to make widespread leagues (let alone national ones) viable. Teams survived on shoestring budgets, with only the best players enjoying under-the-table payments. The AFA seemed to have little interest beyond about two dozen East Coast teams, ignoring the smaller "soccer fish, from sea to shining sea."

In 1911, a new soccer association formed in New York State, purportedly to focus on amateur players (it would not stay amateur for long), calling itself the American Amateur Football Association (AAFA). It chose London-born, German-educated medical doctor Gustav (Gus) Randolph Manning as its first president. Manning was no amateur at organizing. While in Germany, during and after earning a medical degree from Freiburg University, he helped launch the German Football Association. In 1901, he drafted many of the rookie association's bylaws, based on the English model, and became the first secretary of the Deutscher Fußball-Bund (DFB), Germany's Football Association.

Soccer in America now had two national associations: the cagey AFA and the upstart AAFA (which quickly formed its own cup, albeit on a smaller scale than the AFA Cup). Both barely covered one region. And from the start they were at each other's throats. In 1912, AAFA Secretary Thomas Cahill—who would become a dominant figure in the American game—was sent by Manning to a FIFA congress in Stockholm to be accepted as the single footballing authority in the U.S. The AFA also sent a representative, Frederick Wall, with the same purpose. Incredibly, Wall was neither an American nor an immigrant on his way to becoming a citizen. Wall (later knighted) was the then-Secretary of the English FA. There is no evidence he ever stepped foot in America. That the AFA sent Wall as its proxy underscores how little the AFA's "backyard garden" had grown over the previous twenty-five years. The AFA seemed hell-bent on maintaining its immigrant roots and made little progress growing geographically or evolving in purpose. FIFA met with the two groups and told them to get their act together and return with a unified plan.

Following FIFA's mandate, the two bodies met over 1912–1913 at the Astor House in New York City (where more pints of beer should have been imbibed)—and made little progress toward unification. The Astor House (est. 1836), at Broadway and Vesey Street, was one of America's best-known luxury hotels. It featured private dining rooms, a large round mahogany bar, and curved counters along the side walls, all topped by an elliptical cast-iron and glass rotunda. Instead of making material progress under the beautiful accoutrements—which could have provided American soccer a fitting origin story—the two dueling bodies bickered, balked, and threatened walkouts.

The only success was an April 5, 1913, name change for Manning and Cahill's AAFA to the United States Football Association (USFA)—which survives today, after name changes in 1945 (USSFA, with an extra S for "soccer") and in 1974 to the United States Soccer Federation (USSF).* The USFA emerged from the Astor House (which would soon be severed and destroyed by bickering family members) with the most power and momentum and promptly sent an application to FIFA. On the strength of its application—and with Manning and Cahill still on the same page (their relationship would soon sour)—the USFA became a provisional FIFA member on August 15, 1913 (and a full member on June 24, 1914), making the U.S. the fourth country from the Americas to join FIFA (behind Argentina, Chile, and Canada). The USFA, Manning confidently proclaimed, "aims to make soccer the national pastime of the winter in this country." The AFA said as much back in 1884.

Gus Manning also wanted to maintain a true national team to represent the U.S. in the Olympics and other international competitions. With a London birth certificate, a German medical degree, and the experience of drafting Germany's FA documents, Manning was the stately front man.

---

* References in this book to the USFA, USSFA, USSF, and Federation are to the same national governing body that helps develop and organize soccer endeavors in the United States. In modern times, the USSF has claimed the name "U.S. Soccer"—and the Federation's stated mission is "to make soccer, in all its forms, the preeminent sport in the United States." This book will not use the capitalized term "U.S. Soccer" in order to clearly distinguish the Federation from the many U.S. soccer organizations and communities across the United States, from amateur to professional, which are supported by the USSF, but not owned or directly controlled by it. In this book, U.S. soccer is a generic term.

In contrast, Cahill was the industrial blue-collar engine, barreling forward since birth with loads of confidence and optimism. Born in New York, raised in St. Louis, Cahill ran track, played baseball, tended goal for the St. Louis Shamrocks, and eventually (after turning thirty-five) became a soccer promoter for A.G. Spalding & Brothers, the nation's preeminent sporting goods store.

After the USFA was sanctioned by FIFA, the AFA started losing its grip on zones it once influenced. Some Northeastern teams switched allegiances because the AFA, in 1911, had followed orders from the English FA and barred American teams from hosting the touring Corinthians, an English team in a dispute with the English FA. Even states west of the Mississippi, where the AFA never had much sway, joined the USFA. Many in soccer circles felt the AFA remained inordinately tied to the English FA (underscored by never having an American-born or naturalized president)—and it cared too much about a short list of mill and factory teams from the Northeast, and too little about westward expansion. A letter to the editor in a short-lived Harrisburg, Pennsylvania, football paper stressed: "No sport will ever succeed here which is directed [from] across the water, and until the American Association show[s] its independence of foreign domination, soccer will always be regarded as a sport peculiar to Britons in America." But the AFA didn't die. It sputtered through another decade.

The USFA wasted no time attacking the AFA's main asset, the AFA Cup, by setting up and marketing a rival competition in 1913 called the National Challenge Cup—which still exists today as the U.S. Open Cup. In mid-September 1913, USFA Secretary Cahill invited 287 clubs nationwide; forty accepted, from Illinois to Massachusetts. The St. Louis hotbed stayed out for seven years. Meanwhile, the AFA plowed ahead with its AFA Cup.

For nearly a decade, the U.S. had two "national" associations and two "national" cups. The associations were like two Ford Model Ts ("Tin Lizzies") careening down a rough road, navigating long-standing public squabbles and harsh conditions. They plowed through obstacles, which had never been cleared, like inconsistent amateur/professional definitions, horrible refereeing, and outright fisticuffs on and off the field. And horrible weather. Teams faced the insanity of long-distance travel (often during the winter months) along hundreds of miles of Eastern Seaboard—using trains, boats, horse-drawn buggies, and rudimentary cars—often arriving at venues (including soccer pitches that were sometimes not much better than bumpy cow pastures) where nobody knew how many fans would show up.

Outside the cups, the National Association Football League (NAFBL), still semi-regional, chugged along within the Four Corridors in a quasi-professional state. A few of its teams were blowing their steam whistles to turn professional. But many others inched along, with financial difficulties in their own backyards and little to no concern for the feuding of two administrative soccer bodies. It was only a matter of time before the FIFA-backed USFA overtook the lean and getting leaner AFA.

The AFA Cup lost ground to the Challenge Cup each year. In 1923, the USFA added the National Amateur Cup, further diminishing the AFA Cup. The last AFA Cup, in 1924, was won by Bethlehem Steel, America's most successful team to that point. Within a few years, the AFA disappeared completely, along with its Cup, which resurfaced about eighty years later, and today is being held by a private citizen. He reportedly wants $100,000 for the thirteen-inch sterling silver trophy that is crowned (based on old photographs) by a cross-country runner (not a soccer figure) and a ball about the size of a pea—an amateur ensemble befitting the AFA's amateur forty-year history.

From the best players' standpoint, the latter half of the 1910s and much of the 1920s were prosperous. Mill and factory teams backed by individuals with deep pockets continued to dominate. The best players were earning a respectable wage. A 1919 *New York Tribune* article noted that "salaries of professional soccer players—and of some who still pose as amateurs—are approaching the average major league baseball player's stipend in some sections of the country" and that "annual salaries ranging from $3,000 to $6,000 are commonplace in the East." Bethlehem Steel, and several other top teams, were buying up the best players, playing regularly, and drawing crowds approaching ten thousand fans to see late-round cup games and competitions on holidays involving rivalries.

American teams, for the first time, also made three respectable tours abroad. In 1916, Thomas Cahill led a team of "All-American" all-stars (semi-professionals cobbled together from several teams) during a summer tour in Sweden, actually beating the Swedes 3–2, in Stockholm. It was the first roster of men who could call themselves a legitimate USMNT. According to David Wangerin, "The American team proved up to the task: playing before crowds as large as 20,000, it lost only one match of six. Cahill returned to New Jersey weighted down by medals, trophies, and tributes—and utterly convinced of the game's future in America." In 1919, with Cahill once again at the helm, a cohort of players from Bethlehem Steel Football Club toured Sweden and Denmark. And in 1920, Cahill assembled a team entirely of American-born players, mostly St. Louisans. Their Scandinavian tour resulted in seven wins, five ties, and two losses.*

The USFA entered the 1920s cautiously optimistic—with its main rival gone, WWI over, and only baseball firmly entrenched as a professional sport. A new professional league emerged in the early Twenties during a span of time some writers call the "Golden Age of American soccer." While many of the best players would go on to make a respectable wage to play soccer, historians note that a number of players on each team were either unpaid or compensated only partially for playing, often receiving bonuses or stipends from the companies backing their clubs. Nevertheless, as the next three chapters will show, the league was a remarkable—if short-lived—success story. For about a decade, the Yanks were on course to become a world soccer powerhouse.

* The Society for American Soccer History (SASH) website hosts dozens of clips of historical American soccer footage, including clips from some of these European tours, among them the earliest known footage of elite men's American soccer.

6

★★★★★

THE RISE OF AMERICA'S FIRST GENUINE PROFESSIONAL SOCCER LEAGUE

Businesses ignite the Golden Age of American soccer (1920–1925)

"The chief business of the American people is business."

— Calvin Coolidge

The U.S. declared war on Germany in April 1917, joining the Allies who had been fighting the Central Powers for over two and a half years. By then, some newly arrived immigrants in American soccer leagues had already returned to Europe to join the fray. In the summer of 1918, American troops—ten thousand per day—landed on the Western Front, mainly in France, as part of the American Expeditionary Forces. With so many heading overseas and resources being marshaled for the war effort, U.S. soccer leagues slowed to a crawl or disbanded.

Soccer followed the troops. Nearly five million Yankee soldiers were mobilized. Along with military equipment—trucks, guns, helmets, gas masks, flamethrowers, ten thousand homing pigeons, and DH-4 Liberty "bombers"—came seven thousand soccer balls. Over the next year and a half, the American National War Work Council delivered several times that number to troops in the trenches. Only baseballs outnumbered soccer balls. Soccer was easier to play than baseball and safer than gridiron, which needed more gear and caused injuries.

American soldiers embraced the game. In a story for the military publication *Going Over*, Thomas Rice suggested that "when peace is declared, the world will be filled with wanderers from the [Allied] armies, adventuring in the far corners of the earth, and they will carry with them soccer as well as baseball. Soccer will experience an enormous boom in the United States." Rice was right about the latter. Thomas Cahill, still serving as Secretary of the USFA, concurred: "There will be a tremendous growth in soccer popularity, and it behooves those of us who are left behind to keep the game and its organization in such shape that the returning heroes will find their opportunity for indulgence in the game ready for them."

WWI ended in 1918 on the "eleventh hour of the eleventh day of the eleventh month," later Armistice Day, now Veterans Day. Over 116,000 Americans died, many of them immigrants or their sons. Returning soldiers were welcomed with parades and celebrations, tempered by the Eighteenth Amendment (1919) prohibiting alcohol. Six months later came the Nineteenth Amendment (1920) granting women the right to vote. America entered the Roaring Twenties—a decade of prosperity for some, dissipation for others—marked by optimism, technological progress, and new freedoms.

During the Teens, soccer started expanding with lots of help from American businesses of all types. The support continued after the war. Companies were not altruistic. They were motivated by robust sales in their sector, changing state laws, and a desire to avoid labor strife. Company owners formed soccer teams all along the Four Corridors and helped the game spread westward: The Fisk Rubber Company (Chicopee Falls, MA—tires); Hendee Manufacturing (Springfield, MA—motorcycles, such as "the Indian"); American Writing Paper Company (Holyoke, MA—paper);

Robins Dry Dock (Brooklyn, NY—marine sales and repair outfit); General Electric (Schenectady, NY—"everything electric"); Bethlehem Steel Company (steel); Beadling Mine (Pittsburgh, PA—coal); Goodyear Tire & Rubber Company (Akron, OH—tires); Packard Motor Car Company (Detroit, MI—"Twin Six" automobiles); Pullman Company (Chicago, IL—railway cars); Scullin Steel (St. Louis, MO—more steel!); and the Ben Miller Hat Company (also from St. Louis—hats, backed by nifty advertising slogans, such as "Ben Miller wants your head!"). Some of these companies were growing exponentially. In 1916, Goodyear was the world's largest tire manufacturing company, boasting that "more people ride on Goodyear tires than on any other kind." Curiously, Goodyear, the company, was named after but not founded by Charles Goodyear of New Haven, Connecticut, who had patented vulcanized rubber in 1844. Charles's round rubber ball, displayed at the 1855 Paris World's Fair, marked a major step toward ball uniformity—making America the birthplace of the first modern footballs.

Soccer rode the business boom into more fertile fields.

The newcomers to the soccer ranks spiced up the newspaper reports and the box scores (*e.g.*, Robbins Dry Dock versus Bethlehem Steel, or Packard FC versus the Ben Millers). By 1919, attendance at a few competitions involving established teams had bounced back to prewar numbers and had even increased for contests involving top rivals and late-round cup games. Bethlehem Steel's fifth straight Challenge Cup final appearance, in 1919, against Paterson FC, was watched by more than 9,000 fans in Fall River, Massachusetts (a neutral field!). A year later, more than 12,000 assembled at a St. Louis baseball park to watch the Challenge Cup final between local side Ben Millers and Fore River FC, from southern Boston.* The Fore River squad had traveled more than 1,000 miles inland by train. It was not an

---

* American soccer's roots grew from the very soil that produced some of America's finest products and companies. In 1884, Thomas Watson—former assistant to Alexander Graham Bell, the telephone's inventor—founded the Fore River Shipyard, which led to the creation of Fore River FC. Boatbuilders, including some who doubled as soccer players, built some of the world's most sophisticated ships, and entertained, with their feet, Boston and Quincy residents until the mid-1920s.

easy journey for any East Coast team to get to St. Louis, nor for a St. Louis team to get to any venue in the Four Corridors.

The Ben Millers that year—composed of all players born and raised in St. Louis—beat Fore River, establishing three "firsts": the first time a "national" cup had been won by a team not from the Four Corridors; the first time a major soccer cup anywhere on earth had been won by a roster (to a man) of American-born citizens; and the first time a major championship in any sport had been won by a team sponsored by a hat company ("Get under one of Ben Miller's hats"). For several more years, the Hatters were a force to be reckoned with, while St. Louis, for decades to come, churned out some of America's best native-born players.

True, attendance numbers inching past ten thousand for soccer games were the exception. Only college gridiron football (which could not yet be privately monetized) and Major League Baseball (MLB), by then organized under the National and American Leagues (totaling sixteen teams), were drawing more fans. But even the baseball numbers ran the gamut. Between 1919 and 1922, only five MLB teams were drawing more than ten thousand fans on average per game—topped by the New York Yankees (Babe Ruth effect) and the New York Giants. At the bottom of the order, about five teams per year were drawing fewer than five thousand per game. Baseball, of course, involved many more games (140–154 per season during these years) at ballparks that sparkled in the summer sun and hummed in the autumn breeze. Baseball, at the time, was king—sure as the crack of Babe Ruth's bat. But gridiron football, basketball, and hockey, at the start of the 1920s, had no track record in any American market. You would not fault the soccer folk for thinking: *Maybe, just maybe, soccer could carve out a respectable professional home on American soil.*

Thomas Cahill (again) was at the epicenter of the formation of the American Soccer League (ASL), which took its first breath on May 7, 1921, in a bar or a conference room at Manhattan's Hotel Astor. (Note the use of the word "Soccer" in the title, the first professional league anywhere in the world to do so.) Hotel Astor was located a few blocks up Broadway from the site of the severed and soon-to-be totally demolished (in 1926) Astor House (which hosted the feuding USFA and ASL contingents prior to the USFA's revised application to FIFA). Unfortunately, Hotel Astor, like the Astor House, no longer exists. The hotel was torn down in 1967. On the site today sits a massive skyscraper called One Astor Plaza. There is no soccer memento of any kind on either Astor site, which birthed the USSF and ASL, or anywhere in NYC, the original headquarters of the AFA, or Newark, New Jersey, which later became the organization's primary hub from the mid-1890s to the mid-1920s. In contrast, on the exterior wall of a luxury hotel along Great Queen Street, London—the site of the former Freemasons' Tavern and birthplace of the English FA and the Laws of the Game—there is a beautifully engraved commemorative plaque.

During the summer of 1921, Cahill jumped from Secretary of the USFA to Secretary of the newly minted ASL. This was not a financial risk, as his USFA secretarial work was essentially volunteer, though he occasionally earned stipends and honorariums. Cahill's work ethic, toughness, and cheerfulness impressed many, but his strident, bellicose nature undercut relationships and slowed progress. His nickname, "Bullets," could go either way. A recently unearthed St. Louis newspaper article suggests Cahill earned it from a near-fatal encounter with his father-in-law in 1900 during a domestic squabble. Cahill was shot several times but still managed to push his father-in-law down the steps, breaking two of his ribs. Both survived. Cahill's wife, Mary, left Thomas, leading to a custody battle, though they later reconciled. Unsurprisingly, the combative Cahill (perhaps an unrepentant and relentless bully, according to some historians) and the more diplomatic Gus Manning—USFA's main executives in its first decade—clashed over various issues from the start of their professional relationship.

Manning patterned the USFA on the genteel English model, looked to the English FA as an exemplar, and perhaps took directions from them and obeyed their orders. Manning appeared to dislike Cahill's independence, which was maintained by A.G. Spalding & Brothers and its financial interest in spreading the sporting goods company's soccer-related products throughout America—with Cahill's help. Spalding even provided an office for the USFA among the company's offices along Nassau Street in Manhattan. Cahill, for his part, disliked Manning's cozy relationship with the English FA, and instead tried to push the USFA down an American path, which was yet to be agreed upon, let alone developed.

In May of 1921, Cahill seized the opportunity to help establish a professional league and delighted in rounding up backers. According to an article in the *Philadelphia Public Ledger*, investors in the new ASL "were anxious to impress upon [the public] the wonders of soccer, for they hold the belief that game, properly conducted, is the entering wedge of a movement that will soon put soccer in the forefront of American sports." League play began in September 1921 and involved eight teams from soccer's Four Corridors (moving roughly up the coast): Philadelphia Field Club (really Bethlehem Steel), Harrison SC (Harrison, NJ), Jersey City Celtics (Jersey City, NJ), New York FC (NYC), Todd Shipyards FC (Brooklyn, NY), J&P Coats FC (Pawtucket, RI), Fall River United (Fall River, MA), and Holyoke Falco FC (Holyoke, MA). The league required each team to play in adequate facilities, post a $500 appearance bond, publish weekly notices, and show up on time (and with a full roster)—essentially the basic building blocks of any emergent professional league.

The schedule consisted of twenty-eight games, or four games against each of the seven other opponents. David Wangerin observed: "The ASL kept its clubs occupied every weekend from late summer to late spring, often with back-to-back games on Saturday and Sunday. The only exception it was prepared to make—as it might, with Cahill at the helm—was for the Challenge Cup, which retained its status as the official national championship." The arduous league schedule (through the winter) combined with the Challenge Cup fixtures (also through much of the winter, with entry fees and gate receipts flowing primarily to the USFA) would soon become a serious fault line between the ASL and USFA. In any event, the ASL's inaugural season was not a "top bins" success story.*

The first casualty was the well-heeled Bethlehem Steel Football Club (*a.k.a.* Bethlehem, Steelworkers, Steelmen), which didn't make the opening whistle. Less affluent teams said they would not share gate receipts with away teams (the gate being the primary way to make money) and convinced the league to back their plan. The Steelworkers, who were situated in a company-built stadium in a blue-collar town about two hours north (by early-model car) of Philadelphia, never enjoyed much home fan support despite its monstrous success from its founding in 1907† up through its folding in late 1930 (ultimately winning five Challenge Cups, six AFA Cups, and eight league championships spanning the NAFBL and the ASL).

The Steelmen were owned and generously financed by the Bethlehem Steel Corporation, with owner Charles Schwab the biggest corporate soccer benefactor of the day. Schwab and his corporate team never wavered in their desire to assemble the best soccer team on American soil, paying handsomely for the best players they could find in America and pluck from Scotland and England. At the launch of the ASL, the Steelmen demanded a share of the away gate receipts. When the league failed to act, Bethlehem withdrew before the first match, perhaps more out of spite than money. After a decade of churning out massive steel H-beams (a risky bet on an unfamiliar product at the time) that found their way into the Empire State Building, Chrysler Building, Golden Gate Bridge, and Hoover Dam—and tons of steel for boats, cars (and more cars!), and machinery for WWI—the Bethlehem Steel Corporation, by 1922, had become the second largest steel manufacturer in America. The contested gate receipts from an untested

* "Top bins" is soccer slang for a shot that goes into the top corner of the net, just under the crossbar, often near the post, and out of the goalkeeper's reach—a difficult, impressive shot.

† Founded in 1907 with modest support from Bethlehem Steel Company, the team (known then as Bethlehem Soccer Club) gained stronger company backing in 1914, and by 1915 was officially known as Bethlehem Steel Football Club.

multiregional league may not have made much difference to the company's steely bottom line.

The Steelworkers' replacement, Holyoke Falco FC, stumbled through the first season, winning only two games. The Jersey City Celtics folded after five games mainly because its baseball sponsor reneged on its promise to let the soccer team use its park. Several teams did not play the last game or two of the season (once their standing in the league table was locked or irrelevant), a money-saving tactic that plagued the league for years to come. Attendance was generally poor, ranging from low-to-mid triple digits at most games to a few thousand at the best matches. Holyoke Falco FC and Todd Shipyards FC finished the season but said they would not return.

Probably the only success that first year flowed to the team that needed it the least. Philadelphia FC—its franchise purchased a few weeks before the start of the season by a Bethlehem Steel Corporation executive and his brother, who installed virtually the same Steel roster—won the title by five points. Everyone lost money, including Philadelphia FC, which one Philadelphia paper claimed had lost $10,000, probably due to the added cost of ferrying its players between Philadelphia (site of its home games) and Bethlehem, where most of its athletes lived. Cahill, ever the soccer salesman, put some spin on it: "[T]his season, there has been more soccer news printed in New York papers than the entire preceding three years." Soon "every American boy" will be playing soccer "from the time he is able to toddle."

After its inglorious inaugural season, professional soccer could have sunk once again to the relative obscurity of semiprofessional teams in fractured leagues. But it was rescued by Americans and immigrant entrepreneurs who capitalized on booming business in certain industries, lax immigration rules (that would be markedly tightened as the decade wore on), and the age-old desire to beat the competition. For the 1922–1923 season, Bethlehem Steel was restored to its proper home in Bethlehem (a league-wide agreement that away teams would enjoy 20 percent of the gate cooled the Steelmen). The Brooklyn Wanderers were added after receiving an influx of cash (and on-field player help) from a Sheffield-born accountant named Nat Agar. And a restructured Fall River FC (combining Fall River United and Fall River Rovers) arrived on the American scene in a big way, bankrolled by Sam Mark, whose patronage would soon be rewarded by numerous fans and plenty of wins.

Mark built a 15,000-seat stadium for "the Marksmen" (as they would soon be called) and situated it just across the Massachusetts state line and into Rhode Island to escape the Bay State's "blue laws" that prohibited for-profit games and large assemblies on Sundays. "Many regard Mark's stadium [in Tiverton, RI] as the first soccer-specific facility of any consequence to be built in America," opines Wangerin—though that honor should probably go to the Bethlehem Steel Athletic Field, unveiled in 1913, which was built and used primarily for soccer. Mark's addition to the American soccer landscape must have delighted Cahill, who urged, "We need permanent fields and stands of high grade to show our desire to care for spectators and to prove we are a permanent sport in the United States."

Mark wasted no time luring Bethlehem Steel's best player to Rhode Island and adding quality players from Scotland and Canada, and summarily finished the ASL's second season in third place. The following year, in 1924, the Marksmen won the ASL title and the Challenge Cup (the first team to accomplish the double). According to Wangerin:

> The torch was passed [from the Steelmen to the Marksmen] at an epic semifinal between the two clubs in Brooklyn [a neutral ground!], when about 20,000* shoe-horned themselves into tiny Dexter Park to witness the Marksmen surprise 2–0 victory. The final in St. Louis attracted 14,000 to another baseball park, where Fall River beat the local Vesper-Buick club with a defense 'as strong as the proverbial rock of Gibraltar,' in the eyes of *The New York Times*. Fred Morley, a striker with Football league experiences at Blackpool and Brentford, scored twice in a 4–2 win.

* This figure is not cited and is contested by some historians. Independent research cannot corroborate the attendance.

The Marksmen won the ASL three years in a row (1924–1926). They would go on to win the league six out of eleven years (the 1929–1930 season was abandoned with Fall River FC leading); the Challenge Cup a total of five times (their last win, in 1932, was under the New Bedford Whalers banner, but utilized mostly Marksmen, with Sam still at the helm); and the treble in 1930 (ASL title, Challenge Cup, and the Lewis Cup*). These accomplishments elevated Fall River FC to the dynastic status enjoyed only by Bethlehem Steel. Both clubs would sit alone atop Mount Rushmore until the arrival of the North American Soccer League (NASL) and the pulsating five-title run of the New York Cosmos. By the mid-Twenties, many ASL team owners were making money and were looking to expand.

* The Lewis Cup is described in the next chapter.

7

★★★★★

THE GOLDEN AGE OF AMERICAN SOCCER

Growing pains and boom years of the American Soccer League (1924–1929)

"I started soccer in America, and here is where I'll stay."

— Archie Stark, the greatest American goal scorer in the twentieth century

During the 1924–1925 (fourth) season, membership in the ASL increased from eight to twelve teams. The league welcomed Boston SC and the "Wonder Workers," funded by A. G. Wood, President of the Mystic Steamship Company; the New Bedford Whalers, supported by the southern Massachusetts port city known for whaling during the first half of the 1800s and the setting of Herman Melville's 1850 novel, *Moby Dick*; Indiana Flooring, of New York City (really), whose franchise would soon don new names such as the New York Nationals (soccer) and then New York Giants (soccer); Providence FC, from Rhode Island; the short-lived Fleisher Yarn, out of Philadelphia; and the rebranded but perpetually mediocre Newark Skeeters, named after the interminable mosquitoes issuing from the swamps of New Jersey. Thankfully, for several years to come, the fans probably outnumbered the mosquitoes at the various ASL venues along the Four Corridors.

Rivalries and competitive matches were consistently drawing over ten thousand fans. By 1925, the so-called Golden Age of American soccer was in full swing. ASL team owners (businessmen first, soccer lovers probably a distant second), with the help of baseball men, some of the disreputable variety, looked to the baseball model for inspiration—and baseball was ruled by the owners, not some administrative body like the USFA. One baseball man, Charles Stoneham, owner of the New York Giants (and owner, in succession, of all three New York soccer clubs just named), took an outsized role in ASL soccer decisions to come.

Throughout the Twenties, Stoneham oversaw the baseball Giants, dabbled in soccer, and weathered a score of legal battles, including charges of theft, fraud, tampering, and providing false testimony regarding his business dealings with, among others, Arnold Rothstein, the notorious organized crime boss who ran numerous illegal gambling operations and was rumored to have fixed the 1919 World Series. Rothstein was a personal friend of Stoneham, and helped him buy the New York Giants baseball club. A baseball biographer described Charles Stoneham as "a shady stock speculator, ethically challenged businessman, criminal court defendant, serial philanderer, quasi-bigamist [and] easily the worst person ever associated with the Giants"—who nevertheless oversaw the most successful baseball years in New York Giants history. Stoneham was charged with many crimes, but beat the tag each time.

Not surprisingly, Stoneham and most of the other ASL owners disliked the USFA and its Challenge Cup, which disrupted the ASL schedule, and often required ASL teams to travel long distances to play mediocre early-round competition in front of paltry crowds, only to earn nominal gate receipts that barely covered travel expenses. Worse, ASL teams had to return (or travel again) to their ASL matches, often exhausted. Meanwhile, and for over a decade, the USFA had been raking in virtually all the profits from Challenge Cup entry fees and taking a hefty cut of gate receipts from sometimes over thirty major cup games per year, which, by 1921, were growing in popularity in no small part because of ASL teams and talent. It was not a sustainable arrangement.

In August 1924, the ASL told the USFA that ASL clubs would not compete in its Challenge Cup. That year, the ASL hooked up with the St. Louis Soccer League (SLSL), which had long been doing soccer things their own way. Both boycotted the Challenge Cup and instead created the U.S. Professional Cup (also called the "Professional Soccer Championship"). The newly minted tournament required each league to put forth its own winner from an internal competition to compete in the championship, which occurred in the spring of 1925.

Flash-forward to each cup's championship. In the now anemic Challenge Cup, the Shawsheen Indians (based in Andover, MA, and supported by the makers of woolen fabrics) beat Abbot Worsted (Forge Village, MA, carpet yarns) in Sam Mark's near-empty stadium: About 2,500 fans witnessed the final, down from 18,000 the previous year. Over in the brand-new U.S. Professional Cup, the ASL's Boston SC (the Wonder Workers) defeated the SLSL's Ben Millers (the Hatters) in a three-game series that averaged 6,000 fans per match. After this one-year experiment, the USFA capitulated and agreed to reduce its Challenge Cup gate cut from 33.3 percent to 15 percent, which provided suitable financial incentive to the fully professional and seasoned semiprofessional teams in the competition (at least for a while). The cup mutiny was called off. The U.S. Professional Cup was abandoned and the teams in the ASL/SLSL rejoined the Challenge Cup.

Although ASL teams returned to the Challenge Cup series (at least for several more years, before Stoneham demanded another boycott), the ASL decided to offer its own cup, starting in the 1925–1926 season. The Lewis Cup, as it would soon be called, was named after the trophy's donor, Edgar Lewis, Bethlehem Steel Corporation's vice president and proto-athletic director of the Steelworkers. The trophy was awarded from 1915 to 1919 to the winner of the amateur Blue Mountain League located in the Lehigh Valley area of Pennsylvania, whose champion was always (no surprise) the Steelmen. After the U.S. joined WWI in earnest, Lewis put the trophy into storage—and then dug it out and used it during the boycott year (for the U.S. Professional Cup) and then donated it to the ASL.

The ASL ran the Lewis Cup for its ASL teams for five seasons, up until 1930, when the Cup was put back into storage. The Cup was unveiled again in the early 1940s (behind the war effort) and made a steady annual run through 1963. Over the decades, differing bracket formats were used (usually divided into two divisions), and sometimes the Lewis Cup was open to teams outside the ASL. The 1963 winner, Newark Ukrainian Stitch, after beating local rival Philadelphia Ukrainian Nationals, gave the trophy to the Museum of Sports Glory, in Kiev, Ukraine (then *in* Russia). Consequently, no American has handled the Lewis Cup in over half a century. Based on the few surviving photographs, the Lewis Cup stands about two and a half feet tall. It features a square base and a stout, vase-like midsection supporting a shiny globe, roughly the diameter of a size-three soccer ball.

Although hard to judge, the standard of play in the ASL by 1925—at least among the top teams—rivaled the best in any league worldwide. This is not to say the ASL had the best players or was one of the world's top leagues. But the league was trending in that direction. Recruitment efforts stretched all the way to Europe. Though rosters already included first- and second-generation Americans and recent immigrants, ASL owners who could afford it began luring prime players from across the pond. Sometimes they sent telegrams outlining favorable terms; other times representatives appeared at players' homes or local fields with hefty offers. This talent migration was eased by long-standing U.S. connections, as Scottish and English workers and their families were already numerous where the ASL operated.

For the 1924–1925 season, the Wonder Workers snagged Scottish international winger Tommy Muirhead, of Glasgow Rangers, as player-coach, who recruited other top Scottish players to join him. For instance, Alex McNab, active Scottish national team member, who was earning about four pounds a week for first-division Greenock Morton, received a cable from Muirhead's bosses offering him twelve pounds a week and a passage on a transatlantic ship. He was interviewed in transit, and acknowledged: "I jumped at it. Booked my passage. Made no secret about where I was going. And here I am."

Some international players forfeited offseason factory wages, which were considered a gentleman's agreement to play the upcoming year, or flat-out broke their soccer contracts, leaving for teams in the U.S. that were paying two to three times more. "Hundreds of players crossed the Atlantic," according to Colin Jose. "Some, like McNab, made America their home. Others played in the American Soccer League for several years and then returned to Europe." An Irish newspaper observed that "scores of crack footballers" took up positions at American clubs whose owners exhibited no respect for foreign contracts. Some American owners and managers also showed no respect for foreign players (and their families). After several games on American soil, some foreign players who were apparently not up to snuff were dropped, or literally abandoned at railway stations or hotels.

It was not long before the poaching of talent—really, the breaking of contracts—provoked the ire of European clubs and press. British newspapers called it "the American Menace." Some leagues and federations threatened to ban players who hoped to return to their home countries someday. But there was little they could do to prevent a footballer and his family from migrating to America in search of significantly higher wages. In 1927, several European football associations appealed to FIFA to have the U.S. expelled. The threat of being ousted by FIFA, which at that time was not the powerhouse it is today (it had yet to stage its first World Cup), did not have the desired effect on the ASL owners. The league was loath to take direction from the USFA, let alone some foreign soccer syndicate a quarter of the way around the world. The looming crisis was averted when the USFA sent a representative to a FIFA meetup in Finland (FIFA's home at the time was Paris; it wouldn't move to Zurich until 1932) to make amends.

There, after conversations involving larger issues, FIFA strengthened its own regulations regarding contractual obligations and player movement, and the Americans independently made peace with the English and Scottish FAs "to respect each other's registrations and suspensions."

But the Yanks' rookie ASL scared the Brits. For about five years, in the mid- to late-1920s, the European talent drain (especially from the U.K.) and subsequent exasperated responses from foreign clubs and football associations—which had never paid any attention to soccer in the United States (unless to engage in moneymaking international tours)—were special accomplishments for the young American Soccer League.

During the ASL's ten-year run, most of the rosters were heavy with immigrants and professional players from the Old World, a small number in their prime, many others journeymen, bouncing from team to team. This concerned Cahill and others. In 1925, Cahill opined:

> I believe the promising United States players have been permitted to lie idle and go to seed while the foreign player has reaped a harvest . . . The country owes a great deal to the Old Country pioneers who brought the game across and kept it alive during its early days. We need their good players, and their presence in a minor proportion on all clubs is highly desirable. [But] at the present time it is almost impossible outside of St. Louis to assemble an eleven first-class, home-grown soccer football talent.

But Americans on average populated about half of each roster (and maybe even more if you discounted the Steelmen's heavy foreign roster), and some were excellent players who could impress in most leagues around the world. The top three goal scorers, overall, during the league's existence were Americans, with Archie Stark, the best American football player of his era and possibly the greatest American goal-scoring forward in the twentieth century, at the very top.* He scored 260 goals (an average of twenty-six

* According to league statistics compiled by Colin Jose in his wonderfully meticulous and data-driven book *The American Soccer League, 1921–1931: The Golden Years of American Soccer*, the top three leading ASL scorers of all-time were Americans Archie Stark (253), Johnny Nelson (223), and David Brown (189).

goals per year, for a decade!) during his ASL career, which mirrored the life of the league, outclassing his ASL peers of any nationality.

Stark was born in Scotland in 1897 and immigrated to the U.S. when he was thirteen years old. He began his adult soccer career with the Kearny Scots-Americans, where he scored the winning goal—a few months after his seventeenth birthday—in the 1915 AFA Cup final. Archie and his brother Tommy (a midfielder) also played a major role in the Scots-Americans Challenge Cup run that year, falling in the quarterfinals to eventual winners Bethlehem Steel. The following season, the Starks switched to Babcock and Wilcox (maker of steam boilers) in nearby Bayonne, New Jersey, helping them reach the semifinals of the AFA Cup in 1918, before WWI interrupted. Archie spent two years in the U.S. Army with the 77th Division, one of the largest, known as the Liberty Division. After the war, he resumed his career with Erie Athletic Association (NJ), then Paterson FC (NJ), before moving to New York FC for the ASL's inaugural 1921–1922 season. There, on the cusp of his twenty-second birthday, and finally a full professional in a legitimate professional league, he was the leading goal scorer for New York FC and helped them to a second place finish out of eight teams. For the club's 1923–1924 campaign, he was the leading goal scorer in the ASL, notching twenty-one goals.

For the 1924–1925 season, Archie was recruited to the ASL's Bethlehem Steel where he amassed a single-season scoring record that is hard to believe. During his first game in Steelworker colors, he registered four goals in a 7–1 thumping of Philadelphia FC, earning accolades from *The Bethlehem Globe-Times** who called him "a prime favorite." That year he scored a whopping sixty-seven goals in forty-four league games and added three more in the short-lived one-year U.S. Professional Cup. His achievement was all the more remarkable in that it came in the last season before the offside rule was changed to mitigate the stifling defensive tactics that

* In October 1925, *The Bethlehem Times* merged with a local rival to become *The Bethlehem Globe-Times*.

developed in Britain, a move that immediately produced a deluge of goals in leagues around the world, until teams adjusted.*

The sixty-seven goals he scored for Bethlehem Steel has never been threatened as the single-season record in American first-division professional soccer. He scored *eight* hat tricks during the campaign. To put it another way, Archie's final haul that season is thirty-two more goals than the *average* of the other ten years' worth of ASL leading goal scorers' tallies. Only David Brown (another American) came close, netting fifty-two goals for the New York Giants in 1926–1927. Stark's feat is a wonder and a statistical outlier.

On November 8, 1925, Stark suited up for the USMNT and scored five goals in the second half against Canada during a friendly game that resulted in a 6–1† Yankee romp at Ebbets Field in Brooklyn. A *New York Times* reporter noted that Stark's performance "was as brilliant a bit of individuality as was ever seen on an American soccer field." His five-goal

* The evolution of the offside rules, including the tweaks to the rules in the world of the video assistant referee (VAR), could fill a book. Between 1863 and 1925, referees officiating under the rules established by the English FA and, later, the International Football Association Board (IFAB), judged an advancing attacker to be in an offside position if, at the moment the ball was played in his direction, he stood closer to the other team's goal line than three defenders (typically two field players and the goalie). I have yet to meet a soccer historian of any nationality who has adequately explained how it was possible to accurately and fairly apply this three-defender rule with the naked eye—or even with three sets of eyes. Starting in 1881, in England, a central authority figure migrated from the sideline to the actual field of play to become the *center referee* or just plain *referee*. The roaming referee was then assisted by two *umpires*, who stayed on the sideline. The umpires eventually became known as *linesmen* or *assistant referees*, and their primary duty was to run up and down the sideline, equal with the ball, and help the center referee with offside decisions and fouls committed in their vicinity. The offside rules prevent an offensive player from camping out in front of the goal and waiting for a teammate to boot him the ball. Thus, the offside rules encourage fluid play and competitive movements (on and off the ball) from both teams. Other than banning a field player from using his hands, the bundle of offside rules is probably the single most important principle spurring the beautiful game—and fomenting endless debate.

† When stating the final score of an MNT game in this book, the U.S. score will *always be listed first*, regardless of the final score. This convention will appear more frequently in later chapters, especially as we enter the modern era, which I subjectively define as starting in the late 1980s.

sum has never been tied, let alone bested.* It was his second and final cap† for the U.S. Writers of the day observed that Stark "is a great opportunist and given the slightest chance will slip by a defender like an eel," and a player of "wonderful aggressiveness and great speed, together with a natural cleverness which is dazzling." Archie was a winner on every pitch and made every team he played for a contender. Ed Sullivan called him "the Babe Ruth of Soccer," a term that would be applied to other Americans. But Stark was the first. He reportedly turned down overtures from Newcastle United, in England, and other foreign professional teams. "I started soccer here in America," Archie asserted, "and here is where I'll stay." It can be argued that in 1925 he was one of the best footballers on the planet.

Stark was not the only striking success story of the day. In 1926, Hakoah Vienna, the champion of the 1925 Austrian league, embarked on a summer tour of the U.S., drawing unprecedented crowds: 15,000 in Chicago, 25,000 in Philadelphia, 22,000 at Brooklyn's Ebbets Field, and 46,000 at Upper Manhattan's Polo Grounds. In the latter game, the Hakoahs played a Manhattan-based ASL all-star team that was a combination of New York Giants and Indiana Flooring players. The NYC contingent won 3–1. The 46,000 was a record audience "by a yawning margin" for soccer on American

* Some historians claim that Stark scored four goals in this match, or even three, based on several contemporaneous newspaper reports. However, the five-goal tally is clearly described in a November 9th (day after the game) *New York Times* article by Richards Vidmer, a well-known sportswriter. Vidmer's ten-paragraph article takes up nearly an entire column, and it reads like a firsthand account of the game. The article also includes a massive heading, across the entire page, that highlights "Stark's Five Goals." Vidmer's observations were seconded by an article in the *Passaic Daily News* published on the same day that also reads like an eyewitness account. (Passaic, New Jersey, is located about seventeen miles from the site of the international friendly.) However, about a dozen other contemporary unsigned newspaper blurbs state that Stark scored (only!) four goals. Even with digitization, historians face considerable difficulty sifting through documents more than a century old—especially when different reports, sometimes even from the same city or town, state conflicting facts.

† In soccer parlance, a *cap* is earned each time a player suits up and plays (for any amount of time in the game) for his senior national team in any official international match. The term comes from the practice, started by the English FA in 1886, of awarding a physical cap to a player for each international appearance.

soil that would stand for half a century. Over the next five years, teams from England, Scotland, Czechoslovakia, Hungary, Italy, Spain, Argentina, and elsewhere around the globe all kicked a ball on American soil in front of adoring crowds, albeit rarely in front of five-figure audiences. But the big names, such as AC Sparta Prague (1926), Rangers FC (1928 and 1930), and Celtic FC (1931), all drew more than 25,000 people.

The Hakoah's numbers didn't correlate directly to soccer interest. According to Wangerin, "Jews who had become fans of 'American' sports still lacked Jewish idols," and the Hakoah ("the strength" or "the power" in Hebrew) had "tapped into the collective consciousness of a heterogeneous ethnic group." Hakoah Vienna returned the next summer, but that would be it. During their two summer tours of America, nearly the whole squad was poached and paid to stay in the ASL. What started as an awakening and a prideful celebration for an ethnic group turning out in great numbers continued with purposeful assimilation into America's heterogeneous religious and ethnic groups. Pity that such assimilation and growth in the ASL, and swelling interest in good soccer in the Four Corridors, had already reached its peak and was about to experience a dramatic downturn—the result of a one-two punch known as "the American soccer war" and the Great Depression.

8

★★★★★

THE FALL OF THE AMERICAN SOCCER LEAGUE

The bust years (1929–1935)

"Greatness lives in one who triumphs equally over defeat and victory."

— John Steinbeck, *The Acts of King Arthur and His Noble Knights*

Newspapers in soccer's Four Corridors (at the time) and soccer historians (thereafter) called what happened in 1928–1929 the "American soccer war." But this term is a misnomer.* The Yanks, at the tail end of the Twenties, didn't just shoot each other in the foot and then take the gun and turn it on the ball. The ASL's precipitous decline was due to a one-two punch. The first was a nasty uppercut to the chin stemming from a long-simmering disagreement between the ASL and USFA (thus, a self-inflicted blow) that boiled over in the early fall of 1928, causing disagreements and disarray; a rival start-up league; defections, accusations, and

* The American soccer war should not be confused with the 1969 "Soccer War" between Honduras and El Salvador. Sparked by stadium violence during World Cup qualifiers, the one-hundred-hour conflict stemmed from deeper tensions over land, immigration, and nationalism, and left more than three thousand dead, mostly civilians.

lawsuits; and tepid reunification a year later. Then, only a few short weeks after reunification, a knockout punch, in 1929, by the Great Depression, which went to the wallet of American soccer's ownership group and the very heart of America's working-class fan base.

Here comes the roller-coaster ride, so hold on. In the early fall of 1928 and at the start of the new season, the ASL commenced the battle by asking the USFA to move its Challenge Cup out of the ASL two-part season, which was impractical from the USFA's perspective. Further, even if the USFA had agreed to move its Cup, there was no agreement in place that the ASL's teams would enter. The USFA refused to move its Cup. ASL leadership then unilaterally announced that its clubs would not be competing in the Challenge Cup and ordered all ASL franchises to immediately withdraw their applications or not apply. When three ASL clubs (Bethlehem Steel, New Jersey Skeeters, and the New York Giants*) refused, the ASL, on September 24, 1928, fined them $1,000 apiece and summarily suspended them from the league—a vicious and crippling blow to a trio that had long been loyal and important to the ASL, especially the Steelmen. The USFA ordered the ASL to reinstate the three, but Stoneham's ASL leadership refused.

Our soccer Federation, furious, revoked the ASL's membership and branded it an "outlaw league." The ASL went ahead with its schedule and tournaments, not fearing a work-stoppage order from an administrative body. It soon became clear that the ASL desired complete autonomy, underscored by a rumor and then an announcement that it intended to apply to FIFA to govern all of American soccer.

The USFA threw what weight it had behind the three jettisoned teams and a group of five semipro teams from southern New York (that included a new Hakoah All-Stars team) and helped the coterie of eight form a rival league calling itself the Eastern Professional Soccer League (EPSL). Bethlehem Steel was probably the vanguard of this endeavor—the Steelworkers were still smarting from the ASL's decision, the year prior, to disqualify

* Not Charles Stoneham's Giants, yet. Stoneham's New York Nationals would have to wait another season for the New York Giants soccer name to become available, and then Stoneham bought it.

them from the ASL championship bracket at the end of the two-part season for supposedly using an illegal player. It didn't help that the ASL office was located in Boston at the time, and the ASL president was a writer for a Boston newspaper. Additionally, the two teams in the 1928 ASL final were both from Massachusetts.

The Steelworkers had a list of other grievances. "The invasions of the New England states are far too expensive"; "several [ASL] clubs have entirely too much influence directing the operation of the league"; and the failure of Fall River FC to pay the Bethlehem club for a recent player transfer. The Steelmen, through the mouthpiece of the local *Bethlehem Globe-Times* newspaper, threw their support behind the creation of a "new circuit" with all of "the New England clubs eliminated."

This major break unfortunately occurred on Cahill's watch. Since 1921, he had bounced between administrative roles within both organizations—doing more than any other individual in American history to advance American soccer—but by 1928 he had been officially removed or effectively forced to resign as Secretary of the USFA, only to be reappointed, through a series of unnerving and backstabbing events rivaling a soap opera. Cahill had also been passed over for a variety of national team coaching and managing roles during the Twenties. The jobs seemed to always go to people with lesser résumés but with support even more powerful than Cahill's. Cahill had been quietly planning a rival pro soccer league. So, the EPSL may have gone ahead even if the ASL hadn't caused and then embraced its renegade status.

The break quickly caused a rippling effect that engulfed more than the twenty teams involved in the two rival leagues. The Southern New York State Football Association (SNYFA), seeing some of its better teams defecting to the EPSL, struck back, with Nat Agar's help (owner of the ASL Brooklyn Wanderers club *and* president of the SNYFA), and pulled the SNYFA out of the USFA and tried to link up with the ASL. Emboldened and dug in, both rival pro leagues started their respective seasons in the fall of 1928.

After a few months, some teams in both leagues folded. The remaining teams poached each other's players. Some players, confused about their future, switched on their own accord. Each league tried to poach *teams* from the other. The New Bedford Whalers jumped ship from the ASL to the EPSL; then, after eight games, swam back again, reportedly unhappy with the level of competition in the EPSL. Everyone pointed fingers at everyone else. And a few aggrieved parties filed injunctions and lawsuits, always a sign that disagreements had reached a nadir. It was utter chaos. "As the autumn half of the season lurched to an awkward end," observed David Wangerin, "both factions stridently predicted victory and blamed each other for the conflict everyone agreed was ruining the game." FIFA, by December, hadn't done or solved anything but came out strongly in favor of the USFA. Fan attendance for league games suffered greatly across the board.

But the USFA's Challenge Cup championship (a two-game series that year) was a rip-roaring success even without any ASL representation—as the eastern winners, Hakoah All-Stars, squared off against the western winners, Madison Kennel Club of St. Louis. In Missouri, in front of about 18,000 fans, Madison lost to the Hakoahs, 2–0. Then, back in Brooklyn, in front of an astounding 21,583 fans (in a standing-room only affair), Hakoah brought Madison to heel again, 3–0. The second leg in Brooklyn set the record for the largest crowd to see a Challenge Cup final, and remained the attendance pinnacle until 2010 when Seattle Sounders FC defeated Columbus Crew in front of 31,311 spectators (in the renamed Lamar Hunt U.S. Open Cup). Even amidst the roller-coaster ride and chaos, soccer had sizzle.

In late summer 1929, still reeling from a year of siphoning coins from each other's pockets, both leagues prepared to enter their second full season at loggerheads. A writer from *The Bethlehem Globe-Times* put a positive spin on the Steelmen's preseason workouts: "Stark, Gillespie and others can be seen wearing off the surplus avoirdupois* picked up during the sum-

* From the Oxford Dictionary: avoirdupois (n), a-vər-də-ˈpȯiz: weight (humorous); heaviness; *e.g.*, "She was putting on avoirdupois like nobody's business."

mer vacation." By early fall, the feuding soccer cohorts—despite Charles Stoneham doing nothing about his own avoirdupois (based on photographs of the time)—seemed to have quelled their pride and proposed a unification plan. On November 4, the merger became reality. Rifts were papered over by a new league called the Atlantic Coast League (a name that lasted one year before reverting to the ASL). Games were to restart posthaste—the so-called one-year American soccer war over. But no one was quite sure what would happen to the fans who had just endured the worst soccer roller-coaster ride of their lives.

The Great Depression's opening whistle cannot be pinpointed. Historians gesture to a large sell-off of stocks beginning in mid-October 1929. On October 24, the American stock market crashed 11 percent by the closing bell. Actions to stabilize the market failed, and on October 28, the market dropped another 12 percent. The panic continued the next day, on Black Tuesday, when the market fell another 11 percent. Tens of thousands of investors were ruined over the four-day crash, and billions of dollars were lost. Many stocks dwindled to almost nothing. The market recovered 12 percent on Wednesday. But America's investors, industries, and communities, far and wide, poor and rich, were in shock, and collectively about to enter uncharted territory. Though the market recovered somewhat over the next six months, it would dive again and enter a prolonged slump. From April 17, 1930, to July 8, 1932, the market lost nearly 90 percent of its value. Millions of people were affected worldwide. Families in the U.S. were probably hit the hardest, with every economic indicator on life support for nearly three years. By 1933, more than a quarter of the national workforce was unemployed, a statistic keenly felt in the soccer enclaves, with their working-class fan bases.

Soccer communities started to crack and crumble, from the top and from below. Sam Mark and his Marksmen—with Tiverton, Rhode Island, struggling and game attendance in a nosedive, and the town of Fall River just across the bay soon to file for bankruptcy—moved to New York City, in

1930, to take on the glowing name New York Yankees (which didn't work, with Manhattan "no better off than anywhere else"). Before the end of the year, Sam abandoned the Yankees and merged the Marksmen with the New Bedford Whalers, one of the few sobriquets not to get sunk since the Whalers entered the league in 1926. By the summer of 1931, with no end in sight to the dismal economic conditions, and according to Wangerin, Sam Mark "turned his back on the game altogether, to spend most of the rest of his life operating nightclubs."

As to the stadium bearing his name, it continued to serve as a football ground for about two decades. Then it turned into a midget-car racetrack, and finally to a drive-in movie theater. As of 2020, clips posted on the internet show a large overgrown weedy plot tucked between a parking lot and an apartment building, where, during the latter half of the Twenties, more than ten thousand people often assembled for soccer games, their cars parked like sardines around the stadium. There is no plaque or memorial anywhere on-site.

Charles Stoneham survived the Depression comfortably enough and died in a hotel in Hot Springs, Arizona, in 1936. But not before selling off all his soccer interests and giving the New York Giants baseball franchise to his son, Horace—who unceremoniously moved the club to San Francisco in 1958 to become the San Francisco Giants. According to writers for the Society of American Baseball Research, Horace was "a major force in bringing major-league baseball to the West Coast." He also "played an essential role in racially integrating the game" by becoming the third owner to sign Black players. He continued to sign Black and Latino players to the Giants at a greater rate than any other major league club, through the 1960s.

On April 16, 1930—at about the same time Sam Mark announced he was moving his Marksmen from Rhode Island to Manhattan—a writer for *The Bethlehem Globe-Times* reported that Bethlehem Steel (the team, that is) would fold at the close of the season. After a twenty-year run of thrilling fans with spectacular football and accumulating more major trophies than any other soccer team in American history, the Steelmen were history. They played their last game on April 27, away, against the Hakoah All-Stars, losing 3–2 in front of about 3,500 fans. The team then disbanded. Many found roster spots on other teams. Some never played professionally again. The original Bethlehem Steel Athletic Field is now Moravian College's Steel Field. Thankfully, near the stadium steps, there is a plaque commemorating the Steelworkers.

Charles Schwab, President of the Bethlehem Steel Corporation, did not immediately follow his team into the abyss. But he, too, was in a death spiral. A man worth about $600 million (in today's money) by the late Twenties saw nearly all of his fortune erased by the crash and aftermath. Before and after the fall, Schwab was seemingly impervious to risk and reality. Schwab died penniless on January 12, 1939. A writer for a *Time* magazine obituary noted that during the Depression "he continued to pay opera singers to sing at parties he gave at Riverside, his French chateau-style mansion [in Manhattan's Upper West Side] that ate up a ton of coal a month in winter [and] employed Archer Gipson as his private organist to play the classics at $10,000 a year." The writer could not imagine what happened to all of Schwab's money, noting that "whatever the reason, Charles Schwab had left no more to his heirs than if he had kept working at the $1-a-day job in which he entered the steel business in 1881."

Only days after the Steelmen stopped playing, and in April 1930, Thomas Cahill resigned as USFA Secretary, took a vacation, and then took up an advisory role as a "field delegate" to "survey the game's wider terrain and kindle interest in the more forlorn parts of the country"—soccer-administration-speak for being put out to pasture. He served for a stint as Secretary of the St. Louis Soccer League, which was struggling like every other league, and then moved on to Florida, where he had been vacationing, and headed a committee to bring top-level soccer to the southeastern U.S. It didn't work. Families and businesses were still struggling. Prohibition ended on December 5, 1933, with the repeal of the Eighteenth Amendment. And giggle water flowed legally again. But there was not much for the Yanks to celebrate in the mid-Thirties.

For the rest of his life, Cahill, ever the optimist, tirelessly touted the possibility of soccer's success on American soil. In 1947, at a USFA meeting at the Pennsylvania Hotel in Manhattan, Cahill, then eighty-three, rose to speak: "I have given everything from my heart and mind to the devotion" of the sport of soccer. In the decades to come, American soccer struggled to recover from the one-two punch of its internal battle and the crippling effects of the Great Depression. But soccer didn't die. It went dormant. Again. Members of our Federation gave Cahill a standing ovation. And so should we—for Thomas Cahill (despite his many flaws) and Archie Stark, and for all the ASL players and fans within the Four Corridors who witnessed and inspired plenty of fantastic soccer for over a decade. We stand on the shoulders and stout legs of the Steelmen, Marksmen, Wonder Workers, Whalers, Giants, Clamdiggers, Wanderers, Coats, Hakoah, Floorers, and Threadmen. And yes, even the Skeeters.

9

★★★★★

YANKS STUMBLE IN EARLY OLYMPIC SOCCER TOURNAMENTS

Olympic-sized blunders for the Yanks while FIFA picks up steam (1905–1930)

"The past is never dead. It's not even past."

— William Faulkner, *Requiem for a Nun*

The U.S. finished third at the inaugural World Cup in 1930 and beat England in the fourth running of the World Cup, in 1950. But we are getting ahead of ourselves (and the ball) again. In 1930, FIFA was a baby, just learning to crawl, with scant money in its coffers and only several quasi-international Olympic soccer tournaments under its swaddle. FIFA (Fédération Internationale de Football Association) was founded in the "rear of the headquarters" (FIFA's phrase) of the Union Française de Sports Athlétiques, in Paris, on May 21, 1904 (where neither a glass of wine nor a piece of cheese was served). FIFA's charter was signed by representatives from seven European countries: France, Belgium, Denmark,

Netherlands, Spain, Sweden, and Switzerland. Germany joined by telegram that same day but is not considered a founding member.

England was invited more than once but declined, snobbishly stating they could "not see the advantages of such a Federation." Since 1883, the Home Nations—England, Scotland, Wales, and Northern Ireland—had been competing in their own "British International Championship" or "British Home Championship" and saw no point in expanding the game to the continent.

The attendees at the first FIFA assembly hammered out agreements, including recognition of each member's national association. Charter members declared that players could play consecutively (though not simultaneously!) for different countries, and that suspensions meted out by one member would be honored by all (a rule hard to enforce, as the USFA and ASL later proved in the 1920s). FIFA was given power to oversee international competitions and settle disputes—with all members following the Laws of the Game established by the Home Nations and their International Football Association Board (IFAB), created in 1886. The IFAB's mission from the start was to protect and disseminate the Laws of the Game. To this day, IFAB remains the sole governing body for modifications, innovations, and clarifications in world football.*

Membership dues in 1904 were fifty French francs, or ten U.S. dollars ($337 today). No one imagined the economic juggernaut FIFA would become. FIFA's original members elected French journalist Robert Guérin as its first President, and he accepted almost apologetically. Guérin had already made two trips to London to cajole the Brits to join FIFA (unsuccessfully)—British membership was deemed vital for an international body representing a game invented in Britain. Guérin later recalled, regarding his recruitment efforts: "It was like cutting water with a knife." England joined in 1905. A year later, Guérin gladly relinquished the presidency to

* Today's IFAB consists of five constituents (the four Home Nations plus FIFA). Each Home Nation (England, Scotland, Wales, and Northern Ireland) has one vote. FIFA, representing its many member associations, holds four votes. To amend the Laws of the Game, decisions must pass by a three-quarters "super" majority—at least six out of eight votes.

Englishman Daniel Woolfall of Lancashire—who first cut his teeth as an accountant and tax inspector for Blackburn, and later served as the English FA's treasurer.

Under Woolfall, FIFA membership grew steadily, especially in Europe. The first overseas members included Argentina and Canada in 1912, and the U.S. and Chile in 1913. Also in 1913, FIFA was named the fifth (and final) IFAB member, which helped spread the Laws of the Game from top-level competitions down to local leagues in countries around the world. The latter took decades.

But for its first twenty-five years, FIFA was not the most powerful force in world football. That honor probably fell to top footballing leaders at the Home Nations and several officials within early European football associations, who worked in parallel (not always cooperatively) with FIFA and the International Olympic Committee (IOC) to host Olympic soccer tournaments every four years. Team sports hadn't featured at the first three Olympic Games (1896, 1900, 1904). A few club teams played friendlies at the 1900 and 1904 Games, but nobody paid them much attention. (The Olympics did not separate into summer and winter competitions until 1924.) In 1908, Woolfall convinced the IOC to permit the English FA to oversee an Olympic tournament in London (substituting for Rome after Mount Vesuvius erupted the year prior), and the Swedish FA in the 1912 tournament in Stockholm. These Olympic soccer tournaments were minor affairs, "regarded with suspicion," "considered a show, not a competition," and supposedly involved all amateurs per the Olympic ethos of the time.

For footballers, this "amateurism" rule would eventually prove impractical. Clubs around the world were paying players "under the table" for decades. Participating Olympic countries had wildly different interpretations of amateurism. And officials from the IOC and FIFA couldn't police the rule even if they wanted to. Separating soccer amateurs from professionals was about as easy to accomplish as sorting waves from particles in quantum mechanics. And the Olympic and FIFA people were no Einsteins. The 1908 London tournament (six teams) and the 1912 Stockholm tournament (eleven teams) witnessed English amateurs defeat Danish amateurs both times. These two Olympic tournaments were probably the only tournaments to include mostly amateur players. WWI wiped out the 1916 Olympics. No official FIFA meetings occurred in the late Teens, and Woolfall died in 1918. FIFA might have cratered if not for Dutchman Carl Hirschman, a volunteer, who kept FIFA afloat from his Amsterdam office during the war years.

The Olympics resumed in 1920, in Antwerp, with Belgium winning gold. England lost to Norway right off the bat. The U.S. failed to even enter—black eyes for Gus Manning and Thomas Cahill, USFA's President and Secretary. By 1920, both had accumulated over a decade of outstanding soccer administrative experience, including orchestrating tours abroad. Cahill claimed, perhaps correctly, that the USFA lacked money to send a team. The 1920 final match drew 35,000 spectators, the largest crowd ever for an Olympic event. But the game was abandoned in the thirty-ninth minute when the Czechs walked off the field to protest the English referee, forfeiting the medal to Belgium, the original Red Devils.* It was the last Olympic soccer tournament officially limited to amateurs.

Jules Rimet took FIFA's reins in 1921, commencing a thirty-three-year tenure that saw FIFA grow from dark horse to global thoroughbred champion. As early as the Paris Olympics in 1924, Rimet was devising plans "to spit" the Olympic "bit" and gallop toward FIFA's own quadrennial tournament. At the Stade Olympique, Rimet and thousands witnessed twenty-two teams in the first Olympic opening ceremony with a parade of athletes and fireworks. But the parade was sans British and Irish footballers, who refused to attend.

For the 1924 Paris games, the IOC and FIFA had weakened their

* The Red Devils of Manchester United officially raised their pitchfork (on their uniforms) in the early Seventies. United's nickname was popularized in the Sixties by their coach Sir Matt Busby, who credited it not to the Belgians but to Manchester's Salford Rugby Club, located right down the road from Old Trafford (Manchester United's stadium since 1910).

amateurs-only rule and devised a way to permit "broken-time payments" to compensate "amateur" players for lost wages in their "day jobs." However, playing against "non-chaste amateurs" (*i.e.*, professionals) continued to be a deal-breaker for the Brits, who denounced the Olympic soccer contests as "shamateurism." They also loathed facing former wartime enemies. For the next twenty-five years, they ignored the Olympics and FIFA, and focused on their annual Home Championship series. The Three Lions finally emerged from their den, a bit anemic from hibernation, for the 1950 World Cup. They beat Chile but lost to the U.S. and Spain. For all the hullabaloo, England has never won a European Championship and has won the World Cup once, in 1966.

The 1924 U.S. Olympic team was amateur to a T, with no ASL professionals. The team was selected by committee, coached by a journalist, trained by a YMCA director, and untested in warm-ups. The players met for the first time on the dock in New York Harbor. Cahill again raised money for the team but was rebuffed for both manager and coach and did not travel to Paris. Two weeks later, the Americans won their first Olympic match against Estonia, but then lost 0–3 to eventual winners Uruguay (*La Celeste*, Spanish for "light blue").

Uruguay, with a flexible definition of amateurism—and much better preparation methods—had spent months in North America facing professional ASL sides. In the Olympic final, watched by over forty thousand people and broadcast around Europe, Uruguay beat Switzerland, 3–0. Nearly one-third of Olympic revenues that summer came from football.

Four years later, in 1928, the Olympic tournament was held in Amsterdam, Netherlands. The English sat out again. The U.S. team, still amateur and poorly managed, was coached by thirty-two-year-old Elmer Schroeder of Philadelphia, who had no top-level coaching experience. Cahill was again passed over for a leadership role. Ill-prepared, the U.S. was thrashed 2–11 by Argentina (*La Albiceleste*, "white and sky blue")—still the worst-ever defeat of a USMNT. Dent McSkimming (who would become known as the dean of U.S. soccer writers) of the *St. Louis Post-Dispatch* summed it up: "Our puny, half-baked outfit was doomed in advance. Until America changes its 'amateur' definition to conform to European standards, we cannot hope to battle on even terms; and the sending of teams to Europe under conditions like the 1928 team is a pure waste of time and money."

In the 1928 final, Uruguay beat Argentina 2–1 in a replay match* before a packed stadium. The Dutch had received over 250,000 ticket requests for a venue that held only 30,000. Radio carried games across Europe. Uruguay would go on to win the first World Cup in 1930 and again in 1950. And without winning additional World Cups, La Celeste continued to rack up stars above their national team crest.†

The 1928 Olympics proved soccer was ready for the world stage. FIFA's World Cup, always for full professionals, debuted in 1930. Every tournament since—except for cancellations in 1942 and 1946 due to WWII—saw FIFA grow by every metric. Under Rimet (1921–1954), FIFA expanded from twelve members to eighty-five. Rimet saw football as "a universal language." His grandson described him as a "humanist and idealist, who believed that sport could unite the world." From the Sixties onward, this sentiment received a lot of help from TV, which fueled the football explosion. Today, FIFA counts 211 member associations. And its quadrennial World Cup breaks global viewing records with each edition.

---

* Replaying the entire game from scratch (with the score reverting to 0–0) was a common way to resolve ties in knockout soccer tournaments since the birth of the English FA Cup in 1871. Replays offered a second chance and potentially benefited smaller clubs through increased revenue from a second match, particularly if the return leg was at the bigger club's grounds (which often resulted in splitting the revenue from gate receipts). Replays eventually died out. Today, the concept of a *replay* is a thing most people do only with their remote control and TV.

† Stars above national team crests on team jerseys refer to World Cup victories. In 2023, after nearly two decades of dispute, FIFA officially allowed Uruguay to display four stars on their national soccer uniform—to symbolize their two World Cup wins (1930, 1950) and two Olympic victories (1924, 1928), the latter eventually recognized as "world championships." Critics note Uruguay used professionals in those Olympics, while other competitive soccer nations of the time, like Austria, Italy, and the U.S., honored the amateur rules, or, like the British Home Nations, didn't participate.

In stark contrast to the steady growth of soccer during the Twenties and Thirties in Europe and South America, the Yanks' interest was plummeting from a high point in 1928, before the American soccer war and the start of the Great Depression. By the mid-Thirties, soccer had again become marginalized. British-American writer Paul Gardner notes that during this period "there were few places where Americans could discover the game, and its most fertile ground remained the sort of immigrant turf on which red-blooded Americans did not tread."

This rapid decay—or failure to launch—cannot be blamed on a single administrative body, such as the USFA. But the Yanks' Olympic failures during the Twenties (and beyond) and much of the nation's mid-twentieth-century malaise can be attributed largely to poor USFA leadership. From its founding in 1913 through the Sixties, the association was essentially a one-person, one-room organization, perpetually teetering on economic and intellectual bankruptcy.

Our Federation's early history is littered with mistakes, both macro (its role in the American soccer war and early Olympic blunders) and micro. For instance, in February 1931, the USFA, unbeknownst to anyone, changed the kickoff times of its Challenge Cup games. An angry newspaper writer in Fall River, Massachusetts, noted that over a thousand fans were forced to wait for hours "in the biting cold" for the game to begin. And in the cold is where, but for two notable World Cup exceptions (1930 and 1950), many American soccer fans would stand—and wait—for decades to come.

10

★ ★ ★ ★ ★

INAUGURAL 1930 WORLD CUP SUCCESS

Yanks make the semifinals (1930)

"Remember always, that all of us are descended from immigrants and revolutionists."

— Franklin D. Roosevelt

FIFA took the reins of international football at its most senior level from the IOC in 1928. Its first official business was to award the hosting responsibilities for the inaugural 1930 World Cup to Uruguay in recognition of its repeat Olympic victories and to help Uruguay celebrate the centenary of its constitution. There were no qualifying rounds for the tournament (that would start in 1934), and thirteen countries attended. From South America: Uruguay, Argentina, Bolivia, Brazil, Chile, Paraguay, and Peru; North America: U.S. and Mexico; and Europe: Belgium, France, Romania, and Yugoslavia. The Cup fell in a sweet calendar spot for the Americans—the last two weeks of July, during the ASL's offseason. Further, players in the ASL were accustomed to boarding steamships to travel up and down the East Coast for games. Still, if it weren't for Uruguay providing travel stipends for all participants, the U.S. might have sat out, like most European countries.

During the decade leading up to the 1930 World Cup, U.S. soccer experienced its first bona fide boom, with American players populating all the professional teams in the ASL. None of these players, with the sole exception of an unpaid goalie from the Newark Skeeters, had anything to do with the Olympic soccer failures during the Twenties. So, the Yanks' inaugural World Cup squad had the advantage of being seasoned professionals, yet virtually unknown on the international stage. The team was composed of twelve ASL professionals (who would play most minutes in Uruguay) and four supplements from Harrison, NJ; Philadelphia; Cleveland; and St. Louis. They boarded the SS *Munargo* in early June for an eighteen-day journey to Uruguay's capital, Montevideo (site of all games).

The renowned Archie Stark turned down an early invitation to attend the World Cup to focus on opening a garage. He was nearly thirty-three, past his prime. And, most importantly, participation in the first World Cup had no known economic advantage and was probably viewed as a net-negative financially. The endeavor (travel, pre-tournament training in Uruguay, World Cup games, and friendlies slated for after the Final) would require three months away from home.

The American contingent was managed by Wilfred Cummings, an ex-player and coach from Chicago, and long-serving treasurer of the USFA—which may have hastened the retirement of Secretary Cahill from the USFA for good (passed over yet again, for both manager and coach). In those days, the manager of the USMNT oversaw team and travel logistics and wrote a lot of reports, while the head coach blew his whistle and did a lot of shouting.

The head coach, Bob Millar, had a professional playing résumé (and a list of soccer-related fisticuffs) longer than any previous MNT coach at the helm of the "program," if you could call it that. Millar started his professional career with St. Mirren in the Scottish Football League before moving to the U.S. in 1911, at the age of twenty. From 1911 to 1929, Millar played for nearly a dozen teams across America's semiprofessional and professional circuits, eventually becoming a U.S. citizen. He assisted on Archie Stark's second of five goals during the USMNT's game against Canada on November 8, 1925. After the USFA branded the ASL an outlaw league in the fall of 1928, Millar resigned as player-coach of the New York Nationals and hastily sent the ASL office a telegram informing league officials he was siding with the Federation. Just over a year later, the USFA appointed him head coach of the MNT.

American-born players dominated Millar's World Cup squad (10–6). Of the six foreign-born, five were Scottish and one was English. All the early round games in Montevideo were played at either Estadio Gran Parque Central (home to Nacional) or Estadio Pocitos (home, for a few more years, to Club Atlético Peñarol), both grounds that the U.S. had been training on for the first ten days of July. The Cup that year had four groups (one with four countries, and three with three), and the U.S. was placed in group four, with Belgium and Paraguay. Newspaper writers noted that it had been raining in Montevideo for ninety straight days.

On the morning of the U.S.-Belgium match, the pitch was covered in a thin layer of snow (July being winter in Uruguay) that created a "wet, sticky pitch of which many an ASL club would have been proud." In front of about 18,500 fans, the Americans dusted the Belgians 3–0 (the first shutout in World Cup history), with goals from three different ASL wingers and forwards. The Red Devils were unable to match the Yanks' clever flank play, decisive passes, and athleticism—qualities that surprised opponents and fans alike. Prior to the first game, the Americans had been derisively called "shot-putters" by the French team, probably referring back to the rigorously amateur U.S. Olympic soccer squads of 1924 and 1928. The ASL-led victory over the Belgians was no fluke.

Next up was Paraguay (*La Albirroja*, Spanish for "the white and the red"), full of elite footballers. Paraguay had just beaten two-time Olympic champs Uruguay in the 1929 South American Championship (renamed Copa América in 1975), and then narrowly lost the title to Argentina, on points. The top goal scorer in that Championship was the twenty-four-year-old Paraguayan Aurelio González, at the peak of his powers. But the star forward in the U.S.-Paraguay game was not González. It was Fall River, Massachusetts, native Bert Patenaude who clobbered La Albirroja, scoring the World Cup's first-ever hat trick* in a 3–0 victory. Even though contemporary newspapers from Uruguay, Brazil, and Argentina detailed Patenaude's feat (some with diagrams), it would take FIFA seventy-five years to officially confirm the tally. Thanks to the Americans' quick feet and sure hands, Belgium and Paraguay were out of the tournament. The Americans advanced to the semifinals.

Even with the Yanks' 6–0 goal difference in their first two games, you would not fault the U.S. players for being nervous in the hours leading up to the game against Argentina, who had trounced them in the 1928 Olympics, 2–11. Recall Argentina advanced to the Olympic final in Amsterdam, where they lost to Uruguay and took silver. Still hot from this finish, La Albiceleste won their fourth South American Championship in a decade, in November 1929, a little over six months before the start of the 1930 World Cup. The Argentinians and Uruguayans had split pre-tournament votes for the favorites to win it all.

The U.S.-Argentina semifinal took place on July 26, 1930, at the newly completed Centenary Stadium, which had faced many delays. The match drew 73,000 fans, a magnitude of awe even for veteran ASL players who, maybe, had played a game in the ASL or late-round Challenge Cup in front of 15,000 fans. Cummings's report noted the players—dressed in their all-white kits with a generous crest of stars and stripes on their chests—were "cool as cucumbers" entering the stadium. But imagine their true feelings stepping onto the massive, awkwardly wide pitch, before tens of thousands of fans, virtually all of them yelling in Spanish.

In the first five minutes, goalie Jimmy Douglas twisted his ankle and banged his knee in a collision. He limped around the six-yard box for the

* A *hat trick* means three goals scored by the same player in a single game. The term originated in 1858, in English cricket, where a bowler who took three wickets in three consecutive deliveries was celebrated and honored with a new hat. Scoring two goals in one game is called a *brace*, a term from Old English and Anglo-French hunting language, referring to two animals caught or killed together.

remainder of the game. In about the tenth minute, Raphael Tracey was badly injured. He managed to finish the half, but was removed at halftime—a broken leg later confirmed. By rule, he could not be substituted, leaving the Yanks with ten men for the rest of the game. At halftime, the Americans were losing 0–1. In the seventieth minute, Andy Auld received a "kick in the face so hard" that he had to "finish the match with a cloth stuffed in his bloodied mouth." The injuries caught up with the Yanks, and their defense, down a man, crumpled in the second half. Argentina won 1–6. At a hospital after the match, Tracey was given a cast and a pair of crutches—and Auld received seven stitches to rejoin his split upper lip.

The U.S. officially finished in third place, on goal differential. An Argentine reporter summed up the American style, still somewhat relevant today:

> They all are talented athletes who play a smooth game and use their bodies well although occasionally they commit fouls; they have a remarkable domination on high balls which can be paralleled only by the great British and especially Scottish professional teams, whose way of playing perhaps they follow, but without monotonous precision and with much more vitality and enthusiasm. The fullbacks get rid of the ball with power and assurance; the midfield line defends, mixing very well with the fullbacks and giving remarkable help to the forwards, who have a wonderful kick that they utilize for passes and for sending high balls into the goal area to exploit their superior heading capacities.

A week later, Argentina lost the Final* to Uruguay before 93,000 fans. If the 1930 World Cup was FIFA's Initial Public Offering (IPO), FIFA had just made a killing. And its quadrennial tournament, after a few modest iterations, was poised to pay dividends—in perpetuity.

After the Cup, the Americans hung around and played six games

---

* In this book, all references to a specific World Cup Final are always capitalized; other tournaments' finals are not.

against outstanding Uruguayan and Brazilian club sides, enduring partisan refereeing that resulted in ten goals being disallowed. Their South American sojourn ended with a bizarre post-game locker room visit in São Paulo, Brazil, from an interpreter and the head referee to update the Yanks' 4–3 win over Santos FC: "He [the interpreter points to the head referee] has been shown the error of his ways and he has disallowed one of the [goals] after the game was over, and the score officially will be 3–3." The message must have landed at the feet of the "defeated" shot-putters with a thud.

The USMNT returned quietly to America and to an ASL hemorrhaging fans and teams, the Great Depression grinding on. There was virtually no newspaper or radio coverage about what they had just accomplished in Montevideo, and there would be none for decades. The United States was the first country to record a World Cup shutout *and* a World Cup hat trick, and the Americans had reached the semifinal. But nobody seemed to know or care.

History would also be unkind to them. Many historians who should know better, with time and context on their side, and modern search tools at their disposal, declare that most of the 1930 U.S. World Cup roster were "foreigners" who had cut their soccer teeth in professional Scottish and English leagues. Untrue—only one member of the 1930 team, George Moorhouse, had played for a professional team before coming to the U.S., and his total professional experience in England was just two third-division games. According to soccer historian Ed Farnsworth, "Of the six [foreign-born] players in question, two did play professionally in England—James Brown with Manchester United, Brentford, and Tottenham; and Alexander Wood with Leicester City and Nottingham Forest—but not until after the 1930 World Cup. The rest of the players continued their professional careers in the U.S., right where those careers had started."

The Yanks on the 1930 World Cup roster had built virtually all their skills on American soil in front of American fans, primarily up and down the Four Corridors during ASL competitions. Unfortunately, soccer writers from amateur to professional continue to apply a myopic approach to early

U.S. soccer history that is not confined to this narrow World Cup issue. U.S. soccer narratives are full of opinions that are shortsighted about a complex ethnographic issue, which too often contribute to biases (sometimes xenophobia) regarding the "other." Too many writers huff and puff about these exotic, foreign, ethnic, hyphenated-Americans, with their odd ways of doing things and their un-American soccer game.

And yet the 1930 MNT, and the larger contingent of American professional soccer players, had just put in a ten-year shift in the ASL with hundreds of games a year and hundreds of thousands of fans over the course of a season. Those games were drawing more American fans and newly arrived immigrants than all the teams in the rookie NFL and the American Basketball League (predecessor to the NBA), and nearly half the teams in baseball's Major Leagues. And there was virtually no professional hockey on American ice in the Twenties, as only the Boston Bruins had pierced Canada's veil. During the first three decades of the twentieth century, soccer was on a roll toward wider acceptance. Somehow this fact seems to get lost by historians.

Soccer writer Paul Gardner, transplanted Brit—smart, eloquent, and wise about most American soccer endeavors—rudely summed up the American soccer communities during their early years as "a gathering place for immigrants whose devotion to soccer was a pretty good measure of their reluctance to become Americans, and for people who were amateurs in the pejorative sense of the word." Ouch. The sports historians Andrei Markovits and Steven Hellerman concur: "This era was typified by the continued identification by way of ethnicity in the formation of clubs and their followings, as well as the perception of the game as separate from American sports culture by both its practitioners and enthusiasts." But the academics go further, and harder, claiming that, as of 2001, "there is no soccer in the United States" on the basis that the majority of U.S. citizens are not "emotionally attached" to the game. (Imagine my students stumbling across these opinions about the sport they love and are pursuing with every fiber of their being.) These sentiments omit a larger, more important story this book tries to hammer into the back of the net. Like a stubborn player long past his prime, who harbors old-fashioned views and refuses to retire, these conclusions need to be substituted by a more nuanced understanding of American soccer history.

There were plenty of players and fans in the so-called ethnic soccer enclaves, with all their flaws, who were American or striving to become American as soon as possible. Many others may have been guarded in their perspectives, clinging to customs brought from "other" places, but nevertheless were trying to assimilate. It's inaccurate to claim that most of the soccer folk wished to remain separate from the American mainstream. If anything, it was the mainstream, as the decades wore on, that put more distance between itself and them (sometimes consciously, rudely, even illegally).

It's also unfair and inaccurate to paint these people as "amateurs in the pejorative sense of the word." The people in early soccer communities were laborers, machinists, electricians, engineers, plumbers, painters, teachers, students, and later, doctors, lawyers, business owners, entrepreneurs, and investors—American people, blue collar and white collar—who, when they weren't playing or watching soccer, were helping to build and maintain America. Further, the current narrative about soccer history in this country almost always omits the central fact that association football on American soil has always pitched a wide participatory tent. Even today, its canvas covers more of America's true ethnic and religious diversity than its sporting rivals.

Professional baseball leagues, starting in 1887 and for over sixty years, systematically excluded Black Americans (and most Latinos) from their rosters and front offices, *i.e.*, from the entire field of vision. Black players were consigned to Negro leagues, which have their own vibrant history. Baseball's color line would not be broken until Jackie Robinson debuted for the Brooklyn Dodgers on April 11, 1947. Jewish baseball players fared little better. Gridiron football's origin story is no better. It started at elite northeastern colleges, bastions of privilege for rich, white, male students. It spread to colleges nationwide, many of which refused to admit Black and Latino students (not to mention ethnic "foreigners" and the children of first-generation Americans in soccer communities) for decades. NFL owners in 1933 privately banned Black players—and that barrier stood until March 20, 1946, when the Los Angeles Rams signed Kenny Washington.

American soccer history, all along, has been materially different. The rosters of mill and company-sponsored soccer teams in the late 1800s and early 1900s contained players with ethnic and religious diversity, including Black players, while the ASL of the Twenties showcased professionals of African descent. ASL II teams in the Thirties and Forties included Black and Latino players, as well as Jewish-dominated teams. Several all-Black clubs, especially in and around NYC, competed against White teams since the early 1900s. Soccer historians Ed Farnsworth and Brian Bunk have found newspaper accounts of native-born Black players, such as the Watson brothers, in New England, including positive references to integrated teams, dating back to 1894. Farnsworth notes that the Watson brothers "were not Black immigrants coming from someplace else where they learned soccer; instead, they were American kids who grew up in soccer-loving New England neighborhoods."

Ironically, some of these diverse players displayed their soccer talents at Brooklyn's Ebbets Field and at Upper Manhattan's Polo Grounds, entertaining paying soccer audiences that were always more diverse than the baseball owners, players, and fans who prevailed over the same venues during the same era. Soccer embraced plenty of its diversity *decades* before baseball and gridiron did any work to break their color barriers. This is by no means an argument that racism, prejudice, and narrow-mindedness did not exist or does not exist in American soccer circles. They did, and still do. But American soccer was striving for a more perfect union long before its sporting peers.

The 1930 MNT and larger American soccer milieu of the time are illustrative. Among the American players representing the National Team in Montevideo, Uruguay, in 1930 were Adelino Gonsalves, born August 10, 1908, in Portsmouth, Rhode Island, one of seven children. His parents, Augustine and Rose, had moved to the U.S. from the Portuguese island of Madeira (the same tiny island that would later produce Cristiano Ronaldo). In his youth, Gonsalves played baseball and boxed, but his first love was soccer. Dent McSkimming, our persistent soccer reporter from St. Louis, remarked, "I always asked the foreign players the inevitable question, and in total they agreed that Gonsalves would win a place and be a star in any team in the world." At Boston's Fenway Park in 1931, he scored a hat trick in a 4–3 victory over Glasgow's Celtic. He played in the Challenge Cup finals eleven out of fifteen years in venues along the East Coast and in St. Louis. Like Archie Stark before him, he repeatedly turned down offers to play abroad because he wanted to stay in America.

Gonsalves's teammate Bert Patenaude, the 1930 World Cup hat-trick hero, was born in Fall River, Massachusetts, on November 4, 1909, to French Canadian parents. He played for many storied American clubs, among them the Fall River Marksmen—where he netted 114 goals in 158 games between 1928 and 1931 (earning him his 1930 MNT invitation)—New York Yankees (soccer), St. Louis Central Breweries, Philadelphia Passon, Newark Americans, and the Hakoah All-Stars. The Hakoahs drew thousands of fans, sometimes five figures, many of them Jewish, well into the 1930s; virtually all of the players and fans, like nearly everyone else in America, were unaware of the dark clouds forming in Europe.

During the Twenties and Thirties, and spreading westward from soccer's Four Corridors, American teams fielded rosters of so-called traditional American citizens as well as immigrants fast becoming Americans, including more communities of color. They formed patchy networks across the United States. Team names represented the messy melding of ethnic neighborhoods: St. Louis Shamrocks, New York Americans, Philadelphia German-Americans, Cleveland Slavia, Brooklyn Hispano FC, Chicago Bricklayers, San Francisco Scots, Chicago Eagles, Newark Portuguese, New York Galicia, and scores more. The team names serve as a reminder that nearly all of us Yanks descend from immigrant groups or enslaved people—and that we should celebrate our roots, even as we thoughtfully assimilate.

Soccer players and fans in the first half of the twentieth century—when they weren't enjoying soccer—were striving for that elusive but very real American dream for themselves and their extended families, which neither the Great Depression nor WWII would extirpate.

After his professional career ended, Bert Patenaude served in the U.S. Army during WWII, then returned to Fall River and worked as a painter and carpenter until his death in 1977. Today, his grandson, Bertrand M. Patenaude III, lives in California. He is a research fellow and an international expert on Soviet/Russian history, humanitarian studies, and American history at the Hoover Institution, Stanford University—quite the hat trick for the grandson of a first-generation American.

11

YANKS' SOCCER PROGRESS STUNTED BY THE GREAT DEPRESSION AND WWII

But the U.S. team beats England in the 1950 World Cup (1930–1950)

"Man is not made for defeat. A man can be destroyed but not defeated."

— Ernest Hemingway, *The Old Man and the Sea*

You would not entirely fault the American press and public for virtually ignoring the inaugural 1930 World Cup in Uruguay. Starting in late 1929, waves of banking panics had engulfed the U.S. as customers lost confidence and attempted to withdraw their money, precipitating the closure of approximately ten thousand banks over the next three years. The bank failures wiped out the deposits held by millions of Americans (which would not be addressed for future generations until 1933 by the creation of the Federal Deposit Insurance Corporation). Many people lost their life's savings in the chaos, even if they had not invested in any stocks.

Unemployment skyrocketed. No sector had a monopoly on the misery, and virtually all communal experiences were affected. Industrial production dropped by half. An independent environmental disaster called the "Dust Bowl" (also known as the "Dirty Thirties") caused legions of farm foreclosures and a migration from rural areas to cities in search of work that was already scarce or nonexistent. The anemic 1932 Olympics in Los Angeles, California, didn't even feature soccer.

Despite continued hardships, the U.S. team made it to Italy in 1934 for the second running of the World Cup. Thirty-two countries entered the competition, and sixteen qualified for the final tournament. Reigning champs Uruguay sat out, angry that many big European soccer countries had failed to travel to South America in 1930. All four British Home Nations also sat out (again), even though FIFA waived their qualification requirements. Italian dictator Benito Mussolini saw the World Cup as a theatrical stage for his brand of fascism, which by 1934 was palpable and almost in full throat. The head of the Italian Football Federation, General Giorgio Vaccaro, a Mussolini appointee, crowed, "The ultimate goal of the World Cup will be to show the universe what is the true fascist ideal of the sport."

The American team, fresh from their 1930 World Cup success, unfortunately took a U-turn in terms of its management and personnel decisions. For 1934, the president of the USFA, Philadelphian Elmer Schroeder (the same guy who managed the U.S. 1928 Olympic team during its ignominious 2–11 shellacking by Argentina), railroaded himself in as team manager and summarily hired Scottish American David Gould as head coach. Gould played for various American teams over three decades and coached the University of Pennsylvania team for about twenty-three years prior to his MNT appointment. The Penn Quakers, a college team of honest amateurs, couldn't hold a candle to the professional ASL sides that had just enjoyed a decade-long run. Gould had a leg up on the MNT job because Schroeder was undoubtedly already aware of him—Schroeder himself had graduated from Penn's Wharton School (1920) and Law School, and had been serving as a Penn instructor during Gould's appointment. It was another blatant example of unearned patronage inside the early USFA.

Gould and Schroeder held three scrimmages (that doubled as tryouts) for the 1934 World Cup team, two in Philadelphia and one in nearby Newark. Their quickly assembled U.S. team beat the Pennsylvania League All-Stars, 8–0, and the Eastern Pennsylvania All-Stars, 2–0. But in Newark, the MNT lost 0–4 to an all-star ASL II team of semiprofessionals that featured the legendary Archie Stark, who scored a hat trick. Archie was not selected for the team. The unsatisfactory scoreline was a harbinger of dismal results to come.

On the eve of the 1934 World Cup, the USFA was effectively broke and relied on state soccer associations to defray the cost of players from their region selected to the MNT (perhaps the first instance of pay-to-play under the USFA/USSF umbrella). The nineteen-member squad consisted of six players from Pennsylvania; four from St. Louis; four from Pawtucket, Rhode Island; and one each from Cleveland, Chicago, Baltimore, Brooklyn, and NYC.

The USFA's application to FIFA was late. As a result, FIFA required the U.S. to travel to Rome and first play a qualification game against the non-tardy North American qualifier, Mexico. The MNT arrived in Rome on May 14, 1934, and spent the next day playing baseball. Nine days later, the U.S. overwhelmed Mexico, 4–2, with semiprofessional Aldo "Buff"* Donelli, born just outside of Pittsburgh to Italian-American parents, scoring all four goals. Even though the game was played on the World Cup host country's soil only days before the opening World Cup whistle, the match was not deemed an official World Cup match. So, the honor of the first four-goal tally in World Cup history fell to Ernst Wilimowski of Poland, in a 1938 group-game loss to Brazil. The MNT would go nearly fifty-six years without defeating *El Tri* ("the Tricolor," Spanish for Mexico's green, white, and red flag) again in a competitive match.

---

* The name "Buff" was an homage to Donelli's hero, Buffalo Bill (born William Cody), who, at the turn of the twentieth century, was the most recognizable celebrity on earth. Cody's wildly successful traveling show, originally called "Buffalo Bill's Wild West," caravanned across America—and eventually hopped a boat to Europe, conveying to adoring crowds, in a circus-like setting, some of the best and worst of frontier America.

The 1934 World Cup (unlike 1930) was a single-elimination competition. After defeating Mexico, the unlucky Americans drew the host,* Italy, who had bulwarked its team over the prior six months with a core group of Italian-Argentine national team players (under FIFA's lax nationality-switching rules). The Italian head coach, not for the last time that summer, defended his recruitment efforts: "If they can die for Italy, they can play for Italy!" The Yanks got demolished 1–7 by the *Azzurri* ("the Blues," in Italian), with Donelli scoring again. (Buff turned down offers to play professionally in Europe and returned to the U.S., where he coached college gridiron at Duquesne, Boston, Columbia, and even had a stint as the head coach of the Pittsburgh Steelers.) Italy rolled unevenly through the rest of the tournament (many say with help from referees), beating Spain, Austria, and Czechoslovakia. Mussolini attended every Italy match surrounded by his *Camicie Nere* ("Blackshirts"), his thuggish militia. After every battle on the pitch, the "eleven players of the Italian squad dedicated their victories to [Mussolini], their right arms outstretched."

In the Final, the Czechs—who have never won a World Cup—were beating Italy with about nine minutes to go until Italian-Argentine Raimundo Orsi leveled, sending the game into overtime, where another Italian-Argentine assisted on the go-ahead goal, which clinched the victory. Orsi had played thirteen times for Argentina during the Twenties, scoring three goals and winning both the 1927 South American Championship and silver medal at the 1928 Summer Olympics in Amsterdam. Orsi, the next morning, probably couldn't recite, in perfect Italian, the giant headline in the Rome paper declaring: "In the Name and in the Presence of the Duce, the Azzurri Win a New World Title." Beneath the headline were photos of the victors holding the official Jules Rimet World Cup Trophy—a 13.7-inch-tall Art Deco masterpiece portraying Nike, the Greek goddess of Victory, her winged arms raised, and her erect head supporting a decagonal cup, radiating grace and strength.

* Hosting a World Cup appears to result in a clear competitive advantage. As of 2022, six out of twenty-two FIFA World Cup tournaments have been won by the host country (27.3 percent).

Not far away was another trophy, a fascist behemoth. So confident in his team's victory was Mussolini, the architect of fascism, that he commissioned a special trophy called the *Coppa del Duce* ("the Cup of the Leader") for the World Cup event. Standing nearly as tall as the shortest player on the Italian squad, the trophy was pregnant with Roman athletes fighting for a ball under a giant decorative urn. The messy ensemble was anchored by two giant butt-to-butt fasces (axes), their blades ominously facing outward—a feast for fascist eyes.* The English press barely covered the tournament. Four days after the 1934 World Cup finale, Mussolini met with Hitler, the new German chancellor, in Venice. It was the beginning of machinations that would bring war machines and terror to much of Europe.

The U.S. team traveled briefly to Germany for the 1936 Olympics (still ostensibly an "amateur" affair) where they lost 0–1 to a team composed mostly of Italian professional players designated "students" by the Italian FA. With war brewing in Europe—underscored by the belligerent expansionist actions of Fascist Italy and Nazi Germany—the U.S. soccer team, weighed down by politics and lackluster interest at home, sat out the 1938 World Cup in France. Italy won again. Then Europe fell apart.

Less than a week after England declared war on Germany, the English FA, on September 8, 1939, announced that all football activities except football "organised by the armed forces" were suspended "until official notice to the contrary." But the football-loving British soon balked, and the Home Office revised its policy to permit football games and leagues to function in limited areas and within venues holding smaller numbers of fans. Throughout much of the British Isles, football rolled on. With Hitler's Blitzkrieg and WWII carving up Europe, many continental teams suspended their leagues or severely curtailed them. Soccer balls gave way to ball bearings as war machines stormed Europe and North Africa from land, air, and sea.

* Nobody knows what happened to this oversized tribute to a small man who was eventually executed by the Italian people. The trophy is widely believed to have been melted down and sold for its mineral content, or merely destroyed with many other fascist artifacts.

In America during the lead-up to WWII, the USFA's Challenge Cup and revamped ASL league puttered along, but the teams were semiprofessional at best and drew only modest crowds. Teams improvised, teased, folded, and reappeared, often under new names. The renaming continued. After the U.S. officially declared war on Japan and Germany in early December 1941, several storied clubs quickly changed their names. The Philadelphia Germans became the Philadelphia Americans; Brooklyn Hispano became Brooklyn; and the Scots-Americans became Kearny Americans. A few years after the war, many ethnic names returned—and survive to this day (America being the king of free speech). The ethnic names are an intrinsic part of the rich fabric of American soccer history and a nod to the global game. They are also bad for business.

World War II knocked out the World Cup in 1942 and 1946. International soccer resumed in 1948 at the Olympic Games in London. The tournament—still an amateur affair and nicknamed the "Austerity Games"—reflected a Europe recovering from devastation and a world forever changed by modern weapons. European nations were rebuilding. Two footballing countries, Germany and Japan, were banned from participating due to their roles in starting and prolonging the war. Italy, because it defected to the Allies in 1943 (after Mussolini was deposed), was permitted to send athletes—though the Azzurri did not make it past the quarterfinals.

The USFA had recently changed its name to the USSFA (the extra "S" for soccer). But its comical choices during 1948 remained unchanged. Our Federation again sent an unprepared amateur team to the single-elimination Olympic soccer tournament in London (the first international tournament in a decade). The Yanks drew Italy again (bizarrely), finished the match with ten players, and lost 0–9. Sweden won the gold. The victory by the *Blågult* (Swedish for "the blue and yellow") symbolized hope and peace for the world. The U.S. team stuck around Europe for a week and got walloped by Northern Ireland (0–5 in Belfast) and Norway (0–11 in Oslo). The dismal Olympic performance against the Azzurri and results in post-tournament games in Europe—with one notable exceptional win at the 1950 World Cup—presaged decades of domestic indifference and international soccer mediocrity for the Yanks.

With Europe still rebuilding, and with the two World Cups immediately preceding WWII hosted on European soil, the 1950 World Cup was held in Brazil. The U.S. team almost failed to qualify. Four teams from our FIFA region were invited to play in the second edition of the North American Football Championship, in Mexico City, in fall 1949, with the top two finishers earning a berth in the World Cup. Canada failed to attend. The three remaining teams played each other twice. The U.S. squeaked through, losing two times to Mexico (with a 2–12 goal differential), but tying and beating mighty Cuba. With the Yanks' ticket stamped for Brazil, the American Federation divided the ASL (still its top league) into an Eastern team and a Western team, and held a scrimmage in St. Louis that ended 3–3. The final squad chosen to travel to Brazil included six men from St. Louis, four from Chicago, three from Fall River/Boston, and two each from Pittsburgh, Philadelphia, and NYC/Brooklyn. About a third of these players had made the trip to Mexico City the year before—progress from the USSFA, which had customarily sent our quickly assembled team abroad with little more than an uninspiring "give it your best shot" and a slap on the back.

The 1950 MNT was gritty but would still be outclassed by the majority of seasoned professionals they would meet in Brazil. The Americans, to a man, "were part-timers who played in their off hours and gave up their Sundays for the love of the sport." Philadelphian Benny McLaughlin made the U.S. roster but withdrew at the last minute. His boss said he could go to Brazil, but his job would not be around when he returned. St. Louisan Gino Pariani fared better with his predicament. His fiancée agreed to move up their wedding so Pariani could play in Brazil and honeymoon after the tournament (a holy matrimony, to this day, supported by all football-loving spouses).

Thirty-six hours before departing New York for Rio de Janeiro (then the capital of Brazil), the U.S. team scrimmaged a touring All-England team that had scored sixty-six goals while allowing only thirteen in their previous nine games, mostly in Canada. The MNT, with Penn State head soccer coach and icon Bill Jeffrey at the helm for all of two weeks, lost 0–1. Not a bad result for a squad of rugged Americans, a third of whom were WWII veterans. The Yanks endured a post-game dinner with the English, who downplayed the scoreline and blamed it on their arduous touring schedule and the absence of several of their best players who had already joined England's World Cup squad in Brazil. Over the next seventy-five years, touring Brits would pull out the same lame excuse (tired, lacking best players) every time they lost or performed poorly against an American team. The next morning, the Yanks boarded a plane for Rio—the first time a U.S. soccer delegation had traveled to a World Cup by air.

Sixteen teams originally qualified for the Cup, but that number dwindled to thirteen by the opening whistle. The U.K. was granted two spots, but when Scotland lost to England in the final of the Home Nations Cup (doubling as a World Cup qualifying tournament), the proud Scots refused to travel to Brazil. So did several other qualified countries, citing travel costs. The Brazilian Federation reconfigured the brackets and finally settled on four groups, oddly unequal in number: two groups of four (including a group comprised of the U.S., England, Spain, and Chile), one group of three, and one group of two—with host Brazil booked to travel the least amount of distance to its group games by a rainforest mile. The winner of each group would then advance to a four-team round-robin to decide the winner of the 1950 World Cup. It was the first and last time for this patently unfair sequence of contests scripted solely to maximize stadium ticket sales.

First up in the group stage for the U.S. was Spain, with a roster bursting at the seams with full-time professionals drawing respectable wages from FC Barcelona, Real Madrid de Fútbol, Valencia de Fútbol, and other notable teams. In the final ten minutes, Spain overran the U.S., winning 1–3. Elsewhere, England, in its first ever World Cup game, dispatched Chile 2–0 in the newly completed and magnificent Maracanã Stadium (the largest in the world at the time) in downtown Rio. Next up, U.S. versus England, slated for June 29 in Belo Horizonte (Portuguese for "Beautiful Horizon"),* 272 miles north/northwest of Rio, and inland.

The English team arrived four days early and had acclimated to a luxurious hotel on the outskirts of the city, with easy access to a football training ground and a pool. The U.S. team landed the day before the match, did not practice, and retired to the Hotel Amazonas (economy lodging) in the heart of the city. After a twenty-year hibernation and avoidance of all things FIFA, the English team and press were baring their fangs, alert to their 3-to-1 chance of winning it all. The odds for the U.S. team were pegged at 500-to-1. "The only unanswered question," wrote John Thompson in the London *Daily Mirror*, "seemed to be the size of the Americans' defeat." "A band of no-hopers drawn from many lands," growled the *Belfast Telegraph*. "We ain't got a chance against your boys," U.S. coach Jeffrey cooed. "But we're going to fight. Nobody takes us seriously in this Cup, but we came here to learn."

In what can honestly be called a fluke of a game, with American goalkeeper Frank Borghi (St. Louis hearse driver by trade) "standing on his head"—goalkeeper-speak for playing a fantastic game, full of outstanding athletic saves—the U.S. beat England 1–0. Conflicting reports about the Yanks' only goal, scored in about the thirty-eighth minute by Haitian-born Joe Gaetjens (Columbia University accounting student and Harlem dishwasher), persist. The English say it was a lucky goal. Eyewitnesses, including midfielder Walter Bahr (Philadelphia gym teacher), have repeatedly asserted that the goal was no fluke:

> I took a shot from 25 yards out that was moving to the goalkeeper's right. I hit it fairly well, it was gonna be on goal. [Bert Williams, goalkeeper for Wolverhampton Wanderers FC] started to move to his right for my shot. Joe Gaetjens somehow got to the ball. Did he make an honest attempt and head it into the goal or

* Most of Latin America speaks Spanish due to Spanish colonization. But Brazil is the exception because it was colonized by Portugal. Thus, Portuguese is the official language of Brazil.

> did it ricochet off him? He left his feet, he dove at the ball. I'm guessing the ball was five feet in the air. He's in traffic; there are a lot of people in the [eighteen]-yard area. He didn't get a clean head at it, but he definitely made a concerted effort. Joe was a guy who had a nose for the goal. He scored goals where you didn't know how he got to the ball, let alone scored the goals.

Gaetjens landed face down in the grass and never saw how his goal was scored. And neither did many others, aside from about ten thousand mostly Brazilian fans who witnessed the game live. There is no film footage of the goal, and only two legitimate photographs show the ball crossing, or about to cross, the line. There is no discernible data in the background regarding the activity and positioning in front of the goal moments earlier (beware of doctored images on the internet).

According to reports (live radio and follow-up news articles), in the second half a great number of local Brazilians flocked to the stadium to watch the upset unfold, swelling the audience by at least a factor of two. The English continued to pressure the Americans' goal, and Borghi continued to make extraordinary saves. In about the eighty-second minute, English all-star forward Stan Mortensen (Blackpool FC) appeared to be free on a breakaway with the ball near his dominant foot, but was brought down from behind, just outside the penalty box. The culprit was Charlie Colombo (St. Louis warehouseman)—who could always be identified in every game because he wore gloves with the fingertips removed (twenty-five years before Sylvester Stallone donned a similar look in his first *Rocky* movie).

Yank right-back Harry Keough (St. Louis postal worker, later renowned head soccer coach for St. Louis University, who would lead the Billikens to five Division I national championships) recalled: "Colombo wouldn't hesitate to knock a guy on his rear end. If his mother was on the other team, he probably would have kicked her, too." English all-star Alf Ramsey (Tottenham Hotspur FC) took the resulting free kick. He found the head of Jimmy Mullen (Wolverhampton) who redirected it on goal—a downward, bouncing header—before Borghi lunged to his right, reached back, and palmed the ball safely over the endline. Several minutes later, Borghi, backpedaling, punched a looping ball (heading for the inside-top of the goal) up and over the crossbar.

One of the "Kings of English football," the dazzling Stanley Matthews (Blackpool), age thirty-five at the time but still dangerous, wasn't even in Belo Horizonte. Instead, he was listening to the game by radio from his hotel room in Rio, presumably being saved for stiffer competition.

Moments after the final whistle, overjoyed onlookers stormed the pitch and raised Borghi and Gaetjens on their shoulders and carried them off, fans sensing they had just witnessed what the international press would later call one of the greatest football upsets of all time. The fans were also buoyed by the notion that their team might not have to play England later in the tournament. Less than a week later, the U.S. fell to Chile, 2–5, coming in last place in their group, right where everyone thought they would end up. American John "Clarkie" Souza (Falls River loom fixer) was selected to the World Cup All-Star team. England, in its last group game, lost to Spain in the Maracanã, and slunk home, thoroughly embarrassed by their inaugural World Cup run, which had never advanced past a lugubrious crawl. Italy, a two-time World Cup winner, was also ousted in the group stage.

"We didn't think we could win," offered Keough. "We decided to lose by the least number of goals and not give up everything." Bahr agreed. "Our goal was to keep the score respectable. We knew they were better prepared, coached, managed, and in better condition. We were going in as complete underdogs. I don't think any of us went in there thinking we had a chance of winning." All this is retold in a well-meaning but mediocre American film called *The Game of Their Lives* (2005), which was renamed *The Miracle Match* for some distribution channels. Instead of making a movie about this one-off match, as glorious as it was, Hollywood producers and financiers should've made a movie about the first decade of the ASL, which culminated in the MNT's 1930 World Cup run.

The winners of each of the four groups—Spain, Brazil, Sweden, Uruguay—then advanced to a round-robin to determine the overall winner. Brazil, in its first two round-robin games, crushed Sweden (7–1) and

Spain (6–1), amassing a five-game World Cup scoring total of twenty-one goals while conceding only four. Uruguay, for its part, beat Sweden (3–2) and tied Spain (2–2). The Brazil-Uruguay match thus became the de facto Final (with FIFA, decades later, calling it the official Final). Brazil was guaranteed to win the championship so long as they did not lose. According to eyewitnesses and newspaper accounts, the mood of people in Rio the morning of July 16, 1950, was one of absolute confidence that the *Seleção* ("the Team" in Portuguese) would win or tie the game. And the Cup would be theirs for the first time.

Before the opening whistle, every competition sin was committed, which may have offended the soccer gods. "In less than a few hours, [you] will be hailed as champions by millions of compatriots!" bragged the mayor of Rio. Gold commemorative pins—with names, dates, and the inscription "For the World Champions"—were already made and placed in special boxes. A victory song had already been written and practiced. Front pages were already set in type, with headlines raring to go. A sizable majority of home fans packed into the Maracanã, as many as 200,000, still regarded as the largest live crowd in all of history to witness a ticketed team sporting event (as opposed to horse racing contests at giant racetracks or motor racing events along many miles of city streets). Brazil took the lead over Uruguay in the forty-seventh minute, but goals by La Celeste in the sixty-sixth and seventy-ninth minutes stunned the crowd. Brazil couldn't equalize.

After the final whistle, an eerie silence fell upon the stadium, and gloom poured into the streets and settled upon the nation. People called it the *Maracanazo*. Embarrassment bordering on shame lingered in the national conscience. But Brazil soon redeemed itself. Eight years later, in Sweden, the Seleção won their first World Cup, led by the seventeen-year-old Pelé, who would become the face of world football for nearly three decades. Over the past seventy years, Brazil has made the most noise in the tournament, winning five World Cups, more than any other country, the last four clad in their iconic yellow jerseys.

★ ★ ★

The U.S. team returned to the States in late July 1950 to a press corps and a public who, for the most part, didn't know they had left the country. It was eerily similar to the lack of interest shown to the 1930 MNT World Cup campaign. Throughout the 1950s, the soccer Yanks populated semipro leagues, still teeming with immigrants and first- and second-generation Americans, everyone apparently resigned to their fate as second-class sporting citizens. Some enterprising student-athletes matriculated to college, knocked the ball around campus, then graduated to club teams in adult leagues and eventually to sedentary lives. Entering the 1960s, American fans continued to turn up in five-figure numbers to watch foreign touring teams—Real Madrid, Manchester United, Bayern Munich, Juventus, Benfica, River Plate, Santos, to name a few. The athletes demonstrated their soccer skills on the outfields of baseball parks, and, starting in the 1960s, on artificial playing surfaces often covered by gridiron lines within multipurpose stadiums. Many people in America were interested in paying to see good foreign soccer, even in less-than-ideal venues. But were there enough fans willing to support a genuine American professional soccer league?

People were certainly willing to pay money to see the Big Three sports, which significantly widened the gap between themselves and the soccer enclaves. Baseball signed a major national TV broadcasting contract in 1950. Gridiron followed in 1955, and basketball in 1962. Each subsequent deal was sweeter, fueling each sport to greater professional heights and further entrenchments within the American sporting psyche.

In the late Sixties, the Yanks, still in their soccer lull, were roused by a group of enterprising investors and a venture calling itself the North American Soccer League (NASL). The zany NASL, for seventeen years, would shake, rattle, and roll. It briefly disturbed the international soccer cosmos—an ambitious shot that careened off the crossbar and into the night.

12

★★★★★

THE RISE OF THE NORTH AMERICAN SOCCER LEAGUE

The good, the bad, and the ugly (1966–1975)

"Buy the ticket, take the ride."

— Hunter S. Thompson, *Fear and Loathing in Las Vegas*

The wildly successful running of the eighth World Cup in England (1966) fortified American sports promoters' interest in forming an untested bicoastal professional league on American soil. For the rest of the football world, the tournament catapulted the game into the televised stratosphere, where it has remained. But the Brits' hosting endeavors in 1966 did not get off to a good start.

Three months before the opening whistle, the official Jules Rimet World Cup trophy was on display in an exhibition case in Westminster, London, alongside a stamp collection worth (at the time) much more than the soccer trophy. The negligent bobbies were duped by a thief who stole the trophy and legged it right out the back door. Scotland Yard had two unpromising leads—a tall person and a short person—until a man submitted the lining from the trophy and a rambling ransom note to the head of the English FA demanding 15,000 pounds (about 40,000 U.S. dollars at the time). "If the press or police are informed of this, this cup will go into the melting pot."

The head of the FA immediately notified the police, and an undercover cop met the suspected burglar with a briefcase mostly full of blank paper. The burglar said he didn't have the trophy, and they needed to go for a ride. With the cop driving the suspected thief's car, and a van with bars in the back window following, the nervous thief threw himself out of the moving vehicle. He was summarily chased down and arrested. But the trophy was not recovered. The thief claimed he was a middleman and blamed the whole thing on a man called "the Pole." (Incidentally, Poland twice came in third place in the World Cup: 1974 and 1982.)

Lucky for England, two days later, Pickles, a black-and-white collie—on a walk with his South London owner—started sniffing at an abandoned package, wrapped in newspaper and bound with string, lying at the base of a hedge. Pickles's owner tore off a bit of newspaper to reveal a plaque engraved with the names of the most recent World Cup winners—West Germany 1954, Brazil 1958, Brazil 1962. Pickles had found the missing trophy. The Brazilian sports minister called the theft "a sacrilege that would never have been committed in Brazil." But thirteen years later, the same trophy recovered by Pickles was stolen from the Brazilian football federation's headquarters in Rio in much the same fashion as the London fiasco. It vanished without a trace, likely melted down.*

If TV made Pickles a national hero in an instant, imagine what it could do for football. Nearly half the population of the U.K. watched England beat West Germany in the 1966 Final at Wembley Stadium. The game was televised in black and white, the last World Cup match broadcast in the old

* The trophy retrieved by Pickles would be permanently awarded to Brazil in 1970 upon the Seleção winning their third World Cup. After the Brazilians took permanent possession of the Jules Rimet trophy, it was soon replaced by the modern, iconic, stout World Cup trophy—which measures 14.5 inches tall and 5.1 inches wide at its base and near the top. Two human figures hoist up the world, which clearly resembles a soccer ball. Designed by Italian artist Silvio Gazzaniga, the eighteen-karat-gold masterpiece features two horizontal bands of malachite (green mineral) near its base.

medium. Behind the scenes, a film crew had taped some late-round games and the Final in color. Several months later, a twenty-minute full-color documentary called *Goal! The World Cup* was released worldwide. By year's end, several million Americans had watched the film—a level of interest that dovetailed nicely with audiences turning up in five figures to watch foreign touring teams during the 1950s and 1960s. The tantalizing possibility of monetizing an untapped American market could not be ignored.

In 1966, three separate investment groups approached the open-armed USSFA with proposals for a coast-to-coast professional soccer league: The Bill Cox group, the Richard Millen group, and the Jack Cooke group. The USSFA and FIFA—both heavily invested in the outcome—urged the three groups to settle their differences and merge into one. Not surprisingly, that did not happen. The USSFA appointed a committee to review the proposals, with a final recommendation to be made at that year's annual convention. But before the convention, the Bill Cox group claimed FIFA approval (without proof) and unilaterally announced it had formed an eleven-team circuit called the North American Professional Soccer League (NAPSL).

In a history-repeating series of events, the USSFA stated that no league could form without its consent, branding the NAPSL an outlaw league. The USSFA once again urged the groups to merge—or for one group to step forward and agree to financial terms extremely beneficial to the USSFA (4 percent of all gate receipts, 10 percent of all future TV deals, and a $25,000 per team franchise fee—a massive increase from the $25-a-year registration fee ASL teams had enjoyed for decades).

It's easy to imagine what the millionaires thought of the tiny U.S. soccer administration, which had no experience overseeing a profitable pro league. (The ASL of the 1920s operated pretty much on its own accord.) Yet the Federation was acting as if it had a monopoly on professional soccer's future in America. It's also easy to imagine what serious soccer people—especially Yanks raised in the post-WWII soccer desert—thought of the millionaires' slapdash soccer sense. An early league commissioner admitted he didn't "know the difference between a soccer ball and a billiard ball."

The Cox group and the Richard Millen group balked at the Federation's demands. But the Jack Cooke group—calling its circuit the North American Soccer League (NASL)—agreed. The NASL was quickly sanctioned by the USSFA. And overnight it replaced the top echelon of the ASL that had been operating under the USSFA's umbrella for nearly fifty years. The renegade Cox and Millen groups merged and rebranded the NAPSL as the National Professional Soccer League (NPSL). And, incredibly, the NPSL then announced a ten-year TV contract with CBS (albeit with many "outs" for the network) with a million dollars to be paid to the league in its first year. Only in America could two separate professional soccer leagues—with *no* teams and *no* players—materialize out of thin air, with the outlaw league sporting a national TV deal before its opening whistle.

The renegade NPSL was set to commence league play in April 1967, a full year before the NASL. So, the NASL, with our Federation's backing, decided to scramble and beat the NPSL to the pitch with an unusual solution to the no-players/no-teams problem. They decided to import *entire teams* from abroad and place them in cities with supposed corresponding ethnic communities. Ireland's Shamrock Rovers went to Boston (Boston Rovers); England's Wolverhampton Wanderers joined Los Angeles (Wolves); England's Stoke City was assigned to Cleveland (Stokers); Italy's Caliari Calcio went to Chicago (Mustangs); Brazil's Bangu Atlético Clube landed in Houston (Stars); and Uruguay's Club Atlético Cerro wound up in NYC (Skyliners). The NASL marketers then ditched the NASL name and adopted the rudely ironic United Soccer Association (USA) moniker for its potpourri of international soccer talent.

Another irony was that this mass-importation model mirrored the approach the renegade Bill Cox group had exercised over the summers, from 1960 to 1965 (with mixed success), which never fully earned USSFA approval. Now, our Federation was leading the wholly un-American charge. The renegade NPSL quickly assembled its teams by flying around the world to sign virtually all foreign players, too.

For the third time (1894, 1928–1929, 1967), America had two rival professional leagues, fiercely opposed and locked in a death match. The

English FA, astute to the potential harm of "the American menace" this time around (recall the talent drain from the U.K. to ASL sides of the mid- to late-1920s), announced a one-year ban for any players appearing in the outlaw NPSL—a threat most professionals took seriously this time around.

It didn't seem to bother the promoters of both leagues or the executives at CBS that virtually the only Americans on the pitch would be the referees. Some reports claim that fewer than ten Americans suited up across both leagues in 1967. "Anyone could have told the [owners] it wasn't going to work," opined journalist Paul Gardner. "But [they] weren't the sort of guys who were going to back down. They nearly ruined the whole thing before it got off the ground."

Crowds were mediocre across both leagues, typically three thousand to six thousand that first year. Some games drew only a few hundred people. Every team lost money. CBS didn't know how to broadcast soccer. So, referees were reportedly instructed to tell players to fake injuries (and stay on the ground, supine) to permit commercials. The LA Wolves won the sanctioned league, while the Oakland Clippers won the renegade league—the first time in American history that a genuine national professional soccer league was won by a team from the West Coast.

But few people noticed or cared—including players on the actual rosters. According to the English writer Ian Plenderleith in his book *Rock 'n' Roll Soccer: The Short Life and Fast Times of the North American Soccer League*, many of the hastily assembled foreigners had no clue about the geography of the United States. Ex-Newcastle United player and Brit Derek Craig revealed a few years into his NASL sojourn: "I thought [I was playing for] the San Francisco Earthquakes. I didn't know I was in San Jose until I read it on me jersey."

With sparse fans and mounting losses, the two leagues (and the USSFA) began merger talks before the season ended. The dueling parties met in Zurich at FIFA headquarters, where President Sir Stanley Rous attempted to help resolve their disputes. He asked the Americans to leave the room and draft a unification agreement. Hours later, the Yanks returned with a piece of paper but proceeded to argue about its contents. According to

Plenderleith, Sir Stanley was "mad as hell," considered "tearing the sheet into small bits and burying them in the nearest snowdrift," and nearly shut down U.S. soccer for good. Somehow, the parties emerged from Zurich with a unification plan. In December 1967, they merged into one and rekindled the NASL name, which the USSFA quickly approved.

The NASL's first season (1968) involved seventeen franchises, nine in the Eastern Conference and eight in the Western. Top teams performed well: The Atlanta Chiefs beat visiting Manchester City (crowned champions of England, only a few months before) twice before 23,000 and 25,000 fans. Two other NASL teams beat Brazilian giant Santos FC. Crowds, however, were only slightly better than the previous year for the regular season games. For the rookie league championship, the Atlanta Chiefs beat the San Diego Toros. The NASL selected First and Second Team all-stars. But not one was an American. Every team lost money. Again. Some teams squandered nearly a million dollars over a ten-month period. CBS stopped broadcasting games. Twelve teams dissolved at the close of the season—their owners running for the hills, never to utter the word "soccer" again.

The NASL's second season (1969) opened with just five teams and no TV presence. Teams began in rental mode, borrowing entire squads from abroad, again, which allowed time to hire coaches and reassemble rosters. The season had two parts: The rentals competed in the International Cup, while NASL-owned rosters played a round-robin league with no final. Kansas City Spurs won both parts. Average attendance remained around three thousand.

Going into 1970, one team dropped out, and two ASL teams joined, forming a six-team circuit with an even weirder "split" season: One part involved a series of matches against each other; the other was again called the International Cup, and pitted NASL teams against foreign sides, with results against international competition counting in the regular season standings (no kidding). Rochester Lancers, elevated from the ASL, won the championship. Attendance remained bleak, TV absent. Kansas City folded at the close of the season.

Going into the 1971 campaign, two teams from north of the border

(Toronto Metros and Les Olympique of Montreal) and one team from NYC—with the nifty name New York Cosmos—joined the league to form a gang of eight. These teams and their intrepid owners kicked off fourteen more years of professional soccer in America, a turbulent era in which the number of teams and their names never remained stable for two straight seasons—a circus-like atmosphere marked by the good, the bad, and the ugly.

A Welshman named Phil Woosnam quickly became the primary figure in shaping and running the league as the NASL's commissioner from 1969 through 1982. Woosnam (a naturalized U.S. citizen) was a suitable analogue to Thomas Cahill in terms of his optimism and work ethic. He even spoke like Cahill: "The North American Soccer League will be the world's No. 1 soccer league, and it will be the biggest sports league in the USA." Woosnam shepherded the league through the wake of its initial painful merger, slow-moving rookie years, and its spectacular rise in the mid- to late-1970s—before Woosnam himself was cast aside by the owners, in 1982. The early 1980s witnessed the league suffering from the weight of its frenetic expansion, overpaid superstars, and persistent failure to Americanize the game (characterized by its inability to assemble actual Americans on the field of play). After scraping its fuselage across the tops of trees for several years, the league crashed to earth at the close of the 1984 season, returning America to the soccer wilderness. But we are getting ahead of ourselves and the ball again.

From 1969 to 1974, largely thanks to Woosnam's recruitment of owners and nearly Herculean efforts, the NASL kept its feet on the ground and gradually expanded its fan bases and teams—adding zero, one, or two teams per year. Strategic patience was rewarded by incrementally increasing fans and media coverage. With no franchises west of Dallas, travel and accommodation costs remained manageable. Average gates trended upward, reaching 6,000 by 1973. That year the Philadelphia Atoms, with a league-leading six U.S. starters, beat the Dallas Tornado in Texas in front of about 19,000 fans. Dallas's own Yank, Kyle Rote Jr. (son of an ex–New York Giants wide receiver), soon became a household name. Kyle was the league's top scorer in 1973 with ten goals and ten assists—also winning Rookie of the Year—even though he had joined the league late due to college graduation and a wedding. Rote soon appeared on the popular 1970s TV show called *Superstars*, winning the overall contest three years in a row. Curiously, he continued to rack up goals and assists in the NASL, but was never selected to any of the all-star teams.

Far from the hoopla of Hollywood, Commissioner Woosnam was busy growing the league. He was aided and hindered by NASL team owners, ranging from sound businessmen to reckless charlatans. Entrepreneur and team owner Lamar Hunt played a pivotal role in helping the league grow. His business decisions focused on the Dallas Tornado, his main soccer asset. But he also made altruistic choices for the sport as a whole, which continued for four decades, well into the rise of MLS. Pushing the soccer envelope and growing the game certainly weren't being done by the USSFA, which in 1974 finally became the U.S. Soccer Federation (USSF) from its Colorado Springs headquarters. Research can't locate a press release or a news article about the name change. The USSF had yet to hire a full-time National Team coach. The Federation was essentially extraneous to its own sport.

As to the NASL, it took more than Woosnam's enthusiasm and vision, and Hunt's business acumen and money, to sustain the league's initial modest growth and then ignite the league's rapid rise from 1974 to 1979 (from fifteen to twenty-four teams!). It took American ingenuity and spectacle, much of it distasteful from a British perspective. There were tailgaters, cheerleaders, and mascots galore. The Minnesota Kicks, for a while, turned the parking lots outside its rented 49,000-seat Metropolitan Stadium (home of the Vikings from 1961 to 1981) into a "bacchanalian celebration" by offering free parking and a tenuous police presence, which, for a few years, spurred average gates in the 20,000 range.

Once inside any NASL-rented stadium, fans league-wide were often entertained by cheerleaders from the gridiron world. The cheerleading squad names would surely get red-carded by any marketing department today: the Stompers (Oakland), the Shakers (San Jose), the Sting Girls (Chicago), the Vogues (Memphis), the Wowdies (Tampa Bay), the Striker Psychers (Fort Lauderdale), the Honey Dips (Washington, D.C.), and the California Surf Cheerleaders (Anaheim), nicknamed the Surf Breakers (affectionate or sexist, depending on one's point of view). The British press rarely commented on the NASL without using the word "razzmatazz," or a word like it, and referencing the cheerleaders.

One of the first costumed mascots to strut to national popularity, the San Diego Chicken (of baseball's San Diego Padres fame), in a recurring stunt sure to bring a smile to soccer fans the world over, perfected a pirouette move where he'd fall to the ground and thrust his yellow legs into the air—and play dead. After an opposing forward fell (after a nick) during a San Diego Sockers match, and rolled to a stop, clutching his knee in "agony," the chicken ran onto the field and did his pirouette move right beside the "injured" player. Fans went nuts. So did the head referee—who ran over to the home team's bench and screamed, "Get that fucking chicken off the field!" Mascots were summarily banned from the field of play.

But that didn't stop mascots from arriving at NASL games on camels, helicopters, fire trucks, hang gliders, trick bicycles, and cop cars. Cheerleaders and players joined the fun, too. Decked in their cheerleading and playing kits, they entered the stadium astride Harley-Davidson motorcycles and horses, and atop London double-decker buses and wagons. Once the game started, there were cavalry charges up the wings, ducks behind the goals, firecrackers going off, organs, trumpets, and bongo drums accompanying every attack. "The Yanks," observed an English soccer writer, "as usual tend to overdo it."

Many transplanted Brits loved the attention and American approach to sport. "I was interviewed by a woman journalist soon after I got here," reflected Trevor Francis, "and one of the first things she wanted to know was how long I'd been a superstar. I said, 'about three days.'" Foreign salaries were higher, and often came with free apartments and cars. And the crowds were forgiving. "If you made a mistake, there weren't too many people who knew you made a mistake, so you could just get on with it," recalled Scottish defender Charlie Mitchell. "You make one mistake [back home], and 25,000 fans get down on you." English defender Laurie Calloway added: "In England, the attitude is that we are overpaid and under-worked." The NASL was a breath of fresh air for the foreign players.

English football during the NASL's run suffered from hooliganism, dilapidated stadiums, substandard policing, and ineffective crowd control. "If I was a family man, I wouldn't even consider going to a soccer match in England," recounted Seattle Sounders striker Roger Davies. Rodney Marsh in 1976 (in)famously proclaimed: "English football is a gray game played on a gray day before gray people. American soccer is a colorful game played on a sunny day before colorful people." It took stadium disasters in the mid- to late-1980s, renovation of grounds, new policing standards, the creation of the Premier League (1992), and a Sky Sports TV megadeal to curb hooliganism.

Playing in America provided a healthy paycheck, a new perspective, and a sense of freedom. Most of the stars loved relative anonymity, while nightlife attention was never out of reach. Fans were respected. Plenderleith observed: "[Fans] arrived at the stadium two or three hours early to grill hot dogs and chug down beer with mates in the parking lot while listening to ramped-up radio." Marsh recalled: "I found a country that not only celebrated its stars, but enjoyed them too. I felt more relaxed in a place where I could express myself freely, on and off the field."

This suited foreign players, but a decade in, American players remained virtually unknown and irrelevant. The league did little to integrate them. Defender Bobby Smith complained: "Who's looking out for the Americans in the NASL? The owners? They can't get their faces out of the trough long enough to be moral. The coaches? They're so scared of losing games they won't take a chance on us. The foreign players are too insecure with their own starting positions. As a result, we're getting the shaft right here in our own country."

Woosnam, like Cahill almost a half-century before, articulated the central problem clearly: "You don't start with pro soccer and wind up with eight-year-olds playing soccer in grammar school. You start with the eight-year-olds and end with highly competent professional teams. Americans have got to learn the value of playing soccer before they can enjoy watching the finished product." Nobody listened. Shamefully, not one NASL team ever established a fully functioning youth academy. Starting in the late 1970s, the best instruction for teens (often U-16 and older) was stitched together by a smattering of Olympic Development Programs around the country, which appeared for young men long after their basic soccer DNA had formed. Nobody had the will or the patience, let alone the money, to grow the game from within and from below. Woosnam himself eventually capitulated to the money-hungry owners and went for broke. Forget the American problem. Just add teams (just about anywhere) and buy foreign players. It would eventually cost him his job—and destroy the league. But not before a glorious half-decade of shooting for the stars.

The turning point from modesty to spending spree came around 1975 when several team owners started buying aging superstars from South America and Europe. At first, the contracts were modest and the players several strides past their prime. But midway through the 1975 season, the Warner Communications–owned New York Cosmos (under general manager Clive Toye) jilted the cosmos by signing the thirty-four-year-old Edson Arantes do Nascimento, globally known as Pelé, to a three-year deal worth about five million dollars (not including a two-million-dollar Brazilian tax bill Warner covered). The deal, which was built on the grooves of a lot of profitable vinyl records, made Pelé the highest paid team athlete in the world. The NASL soon became the destination for many of soccer's aging international stars. The expensive footrace and increasingly outrageous signings became one of the major culprits responsible for bankrupting the league.

Few acknowledged at the time that Pelé's signing was the beginning of the end, once again, of professional soccer on American soil.

13

THE FALL OF THE NASL AND THE RISE OF TOTAL FOOTBALL

American soccer retreats, once again, while the best in the rest of the world advance the game (1975–1985)

"A nickel ain't worth a dime anymore."

— Yogi Berra

"Total Football is about movement and intelligence. To play well, you need to understand the role of everyone on the pitch. Only then can you make the right decisions."

— Johan Cruyff

Neither the peak of the NASL (late-1970s), nor the precise reason for its demise (at the close of its 1984 season) can be pinpointed, though its dreams and nightmares were always about money. The NASL had long been tweaking the game with gear and gimmicks, from innovative to ridiculous. In addition to cheerleaders, the league experimented with brightly colored balls and jerseys with numbers and names on the back (now ubiquitous worldwide). Early on, the league had no choice but to inherit gridiron-stadium game clocks that counted down to zero, still used (annoyingly) in NCAA soccer games. From 1972 to 1982, the NASL implemented offside lines, thirty-five yards from goal, usually dotted, forming offside-free zones to the halfway line. The zones—a first in world football—had little effect on increased scoring. Defenders just dropped back behind the lines, limiting their ability to join counterattacks. Total Football it wasn't.

From its birth, the NASL awarded teams a bonus point for each goal (capped at three), regardless of the final score. Unlike the offside-free zones, this innovation stimulated more offensive play. Sitting on a one-goal lead ("parking the bus") or throwing in the towel was no longer optimal. The rule also fomented controversy. Five times the nontraditional scoring system gave the regular season title to a team other than the one with the best W-L record.

In 1973, the NASL instituted a three-substitutes rule (the horror!), and in 1974 mandated a penalty shootout (from the penalty spot) to decide all tied games, eight years before it actually appeared in a FIFA World Cup knockout round (1982). In 1977, to appeal to U.S. audiences, the NASL replaced the penalty shootout with a mandatory "dribbling shootout" (from the thirty-five-yard offside line). The shooter had five seconds to dribble toward the goal and score—unless he dribbled too long, missed the shot, or his shot was stopped by the goalie. Each team had five attempts. If still tied, sudden-death shootouts followed. A dribbling shootout win was worth fewer points than a regulation-time win. Many fans loved it. FIFA hated it. Players' feelings were mixed. The shootout lasted until 1984.

In 1975, eight years after the Super Bowl debuted, the Soccer Bowl appeared—a one-game championship* derived from a postseason tournament of playoff teams. Owners, in later years, proposed additional rule

* Except for 1984's best-in-three series, which only needed the first two legs to decide the winner.

changes—some sensible, like limiting the back pass to the goalie; others outrageous, like permitting one field player (designated before the game by giving him a uniquely colored jersey) to swat the ball with his hands anywhere on the pitch. Thankfully, this idea was swatted down by team owners—but only by a narrow margin of votes.

But perhaps the biggest problems tormenting the NASL all along were the poor playing surfaces and mismatched venues, which the league could never jettison for financial reasons. Most NASL games were played on hard artificial surfaces that were dominated by gridiron lines. "Sometimes it was like trying to play soccer on a parking lot." "The ball wouldn't bounce right, and it hurt to fall." "If you slid on Astroturf, you got atrociously burned." Players claimed some burns *never* healed. "The football lines were so distracting that you couldn't tell if it was a soccer match or a Sunday pickup game." Other games occurred on baseball outfields that always included part of the infield. The gridiron lines and baseball dirt were constant reminders to fans in the cavernous stadiums (and on TV!) of soccer's second-class status.

Genuine soccer-specific stadiums did not exist. Fans were always outnumbered by empty seats, sometimes eerily so. "In Europe, we'd play to packed stadiums, full of passion. Here, we had world-class players in a stadium maybe ten percent full. It was surreal." "You'd hear a few fans cheering, and their voices would just echo. It felt like playing in a cathedral, but one where no one showed up for the service." "Going to a game in a 70,000-seat stadium with 5,000 people was depressing. You'd feel part of a failed experiment." "It was a league of great dreams and terrible optics."

Instead of addressing persistent problems, including figuring out a solution to the shortage of actual Americans on the field of play, Commissioner Woosnam and owners started adding franchises rapidly, including putting professional soccer teams in cities and regions ill-suited for soccer. The artificial playing surfaces of Team Hawaii (Honolulu) and the Las Vegas Quicksilvers, during the hottest months, literally melted the rubber soles of soccer boots. Games at these venues were mostly low-scoring, desultory affairs in front of meager crowds with everyone in attendance—players, coaches, stadium staff, even fans—hating the heat. Goalkeeper Alan Mayer recalls: "You'd come into the locker room and dunk your feet, with your shoes still on, straight into a bucket of cold water."

In 1974, eight new teams were added, swelling the league to fifteen teams. The owners started buying increasingly more expensive imports. Average attendance that year was 7,825. Pelé's debut game (an exhibition) in Cosmos colors, halfway into the 1975 season, took place at the outdated and depressing Downing Stadium, located on Randall's Island, NYC. Over 21,000 fans saw Pelé score and assist in a draw with Dallas Tornado. Over 300 journalists attended, as well as a bevy of dignitaries and celebrities. It was a cultural event and the biggest thing to happen to American soccer in its 100-year history. The Brazilian earnestly tendered: "This is not just a game for me; it's an opportunity to help soccer grow in America." Less than a month after joining the league, in Washington, D.C., 35,620 people witnessed Pelé and the Cosmos defeat the Diplomats, a record crowd for a regular-season league game on American soil. This record would not last long. Wherever Pelé and the Cosmos went, turnstiles fluttered—which teased many of the other team owners who saw mountains of money forming in the distance, causing them to ignore problems in their own backyard.

In the second half of 1975, attendance for Cosmos games doubled. With two conferences, four divisions, and twenty teams, Pelé set attendance records at every venue. It became cool to wear a Cosmos shirt, go to a soccer game, boast about a child's youth soccer game at cocktail parties. Attendance at home games in Pelé's third and final season (1977) was four times the gate the year prior to the Brazilian's arrival. That year he helped the Cosmos win one of their five league titles. His retirement game (a non-league friendly) at Giants Stadium on October 11, 1977, drew 77,000 people. Pelé played the first half for the Cosmos, and then swapped jerseys and played the second half for his first professional Brazilian side, Santos FC. Each year during the Seventies—except for a flat 1978 attendance year likely due to the NASL's peak expansion to twenty-four teams (!)—average attendance increased, with the back half of the decade witnessing greater increments. According to David Wangerin, "Pelé didn't just fill seats. He filled hearts and minds with the idea that soccer belonged in America."

The affable and brilliant Brazilian with the infectious smile, together with stargazing owners, triggered an avalanche of signings of aging superstars. George Best, only age thirty upon entering the league, still struggling with alcoholism, was eager to leave a wake of defenders and controversy wherever he went: "I spent a lot of money on booze, birds [women], and fast cars. The rest I just squandered." Also crossing the Atlantic Ocean or making their way up from South America: Eusébio, Geoff Hurst, Rodney Marsh, Bobby Moore, Johan Cruyff, Franz Beckenbauer, Carlos Alberto Torres, Gordon Banks, Ruud Krol, Gerd Müller, Alan Ball, Trevor Francis, and Giorgio Chinaglia (who was the league's all-time leading goal scorer, netting a remarkable 242 goals in 254 games from 1976 to 1983). The list is much longer. Each player deserves a chapter (or more) regarding his NASL days. Many brought skill, talent, showmanship, and flair to the league, making it the world's first professional-sport "melting pot" and a forerunner of modern top European leagues. Ian Plenderleith observed: "The [NASL] was the first truly mobile league, where every team was enhanced, or burdened, by its multinational nature. It was a proving ground for the idea of sport without borders that was finally realized by the English Premier League [which started in 1992]."

The expensive signings were a mixed bag in terms of immediate impact on the gate. Pelé, Cruyff, and Beckenbauer increased attendance, home and away. But few Texans had heard of Bobby Moore—and even if they had, it was likely the one who played wide receiver for the Minnesota Vikings, later known as Ahmad Rashad, who became a sports broadcaster. Eventually the star-chasing tore holes in every owner's wallet, including the coffers of the Cosmos

In the meantime, American players continued to ride the bench, literally and statistically. The league tried to boost domestic presence on the pitch with a rule starting in 1972 requiring two American or Canadian players—commonly a goalkeeper and outside back—on the field at all times. The mandate had little impact, and maybe a negative one once the coaches' biases were confirmed by a quota system. Cruyff cogently summed up the problem: "[The NASL] doesn't have farm clubs or reserve-team schedules. As a cost-cutting move, some colleges are reducing their schedules. Pretty soon no one will be able to afford foreigners. If you bring up your own talent, you don't pay transfer fees. And, besides, in a few years who's going to come and see old stars like me play?" (We'll return to Cruyff a bit later.)

TV, a friend to soccer in Europe and Latin America, carried on doing no favors to Americans by broadcasting games at odd hours and with poor production qualities, including the uncanny ability to cut to a commercial right before a pivotal play. Except for 1968 and 1978, network TV never carried more than nine games, with the other years trending toward low single digits, and some years (especially in the early 1970s) a total blackout. Most franchise owners, at least during the mid- to late-Seventies, kept pouring money into the league, betting their futures on a lucrative national TV deal that never materialized. Several TV networks flirted with soccer, but when ratings lagged (which they always did), they abandoned games and reneged on promises—TV's lawyers always outplaying the NASL's lawyers when it came to negotiating and enforcing contracts. Ironically, from 1976 to 1984, the PBS-produced TV show *Soccer Made in Germany*, which tracked the German Bundesliga, reached more American households than the NASL. It was spotty reception all around for the couch-sitting American soccer fan.

By the early 1980s, teams in small markets folded. Many in larger markets were also hurting. Everyone was losing money. Only the Cosmos could afford to keep hemorrhaging money, and even its Warner Communications owners had a limit. The NASL attempted to expand revenue by entering indoor soccer in the offseason, but scarce dollars were already being vacuumed up by the Major Indoor Soccer League (MISL), operating since 1978. A two-stage recession hit the U.S. in 1980–1982, with skyrocketing inflation and unemployment peaking at nearly 11 percent in late 1982, the highest since the Great Depression.

Paul Cannell, English forward for the Tampa Bay Rowdies, presciently told a *Sports Illustrated* writer in late 1980: “I give the NASL two years. You can’t say that soccer’s arrived anymore. It’s here. But you can’t claim that it’s a major sport either. It’s on some sort of plateau, and if it doesn’t get up and dance this time, I don’t think the public will stay interested.” After ordering a beer, he added: “It needs something new and fresh. Elephants! Pageants! The Village People!”

In 1981, the NASL lost six teams overnight, dropping to eighteen. The following year, four more disbanded. In 1983, the league contracted to twelve squads and attempted to solve its American-player problem by creating Team America and placing them in RFK Stadium. It was billed as a strategy to help the USMNT qualify for the 1986 World Cup. Although logical and well-intentioned, it failed. Many top American players refused to leave their NASL teams. Bob Lifton, likely the only American millionaire still optimistic about soccer’s future, funded the effort. With many top Yanks refusing to assemble in D.C., Team America struggled to field actual American players. So, rules were bent, and some quickly naturalized English-Americans joined. The only thing vibrant about Team America was their colorful flag-looking jerseys, which looked like they had been stitched together in an Eighties home economics class.

On May 20, 1983, FIFA announced that the U.S.—in the running for hosting the 1986 World Cup (after Colombia withdrew)—lost out to Mexico, who had already hosted in 1970. FIFA had been chafing against the USSF and the NASL for more than a decade over the Yanks’ novel soccer rules and arrogance. FIFA, starting in 1981, repeatedly told the NASL to get rid of its thirty-five-yard shootout. But the Yanks refused and kept on dribbling. FIFA also hated the stadium clocks and the point system. FIFA officials may have never been receptive to the Americans’ fairly sophisticated bid to stage the 1986 World Cup tournament. In any event, the Americans’ fate was sealed when a high-ranking representative from the USSF secretly called the FIFA President (after the bid was submitted) and told him the U.S. was not prepared to host. (And maybe America wasn’t ready.)

The lost opportunity deflated the hopes of soccer's dreamers, from the front offices of NASL franchises to fields everywhere in the U.S. where a ball was being kicked. Some blame FIFA for killing pro soccer on American soil. But that criticism mostly misses the mark. The NASL had done a first-rate job of maiming itself over the years.

Team America, at the close of its inaugural season, finished dead last and promptly folded. As 1983 came to an end, Warner Communications reported a loss of $424 million for its first three quarters (primarily due to its struggling Atari video-game division), and sold its stake in what journalists called Warner's "soccer plaything." The best American player on the Cosmos, Ricky Davis, defected to the MISL. Star forward for the Cosmos and league MVP Giorgio Chinaglia negotiated a stake in the Cosmos, but then summarily attacked the entire league. "They're a sinking ship right now, and I refuse to go down with them." Chinaglia then took his money and cache back to Italy to focus on his role as President of S.S. Lazio, the club that helped rocket him to international fame.

Neither Team America nor the Cosmos had any positive residual effect on the USMNT. Even with Mexico already qualified (due to the host-nation automatic-qualification rule) and out of the U.S.'s World Cup qualifying region, the MNT then failed to qualify for the 1986 World Cup, again, for the ninth straight time. This time the U.S. lost to Costa Rica in a July 1985 game where the Yanks only needed a tie to move to the final qualifying round. The game was played in Torrance, California, a venue specifically chosen by the USSF to sell tickets to Costa Ricans. During the halftime locker-room talk, and already down 0–1, the American players couldn't escape the drums and music from the "foreign" fans, causing a young defender to shout: "When are we ever going to play a home game?" Even ESPN, which had bought the rights to broadcast the game, opted to show it (before knowing its final score) on tape-delay, ending at 2:30 AM (for the East Coast soccer insomniac).

The USMNT, under the tutelage of the USSF, was still stumbling around in the soccer desert. From 1953 to 1986, the U.S. lost most of its World Cup qualifying games and never qualified for a World Cup tournament.

Mexico represented the CONCACAF region* six times, El Salvador twice. Even Haiti and Canada made World Cup appearances. The blame went way beyond the athletes. Walt Chyzowych, a two-time MNT coach, adroitly summed it up: A squad—often selected by committee, led by a part-time coach, with little to no training time—was "no way to prepare for international matches." The NASL contributed greatly to the problem by seldom permitting their best American players to join the MNT for matches and tournaments

In the early 1980s, few people were paying attention to the MNT, and enthusiasm for soccer was fading. The NASL entered 1983 on life support and essentially tripped over and then pulled its own plug. The 1983 Soccer Bowl featured the Tulsa Roughnecks and the Montreal Manic. Unfortunately, the talented Roughneck forward Ron Futcher had received a red card in the semifinal match. Recalls defender Bruce Wilson: "Of course, everyone in the world, media and clubs and everyone understands the rule—you're out of the final." But the league commissioner rescinded the red card, claiming his decision was made in the "interest of the sport and the game tomorrow." No amount of sugarcoating dispelled the message to players, fans, and media (whoever was left) that Americans had a "weirdo idea" of soccer's time-honored rules. The Roughnecks won the final, over the Toronto Blizzard, with Futcher scoring one of Tulsa's two goals.

The last game of the NASL was played on October 3, 1984 (down to nine teams), in the second leg of a best-of-three Soccer Bowl series, where the Chicago Sting (named after the 1973 heist film starring Robert Redford and Paul Newman) defeated the Toronto Blizzard. A cynic would say the more ignominious owners had pulled off their own heist after fleecing the fans and fleeing into the hinterlands. Average attendance in its final year slid to about ten thousand, about where the league was in the mid-1970s.

* FIFA created CONCACAF in 1961 and it is still the governing body for the football geographic conglomerate from our region. The mysterious acronym comes from the following letters (even though the second N is omitted): CONfederation of North, Central American, and Caribbean Association Football. CONCACAF currently consists of forty-one football associations. Today, FIFA oversees six such confederations around the world.

One American player made the NASL's 1984 First Team league honors, *one* more American than when the league started seventeen years earlier. The highest attendance in 1984 was for a May 28 league game between the Tampa Bay Rowdies at the Minnesota Strikers, a remarkable 52,621 fans (buoyed by a hybrid event involving a Beach Boys concert). The lowest attendance was recorded by the Tampa Bay Rowdies at the San Diego Sockers, a dismal 2,267. Such was the dichotomy inherent in U.S. professional soccer: devotion and despair. If only the devotion could be monetized, sustained, and tied to the progress and success of American players. Only two teams signed up to play the following year. The league folded. American soccer, once again, sank. But this time it didn't slow its heart rate and hibernate. Instead, it frantically increased its heart rate and went entirely indoors—to artificial oval fields, music blaring, smoke billowing, balls bouncing off walls—an American incarnation that was essentially a stubborn, turf-burned middle finger to Total Football.

While Americans toyed with soccer and the rules for a decade and a half, the best in the rest of the world were making giant inroads in tactics and style of play, which undergird the modern game. In the early 1960s, along cobblestone streets a few hundred yards east of the Ajax football stadium, in Amsterdam, Netherlands, a young teen named Johan Cruyff—with a pair of cleats knotted at the laces and strung over his shoulder, and a cigarette probably hanging from his mouth—emerged from the shadows, turned pro at seventeen, climbed to the top of world football, and changed the game forever. He led AFC Ajax and then FC Barcelona to league titles, domestic cups, and European club championships. He won Europe's highest individual honor, the *Ballon d'Or* ("Golden Ball" in French), three times (1971, 1973, 1974). He led the Dutch to a World Cup final against West Germany in 1974, where the *Oranje* ("Orange" in Dutch) lost by a whisker to *Die Mannschaft* ("The Team" in German).

Everywhere Cruyff went—as a player, and later as a coach—he made vastly better (at least for a while). His Total Football (TF) philosophy, emphasizing positional interchange, fluidity, and technical skill (more specifically defined below), had a lasting impact on both club and international football. As a coach, he revamped FC Barcelona's youth academy, *La Masia* ("the Farmhouse" in Catalan), which produced several world-class players and at least one world-class coach (Pep Guardiola). Cruyff catalyzed change that led to dramatic improvements in youth development worldwide. Commentaries on Cruyff's playing career and Total Football philosophy fill several library shelves (or digital rows on Amazon).

TF is nearly impossible to succinctly define, but it will become clearer below. It wasn't entirely Cruyff's idea. He synthesized ideas percolating for years and articulated (with help from Dutch coach Rinus Michels, two decades his senior) a comprehensive novel approach. Cruyff did this first as a player (orchestrating others during the game, as if he were the sun and all others planets in his orbit), then as coach (the divine architect), elevating teams to empyrean heights. But those heights could not be sustained by Cruyff—or anyone else. Cruyff's tenure nearly everywhere ended in confrontation, often with him leaving before or after getting sacked.

Not many Americans were following Cruyff's journey and the wider adventures of European soccer, not to mention the development of TF. But that didn't mean soccer on American soil for actual Americans was barren. Changes in U.S. immigration policy, starting in the 1960s, led to a broader diversification of the immigrant population, with African and Caribbean communities becoming integral parts of the American social and cultural landscape. Soccer communities started absorbing and enjoying the expertise and "fancy feet" of new kinds of players, often people of color. They formed their own teams or joined teams composed of first- and second-generation immigrants. Some of the better teams were paying players several hundred bucks a game. And they continued operating quietly in the background of the NASL. Further, all during the rise of the NASL, and seemingly unperturbed by the eventual death of the league, American youth soccer and college soccer continued to make tremendous strides in terms of participation.

With the introduction of Title IX in 1972—a federal law prohibiting gender discrimination in any federally funded education program, including college sports—women's athletics (dramatically underrepresented at the time), after a slow start, saw a surge in support. Soccer programs, which were inexpensive to implement and maintain, received a lot of attention and financial backing. Starting in the late 1970s, women's soccer teams materialized and grew rapidly across the nation, their growth rate often outpacing men's teams for decades (the whole point of the law, striving for equality).

Similarly, by the late 1970s, suburban communities had embraced the sport and made youth soccer a mainstream co-recreational activity. Structured youth leagues quickly spread nationwide and spurred pay-to-play club models, which have been almost impossible for American parents to resist due to the lack of alternatives and the appeal of college soccer programs and scholarships. Since the early 1980s, no country has had more youth and college soccer teams than the U.S. The Yanks are winning the participation trophy by a large margin.

Despite soccer's vast reach, with youth leagues in nearly every town and city, and school-sponsored teams at most high schools and colleges nationwide, this network, for decades, did not lead to greater engagement in elite soccer at the international and professional levels. Further, grassroots soccer communities have not experienced a noticeable rise in Total Football concepts. In contrast, players, parents, and fans in soccer-loving countries—because of their deep cultural association with the sport and corresponding "consumption" of elite soccer well into adulthood—have graduated to at least a basic understanding of TF concepts.

Total Football on American soil is easier to define by what it isn't. Every time a coach in America brings players together in a big group, especially before the game, with kids waiting around for one player to emerge from the inert group to take a shot on goal—not TF. Every time a parent yells "great play," "great job," or "great shot" after a fast kid dribbles past slower kids, without lifting his head to pass the ball to the next guy—not TF. Every time a goalie punts a ball into a fifty-fifty situation, a field player kicks a ball down the field and to no one in particular, or a coach tells a player (usually a defender) to "stay back" or "don't cross midfield"—not TF. Nearly every time a coach or a parent rudely yells recriminations or in-game instructions from the sidelines (sure to rob players of the opportunity to play freely and learn from mistakes)—a lot of this, not TF. Indeed, too many youth games and training drills designed by well-meaning parent-coaches (and far too many academy and college coaches) are not based on TF principles at all. It's enough to make parents who truly understand TF concepts run to the nearest corner flag and stab out their eyes.

Further, many parents and coaches remain oblivious to position numbering, which has evolved over 150 years. Modern elite football formations change during the game, according to variables that take a lifetime to master. Tactics have never been America's strong point. This lack of lived experience and tactical knowledge makes having informed discussions with many American fans and players, even some very good ones, difficult. Jonathan Wilson's *Inverting the Pyramid: The History of Soccer Tactics* helps demonstrate how football is as much a mind game as a physical one—a chess match played with boots.

At its highest level, TF incorporates individual and collective techniques and tactics, approaching an art form. Cruyff never articulated TF in a single narrative. But it can be stitched together from anecdotes, interviews, and coaching clinics. His first tenet—"that every disadvantage has its advantage"—was learned growing up. Cruyff lived it on the pitch as a moderately paced pro, and applied it throughout his coaching life: "If you lose the ball [*i.e.*, the disadvantage], you have to press the opponent for 4–5 seconds to get it back." Regaining it often creates a numerical advantage near the other team's goal, leading to more goals as a statistical fact.

Cruyff's players were not rigid cogs. "To play well, you need to understand the role of everyone on the pitch. Only then can you make the right decisions." "The goalkeeper is the first attacker, and the striker is the first defender." Players switched positions seamlessly, creating overloads and surprises, leading to more goals. Sometimes Cruyff's lesson was simple: "When we have the ball, the other team can't score." And yet: "Football is simple, but it's difficult to play simple."

TF emphasizes space and pace: "What do you do when you don't have the ball? That's what determines where the space is. Football is about making space, and then exploiting it." "If you have to defend a restaurant, you defend the front door, not the entire street. You focus on where the danger is." Space, in relation to individual and team movements, became the final frontier for top players: "Football is a game you play with your brain. You have to be in the right place at the right time, not too early, not too late. And for that, players need the freedom to think for themselves."

While people may debate the finer points of Total Football, everyone agrees that the journey to footballing excellence requires years of calibrating the mind and body, and sometimes the spirit. And once a team has mastered it (and that moment will be fleeting—a season or two, if a team has earned it and is lucky), there is only one thing left to do. The entirety of Cruyff's halftime speech at the 1992 European Cup (now the UEFA Champions League) final, which his FC Barcelona team won, was the delightful quip: "Go out and enjoy it." All this is merely the tip of the iceberg. TF has evolved and will continue to evolve for as long as humans play football. Indeed, modern coaches have added to Cruyff's cathedral in ways reminiscent of the various additions to the Sagrada Família (cathedral) in Barcelona, Spain (Cruyff's home city for much of his adult life), designed and begun by the Catalonian artist Antoni Gaudí. The journey continues, and no one has a monopoly on the "right" way to play. In one of Cruyff's early matches as a young coach, when things weren't going well, a defender ran over to the bench to ask for advice. Cruyff barked: "Work it out yourself."

Americans, until very recently, weren't capable of figuring out, on their own, how to play better football. We too often looked abroad, to foreigners, or relied on our athleticism and can-do attitude. But that won't come close to regularly producing world-class players. Cruyff would note that one of the best teachers, all along, for developing football technique and basic tactical movements on and off the ball was right at our feet. Most of our young footballers would be better served if just about every training session and game warm-up involved a rondo (the Cruyffian Yoda) or a variation of it. In these exercises, players—both individually and in small groups—learn how to move, pass, and maintain possession of the ball in very tight spaces, with the coach not doing much more than shagging stray balls.

14

★★★★★

YANKS QUALIFY FOR THE 1990 WORLD CUP, WIN BID TO HOST IN 1994, AND THE BIRTH OF MAJOR LEAGUE SOCCER

Let's get soccer right (1984–1996)

"If you build it, they will come."

— *Field of Dreams*

Several months after FIFA rejected the U.S. bid to host the 1986 World Cup, the U.S. hosted the 1984 Summer Olympics, in sunny Los Angeles.* It was a massive success. Few countries could match Uncle Sam's professional infrastructure, advanced technology (TV production and satellite

* Author's note: The remaining chapters of this book summarize elite-level U.S. men's soccer from 1984 through 2026. Missing are many deserving people, stories, and ideas that could not fit in the lineup. As noted at the start of the book, a writer is really a coach who builds on the work of others and makes thousands of tactical choices along the way. What follows is a good summary, not the whole story.

feeds), corporate sponsorships, and America's brand of commercialism, expertly conveyed by a mascot designed by C. Robert Moore, an artist from Walt Disney Productions. Sam the 1984 Olympic Eagle, with his towering top hat adorned with the Olympic symbol, was a blend of smooth-talking showman and crafty carnival hustler, his yellow beak and googly eyes on the lookout for any wallet in his orbit. Corporations, mostly U.S.-based multinationals, bid for the right to become official sponsors and emblazon the Olympic logo on their products. Thus began a new competition that would venture into all major sporting events and leagues worldwide. Corporate sponsorship, in earnest, began in Los Angeles.

The Olympic soccer tournament drew enormous crowds, including a whopping 78,265 to watch the U.S. Olympic team in an early-round match, and a record-breaking 101,799 fans for the final between France and Brazil at the Rose Bowl, where France won the gold. For the first time since 1932, the Olympic Games posted a profit, a record $225 million. FIFA could no longer ignore America, the cash machine.

By the late Eighties, a whiff of professionalism had begun to infiltrate the USSF. The new administration scraped together a half-million dollars for a 381-page application to FIFA to host the 1994 World Cup. The application was drafted by a talented young attorney, Scott LeTellier, who had a role in the 1984 Olympics, where he got to know top FIFA officials and what they wanted to see in a World Cup bid. LeTellier's application included a thorough analysis of each potential venue, technical details on electronic transmission capabilities, and a heartfelt letter from President Ronald Reagan. Henry Kissinger, former Secretary of State, and an avid soccer fan, lobbied FIFA officials using back-channel diplomacy and overt pleas. So did Pelé, Franz Beckenbauer, and other global soccer icons who had experienced firsthand (during their NASL days) America's modern stadiums, efficient transportation networks, and world-class accommodations. Several major corporate sponsors (Coca-Cola, Visa, Adidas) also backed the bid, virtually ensuring FIFA a lucrative tournament. No surprise, then, that FIFA chose July 4, 1988, to officially announce that the U.S. would host the 1994 World Cup.

FIFA's award had one catch. In order to secure the right to host, FIFA required the U.S. to create a top-tier professional soccer league, which would arrive, after several postponements, in 1996 with Major League Soccer (MLS). But we are getting ahead of ourselves and the ball again.

Immediately after FIFA's announcement that the U.S. would host in 1994, the pressure to qualify for the 1990 World Cup was palpably felt throughout the U.S. soccer system. "Reaching Italy for the 1990 World Cup was now imperative if the U.S. were to carry any credibility as a host," noted David Wangerin. But in 1988, four years after the demise of the NASL, soccer at its highest level across the U.S. was rickety and disconnected. That year, five teams in the Major Indoor Soccer League folded. Many players found their way to respectable outdoor teams within one of two decent leagues on opposite coasts, operating on a semiprofessional basis, at best. Very few Americans at the time were playing professional soccer on real grass anywhere in the world. With the hosting duties and an automatic berth in the 1994 World Cup in their back pocket, could the U.S. men qualify for the 1990 tournament on merit?

The Americans' qualification journey for the 1990 World Cup began poorly. The MNT tied Jamaica in Kingston 0–0 on August 18, 1988. In the return leg,* in St. Louis, with the game in the sixtieth minute, the Yanks and the soon-to-be-dubbed Reggae Boyz were tied 1–1. The Americans were on the verge of another World Cup extinction.

But then the game plan shifted. The U.S. team scored four unanswered second-half goals to win 5–1, clearing the first qualification hurdle. Hours after the victory, the USSF announced it would begin signing players to

* *Return leg* or *second leg* are soccer terms for the second match in a two-game series in a tournament that requires two teams to play both home and away—with the aggregate score determining the winner. In some tournaments, particularly those that involve a larger group of teams (three or more), with each team playing one another home and away, the aggregate scores go toward a larger point tally involving all the teams in the group. The latter scenario applies to many modern World Cup qualification rounds.

modest contracts—securing their commitment to the MNT while allowing loans to other clubs. Some players left their clubs entirely; others used the income to supplement their professional or semiprofessional salaries. The USSF also ditched its part-time coach and hired the forty-seven-year-old, Hungarian-born Bob Gansler, whose father had been imprisoned by the Soviets during WWII, before emigrating from Budapest to Milwaukee, Wisconsin.

Then the U.S. team caught a lucky break. In June 1988, FIFA announced that Mexico, long the U.S.'s main CONCACAF nemesis, was disqualified from entering the 1990 World Cup because El Tri had knowingly rostered and played at least four overage players during an April 1988 FIFA World Youth Championship qualifying tournament. But even with Mexico out of the qualification cycle, the U.S. still struggled. Infighting continued at the USSF, and injuries followed. Meanwhile, support for the MNT at "home" games continued to be challenged by many first- and second-generation Americans and immigrants—who seemed to take pleasure in showing up at American venues not just to cheer their native country, but to jeer the U.S. team. A public address announcer during a 1989 qualification game in a St. Louis suburb urged the crowd to "remind the players what country the game is being played in." During its second and final qualification round, the U.S. collected three wins, one loss, and three ties, leaving the U.S. needing to win their final game against Trinidad and Tobago (T&T), away, in order to qualify.

This was not an easy task. T&T only needed a draw to qualify for their first-ever World Cup. The game was held on November 19, 1989, in Port of Spain, T&T's capital, in front of about thirty thousand jubilant fans, most decked out in red, the largest "away" crowd for any World Cup qualifying game for the MNT in forty years (barring two matches at Estadio Azteca, Mexico City). The Federation had borrowed heavily to finance the team. To help cover training costs in Florida ahead of the T&T match, USSF president Werner Fricker took out a sizable loan from his own construction company, effectively out of his own pocket.

The stakes were massive and the pressure on the young team enormous.

Years later, in the 2023 film documentary *The Billion Dollar Goal* (*TBDG*), several players admitted that anxiety was palpable in the days leading up to the T&T match. "We had to qualify," reflected midfielder Paul Caligiuri. If we failed, FIFA might "pull the next World Cup, that was legitimate, FIFA has the ability to do that." Caligiuri asked rhetorically: "What was soccer going to become in our country?" "Qualifying on our own was the springboard we needed to get to the next level," added goalkeeper Tony Meola. "Not having the 1994 World Cup would've been sport destroying."

It is easy to forget that the team arriving in Port of Spain was composed of players only a few years out of college, or still in college (Meola had just entered his junior year at the University of Virginia)—kids, really. Before the game, new captain Mike Windischmann—plucked from the semiprofessional ranks of the ASL's Albany Capitals—wryly observed: "Don't you realize, if we lose, some of us will have to go out and get jobs?" As told in *TBDG*, Meola, on the eve of the game, imagined a newspaper headline: "*Caligiuri Scores, Meola Pitches a Shutout.* We go to the World Cup! Sure as sh–, that's exactly what happened."

The game was close, tense, hard fought. The Yanks dodged an early bullet in a no-call on a clear penalty by an American defender. Then one of the most important goals in U.S. soccer history spontaneously and gloriously combusted. American sportswriters later called it "the shot heard around the world" (a phrase popularized by Ralph Waldo Emerson in his 1837 poem "Concord Hymn" about the Revolutionary War). Nearing the end of the first half, Caligiuri—in a clean white jersey tucked neatly into his Old Glory Blue shorts—received a bouncing square pass from Tab Ramos (one of the most skilled U.S. players in history). Caligiuri pivoted, chested the ball down, juked a defender, and pushed the ball into a pocket of free space. And then he took a shot from about twenty-five yards out—outside of the penalty box—a glorious looping long shot that found the top bins of the net. The goalie dove but there was nothing he could do. A toenail-biting fifty-three minutes of football ensued. T&T almost scored on three occasions. But the game ended 1–0, guaranteeing the U.S. their first World Cup appearance since 1950.

At that moment, the USMNT and larger program, a phoenix (or a battered, broken eagle, according to some people), started its wobbly yet inexorable rise. But the Yanks' rise to respectability among the world's elite was slow. A country can't make up for forty years of mediocrity overnight. Imagine the pressure once again on the American team, who arrived in Italy in the summer of 1990, about seven months after Caligiuri's goal, with a roster of mostly semiprofessionals, whose average age was twenty-three, including three active college players. The English football journalist Brian Glanville unfairly dismissed the U.S. team as a "galumphing side of corn-fed college boys," a comment reminiscent of the derogatory "shot-putters" term the French had used for the Americans leading into the 1930 World Cup, sixty years prior.

Truth be told, high-level soccer in the U.S.—from a pure athletic-pursuit standpoint—had been hindered for decades by NCAA rules requiring players to maintain strict amateur status at all times leading up to and including all four years of college. Further, the rules severely limited the number of training days and games a coach could orchestrate per academic year. From its inception, the NCAA took the British maxim "a gentleman never plays for money" and codified it—"no student shall represent a College or University in any intercollegiate game or contest who is paid or receives, directly or indirectly, any money, or financial concession"—and strictly enforced it with byzantine rules.* The regulations may have been

* To paraphrase just one example from the modern 433-page NCAA Division I Compliance Manual: a teenage high school soccer player who receives a few hundred dollars—or even a bag of soccer balls—for participating in a one-day tournament forever forfeits his chance to play NCAA Division I soccer. Yet that same athlete could still kick field goals on an athletic scholarship for the gridiron team. Critics have noted that student-athletes often need a lawyer just to navigate the regulations, which is why nearly every reputable college athletic department employs multiple compliance officers to ensure coaches and athletes don't run afoul of the rules. The recent advent of NIL (Name, Image, and Likeness) rights, which allow athletes to profit from their personal brand without jeopardizing their amateur status, is an improvement. Notwithstanding NIL and several more recent proposed changes, soccer players—and most other college athletes—for over a century, could not accept payment ("above actual and necessary expenses") for playing their sport in nearly any context, for fear of forfeiting their NCAA eligibility.

aimed at protecting the student in the student-athlete equation, but the system made it effectively impossible for American college soccer players and their coaches—a large network of hardworking people who had been carrying the water for the USSF and NASL for years—to even remotely keep up with an average soccer country's semipros and full professionals.

During the World Cup summer of 1990,* the spirited young Yanks lost to Czechoslovakia (1–5), Italy (0–1), and Austria (1–2), against fully professional, polished pros. None of the players from these powerhouse national teams would know (rightly so) a college textbook if it fell out of their locker in Rome. West Germany beat Italy in the Final, concluding a relatively lifeless, defense-heavy tournament plagued by low scoring (the worst in tournament history) and minimal creativity, aptly symbolized by the 1990 World Cup mascot called *Ciao* ("Hello" and "Goodbye" in Italian), an anemic stick figure composed of square blocks and a soccer-ball head.†

After the Azzurri match, some Italians gave the Yanks an ovation for their gritty performance. David Wangerin underscored the team's "indomitable spirit." The Americans, still without a true professional league, had held their own among football veterans who had over a half-century head start. "That team changed everything," recalled U.S. striker Bruce Murray. "We showed this country what soccer was all about. We even got the TV people at ESPN and TNT to care." The American writer Hal Phillips called the members of the 1990 MNT, and others within striking distance of the

---

* Most modern World Cups last twenty-eight to thirty-two days, straddling June and July. But the 2026 World Cup is slated to last thirty-nine days to accommodate the expanded field of forty-eight teams (up from thirty-two). In the 1990 World Cup, there were twenty-four teams.

† The product on the field was so poor that the International Football Association Board, at FIFA's request, made three major rule changes: (1) a player who was even with the last defender was deemed to be onside (not offside, as it had been for over a century); (2) a goalie, upon receiving an intentional back pass from a teammate's foot, could no longer touch the ball with his hands; and (3) a team victory during group play at a FIFA competition would be awarded three points (not two) to incentivize goals and wins over scoreless draws and defensive play. A delegation of Americans and next-host people, tagging along with FIFA officials at Italy 1990, also took note of everyone's desire to make the game more appealing to the global audience.

roster, *Generation Zero* in his book by the same name. These intrepid athletes set the groundwork for soccer's re-launch. After the Yanks' exit, the international press was lukewarm: outclassed but determined, too reliant on physicality, tactically naive, future hosts with potential.

It was soccer potential, of course, that had been dogging the Americans for decades. Planning for the 1994 tournament on American soil had been sluggish. Pressure from FIFA for new leadership and assurances mounted, even as the 1990 Cup wound down in Italy. Alan Rothenberg, a high-powered Los Angeles lawyer with NASL ownership experience and soccer-organizing chops going back to the 1984 Olympic Games, emerged from a three-way election in August 1990 (with FIFA's backing) to take over the USSF and the World Cup USA 1994 Planning Committee. Rothenberg accepted the mantle gracefully. With confidence akin to that of a newly elected public official, he declared: "Together, we will take soccer in the United States closer to the goal we all share of worldwide preeminence." Behind the scenes, however, there was a lot of doubt and a massive amount of work to be done.

Rothenberg cleared out the volunteers and hired salaried administrators and professionals, who hired other professionals, before letting the volunteers back in. More than 1,500 volunteers would be recruited to assist the 1994 World Cup host cities. USSF set a six-figure-salary record when it hired Hank Steinbrecher as secretary, who underscored American soccer's new mantra: "What we want is mom and dad, family income of $40,000 with a minivan and two kids who play on Saturday." The U.S. Soccer Federation had been a mom-and-pop store for decades. It had finally incorporated. The World Cup Organizing Committee set about getting a lot of ducks in a row, coast to coast, and would soon assemble formations in nine venues* (culled from a list of twenty-seven applicants), with the chair of

* The Rose Bowl in Pasadena, California; Stanford Stadium in Palo Alto, California; Soldier Field in Chicago, Illinois; the Pontiac Silverdome in Pontiac (near Detroit), Michigan; the Cotton Bowl in Dallas, Texas; the Citrus Bowl in Orlando, Florida; RFK Stadium in Washington, D.C.; Giants Stadium in East Rutherford, New Jersey; and Foxboro Stadium (now Gillette Stadium) in Foxborough, Massachusetts.

each city leading an enthusiastic flock of paid people and volunteers on how to host and broadcast world-class soccer.

From the start, the Committee's tasks were fraught with technical challenges, logistical concerns, and relentless pressure from the international community. Even our own press piled on, which from a U.S.-soccer-fan standpoint was not surprising. For nearly a century, America's sportswriters and garden-variety pundits—and their editors, and later, radio and TV hosts—what the American journalist Franklin Foer has called the "anti-soccer lobby"—have never hesitated to cough up and spit out ill-informed soccer diatribes. We American soccer fans, players, parents, coaches, all of us, roll our eyes whenever we come across this dreck, which is thankfully receding each year. We recognize the lobby and trolls as careless and confused people who, if they don't convert, will go to their graves clutching, in their wizened arms, the belief that America is so narrow that it cannot accommodate the beautiful game.

Rothenberg and FIFA had a huge challenge. No host had ever tried to run a tournament simultaneously in nine cities across three time zones—2,760 miles, as the crow flies, from Pasadena to Boston—in a country that neither had a functioning professional league nor a single adequate soccer-specific stadium. All nine World Cup stadiums had to be reconfigured. The directors of Giants Stadium (now MetLife Stadium) balked at having its hallowed gridiron playing surface modified, and publicly worried that its anchor tenants, the New York Giants and Jets (which had abandoned Shea Stadium), might be upset. The proposed modification boiled down to adding, temporarily, "a platform, which will reach the level of the first row of seats (about 10 feet above the football field) [to] support 6 to 10 inches of soil and natural grass." Nobody wanted to do it or fund it. FIFA, in response, drilled a shot right at Uncle Sam's chest: "If in the United States, the land of all possibilities, this is not overcome, FIFA shall not bring the World Cup to New York."

When FIFA was told that the platform would cost about $5 million, and that none of the constituents involved—the state authority that oversaw the stadium, the taxpayers of New Jersey, the USSF, FIFA's 1994 World

Cup company sponsors—would pay for it, FIFA backpedaled, likening the kerfuffle to "haggling over a few centimeters." Games went ahead in the Meadowlands on a pitch only seventy meters wide, five meters narrower than the FIFA minimum. As an illustrative example of how far public enthusiasm for soccer has come in thirty years: MetLife stadium, for the 2026 World Cup, removed tens of thousands of pounds of concrete and about 1,750 seats to accommodate the full dimensions of a FIFA World Cup pitch. This time, there was nary a peep of complaint from anybody.

What New York and New Jersey lacked in soccer etiquette on the eve of World Cup 1994, American ingenuity made up for in Detroit at the late "great" indoor Pontiac Silverdome. The main challenge for this venue was not so much with the field dimensions (though that was an issue), but with getting grass to grow and stay green and stable indoors for the life of the tournament. Scientist Trey Rogers, a professor of turf grass management at Michigan State University, and his team spent more than a year and a half figuring out how to grow grass, move grass, and keep it alive inside the Silverdome for a month. It worked. Once inside the Silverdome, the transplanted grass had to be coaxed with artificial grow lights and cooled by fans. A new industry emerged: cultivating grass off-site in movable trays or dense sod panels. These were then delivered to stadiums (most of which were open to the sky) and rolled out and installed, with drainage layers, over artificial turf.

A World Cup game had never been played indoors before, let alone on a surface composed entirely of transplanted natural grass. "The pitch is perfect. You look up and expect to see the sky and the sun but you see only the dome," observed England's John Barnes, during U.S. Cup 1993, a trial-run tournament held in several host cities. (FIFA soon embraced the American idea of World Cup hosts running major international regional tournaments during the summers leading up to a particular World Cup.) Nearly a century and a half after Charles Goodyear's rubber ball advanced the game, Michigan State's scientists and researchers played a pivotal role in improving another important accoutrement of the sport: portable (real) grass.

Not to be outpaced by the World Cup organizers and behind-the-scenes scientists, about thirty athletes on or within sniffing distance of the MNT transplanted themselves and their families to greener pastures abroad. Many ended up in the middle divisions of Germany and England. But those pastures weren't always so green. Paul Caligiuri went to Hansa Rostock, then in East Germany, and waited over ten weeks for the club to find him a steady place to live, and then endured a Spartan existence his wife surely did not sign up for. Steve Trittschuh joined up with Sparta Prague, in Czechoslovakia. When the weather turned dour, he found it difficult to find food. Lucky John Harkes, with a British passport by way of his father's Scottish birth, ventured to Yorkshire, where he eventually broke into the Sheffield Wednesday side. Harkes became the first American player (after the passing of 120 years) to appear in an FA Cup final, at London's iconic Wembley Stadium. Wednesday won 1–0.

Imagine the sheer audacity and chutzpah these daring athletes exuded, and the difficulties they faced on the other side of the pond—pre-internet, utter blackout on American television (and in print) of their very existence, fighting for positions on teams where anti-American bias for footballers was near universal and rock hard. "Saxifrage is my flower that splits the rocks," wrote the New Jersey poet and pediatrician William Carlos Williams back in 1921. He was talking about poetry. But his words about the power and persistence of an underdog wild plant called saxifrage—which can find a crack in a rock and eventually split it open—could just as easily apply to any Yank who has ventured abroad to fight stereotypes and pry his way into the lineup of any foreign professional soccer team. It was, and continues to be, an extraordinarily difficult task.

On the home front, and in March 1991, Rothenberg appointed the itinerant Serb Bora Milutinović, the "miracle worker," as head MNT coach after he had led Mexico to the quarterfinals of the 1986 World Cup, and Costa Rica to the knockout round of 16 in 1990. Milutinović's initial roster of Americans quickly rewarded him by winning its first major international trophy at the first iteration of the CONCACAF Gold Cup. The Yanks beat Mexico in the semifinal (our first meaningful victory over El Tri since 1934) and Honduras in the final.

The USSF's MNT program, rendered flabby during its long history of mediocrity and inactivity (spacing out MNT games to save money), flexed its newly forming muscles and started churning out fixtures and caps for its young Americans. The USSF set up two years' worth of summer U.S. Cups (four teams each), dry runs for the players, teams, and some of the 1994 World Cup venues. The mini-tournaments attracted several top national teams. The Yanks won it in 1992 and placed third in 1993 where the U.S., incredibly, beat the Three Lions in Foxborough, 2–0. The popular London tabloid *The Sun* lambasted the English team with the snarky headline: "Yanks 2, Planks 0." The Planks then buckled even more, eventually tying the Netherlands, on November 17, 1993, in a game they needed to win, and collapsed into the pile of teams that did not qualify for the 1994 World Cup. With the final whistle in Rotterdam, and in a flash, the English Menace—largely manifested by their traveling hooliganism problem, which had reached its ugly apex in the late 1980s—had been eliminated from the planning metrics inherent in Rothenberg's calculus.

With Rothenberg's careful planning leading to increased excitement as to the upcoming main event, nobody could figure out head coach Milutinović's rationale for roster decisions. In the many "friendly" games between his appointment and the opening of the 1994 World Cup, he made a dizzying array of unpredictable team selections, which "hinted at panic more than experimentation." While the MNT had performed well in the 1991 Gold Cup and 1992 U.S. Cup, the MNT under Bora had amassed a 1–2–7 record in games against actual World Cup finalists (*i.e.*, countries that had participated in a prior World Cup). Fifteen months before the World Cup opened, the U.S. lost to Iceland (population: 260,000), in San Diego, in front of an overwhelmingly friendly American crowd.

When accosted by the press, the inscrutable Bora Milutinović swatted aside questions and naysayers. "My job isn't hard," he offered. "You're the ones with the difficult job—trying to get me to tell you something. I speak five languages, but English is not chief among them." Then he might dance a jig for the reporters. A *New York Times* writer called him a nutty professor. He was goofy, weird, mysterious. Sometimes Bora just left the bench area (early), or returned from the locker room (late), while the game was going on. His assistant Steve Sampson (who would eventually take over the head coaching job and lead the U.S. team through the 1998 World Cup cycle) recalled: "One day I asked him: 'How come you never let us know what you're going to do for training?' He said: 'My friend, I must smell the grass to know exactly what the need is every single day.'" With three weeks to go before the opening whistle, Milutinović finally settled on his twenty-two-man roster. Only eight had been a part of the Italy 1990 squad. And, in keeping with every subsequent MNT World Cup squad, Bora had an affinity (understandably) for players with professional European experience.

Bora wasn't the only bizarre thing to appear on the road to the opening whistle. Outside a Las Vegas casino resort, on December 19, 1993, a giant soccer ball descended to earth—which was supposed to imitate Times Square's New Year's Eve "ball drop"—but succeeded only in looking like a foreign object had landed on the Strip, which is exactly what Rothenberg's World Cup Planning Committee wanted to avoid.

Inside, at a nearby casino convention center, a weird ensemble of FIFA people, Hollywood movie stars, athletes from both sides of the Atlantic, and one very funny American comedian began pulling blue and yellow balls out of glass jars and lighting the names of selected countries on a giant electronic grid. The goal of the World Cup "Draw" was to place the twenty-four qualified teams into six groups of four to play a round-robin group stage the following summer. In mid-June, the top two teams from each group, along with the four best third-place teams, would advance to a single-elimination tournament to determine the overall winner. FIFA's goal with the balls and lights was transparency. What millions saw on TV was clumsiness and discomfort exuding from just about everyone onstage.

To MC the event, FIFA chose Sepp Blatter, then FIFA's second-in-command, who had about as much personality as the nearest cactus. He paced back and forth onstage, his waxy head protruding from a stiff, angular suit, and fumbled his way, in imperfect English, trying to explain the balls and the electronic grid. The whole proceeding was finally rescued by the appearance of the American comedian Robin Williams, who repeatedly called Sepp "Mr. Bla*dder*," and passed him blue balls, then yellow, while wearing a surgical glove and cracking jokes—not about the sport of soccer—but about the balls and the board. Blatter was noticeably uncomfortable. But probably not as uncomfortable as he felt twenty-one years later, starting in 2015, during his fall from FIFA President to a member of FIFA Team Infamy, a large, ugly recalcitrant fraternity. Team Infamy has been growing for decades, like a noxious weed, and today includes people of many nationalities who took bribes or kickbacks in exchange for votes to award hosting rights for World Cup tournaments, among other crimes.* After all the balls had been accounted for, the U.S. found itself in a moderately tough group with (in fixture order) Switzerland, Colombia (one of the favorites to win it all), and Romania.

Virtually all tickets had been sold before the first game. All nine pitches were immaculate. Ted Koppel, the host of ABC *Nightline*, confessed that he "would choose to watch a good soccer match [over] baseball's All-Star game any day of the week." Striker, the giddy 1994 World Cup dog mascot, designed by the animation team at Warner Bros.—resembling Scooby-Doo's athletic cousin on soccer scholarship—was doing his happy dance on TV and posters everywhere. Notwithstanding the positivity, the international press "took endless delight in corralling the American-in-the street and waiting for the inevitable response to their question: The World *what*?" Yankee journalists piled on with shotgun-articles spewing buckshot in all directions about how "dreary and incomprehensible" this game of soccer is, and the hooliganism problem, and its potential to destroy American

* Team Infamy also includes people who laundered FIFA or sponsorship money, engaged in unreported or ghost contracts, deliberately "cooked the books," colluded in FIFA-related contracts and decisions for personal gain, stole or misappropriated FIFA funds earmarked to improve youth development at the local level, obstructed justice, destroyed documents, lied to investigators, intimidated witnesses—and all those who ignored the accumulation of crimes while standing on the sidelines, hands in pockets, mum. It's a deep bench.

cities. Which, like Y2K (Millennium Bug), didn't happen. The naysayers on both sides of the Atlantic failed to realize what the majority of Americans failed (and still fail) to realize—that there is a sizable number of very spirited people in America, millions deep, that continues to grow, who adore soccer and will repeatedly pay to see good soccer.

ABC and ESPN earned some soccer stripes by agreeing to show (and not reneging on showing) all fifty-two matches, live, and without commercial interruption during gameplay. It was a glorious day (month) for the virtual American soccer fan, who witnessed "more live coverage" than the country "had seen from the past fourteen tournaments put together."

From a marketing standpoint, the opening match at Soldier Field in Chicago on June 17, 1994, got off to a bumpy start. Oprah Winfrey served as the master of ceremonies and nearly fell off the stage. Diana Ross sang four songs, in a red jumpsuit, beginning with her hit "I'm Coming Out," which she sang as she strutted down the field, from one goal mouth to the other, the soul singer's movements and lyrics meant to roll soccer right into American living rooms. In the midst of the song, she took a penalty kick against a fake regulation-sized goal, but missed wide. Then the goalposts and nets purposely tore away at midpoint, permitting her to jog through the goal mouth to mount a stage.

The anti-soccer lobby loved it, wrongly claiming that the goal just toppled over. Further, anyone can miss a penalty kick, as the Italian legend Roberto Baggio would soon attest, several weeks later. The 1994 World Cup began and ended with a missed penalty kick. The opening match saw Germany beat Bolivia in front of a near-capacity 63,117 fans—a large jump from the average 48,400 fans for the 1990 World Cup tournament, in Italy.

The games at all nine U.S. venues rolled forward.

Cheered on by 73,425 mostly American fans, the MNT kicked off their campaign against Switzerland on real grass at the Pontiac Silverdome. It was the largest partisan Yankee crowd ever assembled for a soccer game. The stadium was decked out in red, white, and blue banners. The MNT colors, together with the stars and stripes of thousands of T-shirts and flags of all sizes, were being flaunted and waved by throngs of giddy

American fans of all ages. Many took great pride in spontaneously chanting "U-S-A" over and over. The MNT over the next thirty years spread its wings and reached loftier heights, onward and upward, bolstered by chants of "I-believe-that-we-will-win!" and "Oh-when-the-Yanks! Go-marching-in!"—only to revert to the base beat: "U-S-A! U-S-A! U-S-A!"

While the MNT has improved its game and tactical rhythms over the ensuing decades, U.S. soccer chants still rank dead last among serious soccer nations.

The Swiss took the lead in the thirty-ninth minute off a free kick. The Americans quickly equalized off a lovely long-range, over-the-wall free kick from Eric Wynalda, which banged in off the crossbar, right at the near post. During the second half, the giant indoor terrarium of the non-air-conditioned Silverdome, with the temperature at pitch-level inching toward 106°F (41°C) and a humidity level of 71 percent, slowed the pace of the players and the action. The game ended in a 1–1 draw. The United States claimed its first World Cup point in forty-four years.*

Next up were the colorful Colombians represented by the iconic light-yellow, lionesque Afro (a few shades lighter than the team's bold yellow jerseys) of captain Carlos Valderrama, one of the world's best midfielders. Soccer pundits predicted Colombia to reach the final four, maybe even win it all. The Yanks were represented by their own flamboyant center-back, Alexi Lalas, sporting a mane of fiery red hair and a well-coiffed dagger-goatee. Lalas, bold and defiant, proved to be an unabashed supporter of U.S. soccer at all levels over the years, but has been criticized as boisterous and bombastic. Fans often forget he represents the tail end of the first generation of the modern American professional player—athletic, free-spirited, barreling forward—one of the first down the chute and into the unknown. He and many others in the first two generations of modern American players went on to shape the U.S. soccer landscape at elite levels, mostly for good, as players, coaches, technical directors, managers, owners

* In all World Cup group-stage matches from 1994 onward, a tie earns a team *one point* while a win earns *three points*.

of lower division teams, TV pundits, podcasters, and fathers of next-generation great players (men and women). Their soccer lives over the last three decades often epitomized Ralph Waldo Emerson's model of self-reliance and the not always likable habit of speaking "the rude truth in all ways." These chapters cannot plumb those depths (and heights) in detail. But their DNA is in this book.

A record crowd for a USMNT game of 93,194 fans had packed into the Pasadena Rose Bowl to witness the Yanks take on Colombia, nicknamed *Los Cafeteros* ("the Coffee Growers" in Spanish). For thirty minutes, the teams traded deep attacking salvos, adrenaline surging on both sides. Then a mistake by the Colombian defender Andrés Escobar (unrelated to the drug czar) put the U.S. up a goal. Escobar, tracking back to defend his own goal, slid to intercept an American low-cross to the back post. But his outstretched foot redirected the ball into the only place on earth Escobar didn't want it to go. The U.S. doubled its lead in the fifty-second minute when "the fleet-footed Earnie Stewart latched onto a lofted pass from Tab Ramos and clipped it into the net." The Colombians pulled a goal back in the eighty-ninth minute. But the U.S. held on to win the game, its first World Cup win since the Yanks' dispersal of the Three Lions back in 1950.

It was disaster for the Colombians, who couldn't control their destiny and were out of the tournament. Escobar penned a heartfelt apology to his countrymen. After he returned to Colombia, and while the tournament in the States advanced to the knockout rounds, Escobar was brutally murdered in a parking lot of his home city, Medellín. Precise motive and details surrounding the killing (six shots to the body) remain unclear. Almost on cue, the American anti-soccer lobby inked a bunch of stories about the murder, ignoring the great and joyous things unfolding right before their eyes on American soil. Like the slugs that hit Escobar, they berated soccer as a vicious, violent foreign sport.

The Americans entered their third and final group game confident they would advance, which they did, even with a 0–1 loss to Romania in front of yet another record crowd (for an MNT game) of 93,869 fans. Romania advanced, beat the Maradona-less Argentina (Diego had been ejected from the tournament for failing a drug test), and then fell to Sweden in the semifinals. The Yanks advanced to their first-ever modern knockout round against mighty three-time winner Brazil, on Independence Day, a hot July Fourth, before another record 94,194 fans (another twenty-eight million Americans watched on TV).

But it was not a full-blown celebration for the MNT. The Americans defended well and occasionally countered well—highlighted by an audacious long-range bicycle kick from U.S. defender Marcelo Balboa that zoomed past the near post, a few inches wide. But the Yanks ultimately lost 0–1 to the better team. The Brazilians were reduced to ten men for just over half the match after a brutal elbow from defender Leonardo fractured Tab Ramos's skull, ended his soccer day on the spot, and sidelined him for months. After the final whistle, America's tournament dreams fell to earth, like floating embers drifting down. It had been a gritty performance and a pretty spectacular run for the young team.

Brazil went on to win the tournament, in penalty kicks—after the Italian Roberto Baggio, a devout Buddhist, sporting a long, dark, divinely braided ponytail, skied his penalty kick (it wasn't even close). The miss sealed the win for the Seleção. Baggio stood at the penalty spot, bowed his head, and kept his ground, while the Brazilian players, in wild celebration, stormed the area near him, celebrating. It was a soccer diptych at the highest level: utter joy and utter despair. Baggio's feet seemed to sink into concrete. The image became known as "the man who died standing"—an apt description for that instant. And yet it didn't capture the life Baggio had given the Azzurri. Italy would've never made the Final without him. Imagine the inner turmoil moments after the miss, and the malicious memories and thoughts, elbowing their way into Baggio's mind for the rest of his life. Śāntiḥ śāntiḥ śāntiḥ. Peace.

America had succeeded in putting on a great show for the world's best footballers and international fans, and had, themselves, witnessed firsthand the brilliance and personalities of the best in the game. Millions of American kids got to see soccer played at its highest level, on pitches where nary a blade of grass was out of place, by superb athletes of all sizes, religions, and ideologies—with snazzy hair of all kinds (and even no hair, like the ultra-smooth baldness of the Bulgarian Yordan Letchkov).

God, we love this beautiful game.

Everyone made a ton of money. Had FIFA a mascot, it would have happily run right up to Striker and thanked him with a kiss on his wet nose. By all objective metrics, USA 1994 was a rousing success. Ticket sales alone generated $210 million. Nearly 3.6 million fans attended the fifty-two matches, packing America's giant gridiron stadiums to 96 percent capacity (an average of nearly 69,000 fans per match) and setting attendance records that are expected to last until 2026.*

For American soccer fans, World Cup 1994 was a turning point. Before the tournament, and for about a decade, soccer fandom in America was virtually off the grid. The evangelists could be identified by a little soccer ball dangling from a rearview mirror, or a sticker on a bumper, which would elicit a nod or wave (or even a beep) from one supporter to another. But after 1994, people outside the sport, or on its periphery, started to come into the tent. And that tent has continued to expand, not by leaps and bounds, but bit by bit, pretty much year by year, right on up and through the 2026 World Cup.

But as we're about to see, the tent almost collapsed several times, especially during the birth and rookie years of America's new soccer league.

Behind all the buzz and excitement of the 1994 tournament, a small group of planners were busy trying to figure out how to build a pro league (as promised to FIFA and American fans). The original architect was a young associate attorney named Mark Abbott, working in a fire closet in a suburban Los Angeles office park, toting around his yellow legal pads with the outlines of a soccer league founded on a unique single-entity idea (more about this in the next chapter), which had begun taking shape from conversations with his boss Alan Rothenberg. Abbott, only twenty-seven

* The 2026 World Cup is poised to shatter stadium attendance and electronic viewership records (home and internationally), driven by its unprecedented scale, expanded format, enthusiasm surrounding its three North American hosts (U.S., Mexico, and Canada), and football's continued and unmitigated global dominance.

at the time, set about drafting the original business plan for a league that would need to become the main tent poles and canvas for the entire U.S. soccer canopy.

The league had to be vibrant enough to attract investors and fans, strong and flexible enough to withstand the inevitable anti-soccer winds blowing across America's landscape, and smart enough to escape death, which pro soccer on American soil had failed to do on three previous occasions. How fitting that MLS was forged from the minds of entrepreneurial American lawyers and propelled by the swift feet of America's best soccer athletes. The latter had proven for years—even before anyone was paying much attention—that they deserved a place on America's professional sporting stage. Today, the league is up to thirty teams and breathing down the neck of the top ten football leagues in the world. But the storms! They shook the tent during the early years.

15

★★★★★

MLS ARRIVES, MEN ADVANCE, WOMEN DOMINATE

Base camp, gathering gear, and strategizing (1995–2002)

"Once Everest was determined to be the highest summit on earth, it was only a matter of time before people decided that Everest needed to be climbed."

— Jon Krakauer, *Into Thin Air*

The USSF had publicly stated it would sanction only one professional "Division I soccer league" in America and would look askance at any ownership group loaded for bear and eager to relive the past by bypassing the USSF and going out on its own. Behind the scenes of the run-up and hosting of the 1994 World Cup, there was a lopsided race to organize and submit the best project for structuring a new league and recruiting owners. As Mark Abbott tells it, he was a third-year associate (rookie lawyer) at a large Los Angeles–based firm when he overheard senior partner Alan Rothenberg (and USSF president) on speakerphone saying he needed someone to write a business plan for a new pro soccer league. "I ran into Rothenberg's office and said, 'I'll do it,'" Abbott recalled. "And Alan said, 'You'll do what?'" Despite Abbott admitting he had never written a business plan before, Rothenberg gave him a shot. "I knew he was great and I knew he loved soccer," Rothenberg recalled. "So next thing you knew he came to work on our incipient project" that hadn't even been officially announced.

There were two main rivals to the unnamed Rothenberg-Abbott project (which had a major advantage with Rothenberg at the helm of the USSF). The American Professional Soccer League (APSL), which had evolved from bicoastal regional leagues, urged the USSF to elevate it from Division II status. The APSL, unlike the other candidates, was actually playing outdoor semipro soccer largely under FIFA rules—despite having shrunk to five teams in 1992. The APSL's application didn't move the soccer needle. It was an uninspired attempt to distance itself (not remake itself) from a decade-long life of scraping its belly along tufts of grass and dirt, like an inchworm, across fields in the U.S. and Canada. It was full of many good people, no doubt, but it was never going to turn itself into a butterfly. The USSF, predictably, sniffed at the proposal.

Then there was a really stupid idea from Chicago businessman Jim Paglia called League One America. Paglia claimed he would rekindle multipurpose stadiums and transfigure fields "into zones marked with chevrons limiting players to specific zones for an entire period." Players would be outfitted with four different colors of uniforms and an electronic device that would tell the referee when a player exited his prescribed zone. There were not two goals, but four, with the larger ones built around the regulation-size goals. A multipoint system was tied to the origin of the shot (by zone) and its ultimate destination (by goal). FIFA invited Paglia to Switzerland to discuss it—probably out of deference to Rothenberg, who was busy planning for the 1994 World Cup, and to insulate Alan from the bid process early on. Rothenberg's team eventually met with Paglia and rightly concluded it was merely "an idea" with no "substance behind it." The business plan combusting in Abbott's fire closet, soon to be christened Major League Soccer (MLS), was the only bid with legs and legitimacy.

At the core of the bid was Rothenberg's single-entity idea, which Abbott built into a league-wide plan with structure, symmetry, checks and balances, and protections to tamp down the selfishness and avarice among the ownership group that had doomed pro leagues in the past. "The idea was when you 'buy a team,' you are buying a share of this limited liability company [Major League Soccer, LLC], and the right to operate a team in a particular market," Abbott explained. "So, you're incentivized at the league level, by your ownership of part of the league. And you're incentivized at the local level through the revenue-sharing formula set forth in the operating agreement." If teams are going to climb a tall mountain (again) and stay up there among rocky terrain and unpredictable weather, you can't have some owners behaving inimical to other owners and endangering the whole enterprise.

The single-entity framework has evolved over the three-decade life of the league to accommodate exceptions and modifications, like the Designated Player Rule (clubs can currently pay up to three elite players above the salary cap), Homegrown Player Rule (clubs can directly sign local talent, bypassing the draft, with certain salaries exempt from the cap), and significant club autonomy in branding, merchandising, and stadium oversight. Other carve-outs, exceptions, and profit-sharing metrics are constantly negotiated by the owners (and their lawyers), many of whom love winning almost as much as the players. The league has matured and stabilized. It is still a single-entity structure, but now operates more like a quasi-franchise model with ample financial and operational autonomy.

To invoke a biological metaphor: The thirty current franchises function like the busy proteins within a single red blood cell, which lacks a nucleus, but whose proteins operate in tandem to keep the cell (and the whole body) alive by sharing resources and working to keep costs down. Unfortunately, the evolution of the single-entity structure has not mutated enough to slough off its locked-league (no promotion or relegation) framework—meaning teams don't get added or dropped based on the table at season's end. Most American sports fans who don't follow soccer likely don't care about the promotion–relegation debate, because all U.S.-based pro leagues (NFL, NBA, MLB, NHL, and MLS) are franchise-based. Team owners buy into the league, and once they're in, they can't be dropped for poor performance. Finishing last doesn't mean going down a league or getting ousted. Instead, it might mean better draft picks. No other soccer-loving country follows this locked-league model.

In much of the world where soccer is central to public life—especially in England—and where professional leagues have operated for decades, sometimes over a century, promotion and relegation are deeply woven into both fandom and the business of the sport. Fans and owners are accustomed to multitiered leagues in which (usually) three teams move up and three move down at season's end based on performance. The notion that a club could fail year after year and never be relegated or replaced—paired with the idea that a small-market team could never earn its way into the top league—is antithetical, even blasphemous, to many soccer people worldwide.

For the Yanks in MLS, however, it appears that the locked-league framework is legally airtight and here to stay. And it makes perfect sense to any rational human being genuinely trying to imagine life as an MLS team owner*—as opposed to the life of the rest of us mere mortals who waste enormous amounts of hemoglobin arguing about how cool, competitive, and wonderful it would be to have promotion and relegation. All thoughts of MLS moving to such a system, or even a modified one, as of 2026, may not be a chimera, but is akin to entering a birthing room with a decapitated lion, hornless goat, and tailless snake. It's DOA. So let's stop arguing about it.

But—but—pressure is coming. In 2027, the United Soccer League

* In May 2023, the ownership group for the most recent addition to MLS, San Diego FC, forked over $500 million for an expansion franchise—and not one dollar of that fee goes to move a stone, buy a player, or hire a coach. Owners (and their lawyers) would never pay this sum of money to enter an American soccer league if the basic framework could be altered in the foreseeable future. To even consider it, they would need enormous safeguards and a big cushion of time.

(USL), designated Division II by the USSF, plans to launch a new USL Division One, which will sit atop its existing USL Championship (Division II) and USL League One (Division III). All three leagues will be interconnected through a structured promotion and relegation system, where more matches matter, rewarding performance and affording new opportunities for clubs, players, and fans. This is good news for the American soccer nation. Anyone who has been to a high-level USL match can feel the excitement brewing and its potential to reshape the future.

Back in 1995, the nascent MLS had to wheedle and cajole investors, and ultimately decided to put some time and distance between the packed houses of the 1994 World Cup and the opening of the new league, which MLS organizers knew would draw fewer fans and fanfare. The league did not kick off in 1995. Instead, it waited until spring 1996. It turned out to be the right decision. Mark Abbott became the league's first employee. Alan Rothenberg remained president of USSF and added the title "chairman of the MLS Board of Directors" to his duties. In 1995, the board appointed Doug Logan, a bilingual (English, Spanish) sports and entertainment promoter, as the league's first commissioner. For once, a professional league and the Federation were aligned, with all the major constituents ultimately accountable to Alan Rothenberg. This required team owners to demonstrate genuine respect for the global game beyond their own interests.

The investors were also compelled to show healthy respect to Rothenberg, who had just pulled off the most successful World Cup in history and had promptly paid himself a hefty $7 million from the $60 million surplus generated by the tournament, characterized as bonus payments and deferred compensation. The windfall irritated a bunch of people—but not the MLS owners Alan was busy rounding up, who were well-schooled in being financially rewarded for a job well done.

Lined up in the stadium tunnel leading into spring 1996 were ten MLS teams and venues culled from a list of twenty-two bidding cities.* The teams emerged from agreements among a small group of "investor-operators" (capitalized in the original league documents) who, when push came to shove, ponied up the $5 million per team buy-in fee. These intrepid investors included Robert Kraft (and family), Peter Guber, Dan Miller, George Soros, John Kluge, Stuart Subotnick, Phil Anschutz, and Lamar Hunt (the latter three reached even deeper to support an additional team, getting the league from seven to ten teams), and several other bundles of investors standing behind corporate names.

The league decided on mostly FIFA rules, with some exceptions that irritated purists: The clock would count down (not up), even though the head referee still controlled the time from his wristwatch (so the stadium clock would freeze at zero); substitutes were capped at four, not three, so long as one sub was a goalkeeper; and all tied games at the end of regulation would conclude with an NASL-style thirty-five-yard dribbling shootout. Notably, within a few years, all of these rules reverted to the FIFA norm.

The league, which owned all the players' contracts (a provision later revised for some team flexibility), allotted four marquee players per team, then built out the rosters with a gridiron-like two-week "combine" at the University of California (Irvine campus) culminating in a draft, and then a month later, a supplemental draft. Most Americans sojourning abroad returned home, and scattered (for parity and marketing purposes)—or

* The original teams included the New England Revolution, New York/New Jersey MetroStars (now New York Red Bulls), D.C. United, Tampa Bay Mutiny, Columbus Crew, Colorado Rapids, Dallas Burn (now FC Dallas), Kansas City Wiz (now Sporting Kansas City), San Jose Clash (now San Jose Earthquakes), and the Los Angeles Galaxy. The names of the original teams reflected the sports marketing blitz of the time, which tried to capture the excitement of movies, rock bands, and giant creatures. The Gotham Golems (fictitious) would not have been out of place in the mid-1990s, on a court with the Toronto Raptors (named after the original *Jurassic Park* movie). The Raptors, of course, survive today. So do the Revolution, Crew, Galaxy, and Rapids. The rest of the MLS franchises—and the new ones—eventually gravitated to the international football mean. They ultimately named (or renamed) themselves after their host city or geographic region, often with one of the following appendages: FC, City, United, or Union. Similarly, to align with the FIFA/European calendar, MLS is adopting a summer-to-spring schedule, beginning in 2027.

more accurately, they were unilaterally assigned by MLS deputy commissioner Sunil Gulati—around the country. The player pool was predominantly American, enriched by Latin and African flair, while coaches came largely from Europe or represented the old guard of American soccer. Only two coaches were American-born: Bruce Arena (University of Virginia) took the helm at D.C. United, and Dave Dir (APSL's Colorado Foxes) led Dallas Burn.

The first game in MLS history was played on April 6, 1996, in San Jose, California, with the San Jose Clash hosting D.C. United. A sellout crowd of 31,683 witnessed the Clash secure a 1–0 victory at Spartan Stadium. The lone goal was scored by Eric Wynalda in the eighty-eighth minute. It was a tepid match that began only after a giant white MLS logo in the center circle had been triple-coated with green paint (by fiat of league execs who had arrived before the match). The league's VIPs were not soccer purists, to be sure. But from the start—and in contrast to most of the NASL bigwigs—they envisioned real grass, minimal gimmicks, and soccer-specific stadiums (which would come much later), with the gear and guiding principles all growing toward the light.

The spirit of the league was not necessarily Spartan, but it was American at its core and multicultural, with a tinge of modesty undergirding the whole enterprise (notwithstanding the original flashy Nike-designed uniforms across half the league). The tone was set on day one. A week later, 69,255 people turned out for a Los Angeles Galaxy home game at the Rose Bowl against the MetroStars, a crowd buoyed by the signing of the Mexican hybrid goalkeeper (and forward!) Jorge Campos. In June 1996, MLS announced it would relocate its headquarters from Los Angeles to New York City, positioning itself alongside the offices of the four other major North American professional sports leagues. Major League Soccer was off and running. But would the tent stakes hold, and would the canvas grow?

On the National Team side, Milutinović had moved on to coach Nigeria—Bora said he was fired; the USSF said he resigned. Bora's assistant Steve

Sampson took over MNT duties in August 1995 on an interim basis. Since the start of the Word Cup era, Steve was only the second native-born MNT gaffer* in Federation history, following Walter Giesler (1957–1964). Sampson had learned his trade as a successful college coach and an administrator at both the 1984 Olympics and the 1994 World Cup. During the latter, Sampson served on one of the World Cup's organizing committees and as one of Bora's assistants. The sexy choice for the top spot he was not.

Sampson's debut tournament in charge—like Bora's inaugural outing—was a success. The Yanks won the 1995 U.S. Cup with a hallmark victory over Mexico, 4–0, which was "a coming out party" for a young Yank named Claudio Reyna, who would go on to be a midfield mainstay for over a decade.

Later that year, the U.S. earned an invite to the 1995 Copa América as one of two guest nations. The U.S. came in fourth place out of twelve. They upset Argentina (a downscaled squad, since La Albiceleste didn't need to win), 3–0, to top the group. Diego Maradona, who did not play in the match (though still playing for Boca Juniors and publicly fighting a drug problem), appeared in the U.S. post-game locker room, shook everyone's hand, and emotionally acknowledged how well the Yanks had played. "I'm not crying because Argentina lost, I'm crying because it was so beautiful to see the Americans play so well." The U.S. advanced, beat El Tri in the next round, but fell to Brazil in the semifinals. Uruguay went on to win. Sampson's interim label was removed, but he was put on an annual contract, underscoring Rothenberg's hedging strategy and visible desire for a last-minute internationally acclaimed coach. Three years later, in the 1998 CONCACAF Gold Cup semifinal, the U.S. beat Brazil (a strong team, but not its full arsenal), 1–0. Keeper Kasey Keller delivered one of the most remarkable goalkeeping performances in USMNT history. It remains the Yanks' only victory over the Seleção. The U.S. lost to Mexico in the final. Progress.

* In British English, the term *gaffer* is an informal and respectful way to refer to the head coach (also called the manager) of a football team. It probably originated as a contraction of "godfather," a term of respect for an older, experienced man, and later evolved to describe a boss or foreman in working-class British slang.

The MNT made it out of the first round of qualification for the 1998 World Cup and into the frying pan of the final qualification round. It was a rough road for Sampson, who had to contend with tough games and inconsistent support from Rothenberg. Behind the scenes, a multifaceted pay dispute advanced by MNT players against the USSF—plus a separate antitrust lawsuit between a wider group of players and the USSF and MLS (more about this later in this chapter)—extracted time and energy from the athletes' training regimen and playing schedule.

The gist of the pay dispute boiled down to the fact that the USSF, which had gone corporate and was "the bank," was paying the players, who never had a union or much legal representation, peanuts. Former MNT players from the 1990s and well into the 2000s often depict USSF executives as paternalistic, condescending, and controlling. Frustrated by unequal and unpredictable pay, the players founded the U.S. National Soccer Team Players Association (USNSTPA) in 1996 to secure a collective bargaining agreement (CBA), with negotiations kicking off in 1997. The USNSTPA (for the men) still exists today. In August 2022, it, together with the United States Women's National Team Players Association (USWNTPA), signed historic CBAs that run through 2028, which achieve equal pay for both teams through identical economic terms and revenue sharing mechanisms.

Qualifying for the 1998 World Cup out of CONCACAF required the MNT to advance from a first-round tournament into a six-team group, nicknamed "the Hex" (short for Hexagonal). At the end of the ten-game schedule, the top three teams in the Hex automatically qualified for the World Cup. This format lasted from 1997 through 2018. And just when a critical mass of fans was getting used to it, CONCACAF switched to a different format for 2022. In 1997, the U.S. finished its Hex campaign with a 4–5–1 record, good enough for second place and a berth in the 1998 World Cup in France.

The MNT that arrived in Paris was no longer a bunch of college kids—it was a squad of mostly MLS pros (sixteen of twenty-two) with two solid years of regular play under their baggy polyester shorts. Fans had high hopes for 1998. The Yanks were grouped with Germany, Iran, and Yugoslavia.

On the eve of the tournament, Sampson cut veteran John Harkes after learning he was having an affair with Eric Wynalda's wife. Wynalda, then and now (as incredible as it may sound), maintains he forgave Harkes (at the time) and would've been OK playing alongside him because the team needed his expertise in France. The story stayed out of the press for years.* Meanwhile, Sampson and the Federation fast-tracked the citizenship of a French defender who had joined the roster just five weeks earlier. Once in France, Sampson secluded the team two hours outside Paris, let players and families mix freely, housed players and coaches separately, and kept tinkering with tactics and the lineup.

Against Germany, the MNT fielded seven World Cup rookies. Most veterans were benched for the whole tournament. Germany controlled much of the first half, scoring early through a double-headed goal—Jürgen Klinsmann to Andreas Möller, with the ball somehow sneaking past a covering defender at the post. Claudio Reyna and Eric Wynalda struggled under tight marking. The U.S. showed attacking promise early in the second half—Frankie Hejduk came close—but momentum faded. And Klinsmann sealed the 0–2 win in the sixty-fifth minute.

The U.S. vs. Iran match on June 21 carried symbolism and tensions beyond soccer with the Iranian Hostage Crisis less than two decades old. Despite being favorites and creating multiple chances with a new 3–5–2 formation, the MNT fell behind to a well-timed header from Hamid Estili. The atmosphere between fans stayed friendly. In the second half, the Yanks hit the post four times but couldn't score. Iran extended their lead late. Brian McBride scored in the eighty-seventh minute, but the U.S. lost 1–2, and, as other games concluded in their group, the Americans had virtually no mathematical chance of advancing.

The U.S. entered its final group match against Yugoslavia on June 25, 1998, amid political tensions related to the Balkans, and growing internal MNT discord. Alexi Lalas revealed rising frustration, and Sampson again

* Harkes became a key figure in Major League Soccer and later transitioned to coaching, eventually establishing himself as a respected TV analyst and an exceptional ambassador for American soccer.

altered the lineup. Despite the U.S. delivering their strongest performance, an early rebound gave Yugoslavia a 0–1 win. The U.S.'s World Cup campaign had resulted in three losses and a single goal, leaving them dead last out of thirty-two teams. American TV coverage nosedived and stayed low for the rest of the tournament. Host nation France, nicknamed *Les Bleus* (French for "the Blues"), led by Zinedine Zidane and a diverse roster, advanced through the tournament and won the Final, defeating Brazil 3–0. Their success gave Footix—the Gallic rooster and World Cup mascot—reason to puff out his chest and embrace his country's ethnic soccer roots (though the diversity was not without some far-right French crowing).

Nobody in the American camp was happy. Players were furious, and their anger was directed the whole way to the "U.S. Soccer House," USSF's two (adjacent) mansions in Chicago, in the historic Prairie Avenue District, center of soccer administrative operations from 1991 to 2025.* An Associated Press writer summed it up: "They stunk. And they hated their coach." While the tournament was still underway, USSF president Alan Rothenberg met Sampson for dinner in Paris. Sampson resigned before the bill arrived. Most of the American team returned home and continued their soccer careers in MLS. Many still speak of France 1998 with bitterness.

Joy and soccer excellence prevailed on the women's side. Less than a year later, the USWNT won their second World Cup on July 10, 1999,

* In 2026, the Federation will consolidate all of its administrative and training operations and situate them within a brand-new, state-of-the-art National Training Center in Fayetteville, Georgia, which is being built and unveiled (at least phase one) as this book is going to print. This new facility will house all USSF operations and will serve as the hub for the entire U.S. National Team system, which includes senior men's and women's teams, a full ladder of youth teams, and various disability and inclusion teams. The Center is being heavily financed by Arthur Blank, Home Depot's founder (and owner of the Atlanta Falcons and MLS's Atlanta United), and the Coca-Cola Company. The soccer hub, incidentally, is being built adjacent to the Town at Trilith, home of Trilith Studios and associated artists whose blockbusters most recently include *Spider-Man: No Way Home* (2021), *Black Panther: Wakanda Forever* (2022), *Black Adam* (2022), *Guardians of the Galaxy Vol. 3* (2023), *Captain America: Brave New World* (2025), and *Superman* (2025). How fitting that all the National Teams (men, women, youth, and disability and inclusion participants) will play in the foreground of America's pop culture. And that the ball, for years to come, will bounce and roll along the lush year-round grass of Georgia.

at the Rose Bowl before 90,000 mostly American fans—the second-largest live crowd for a women's sporting event in history. The largest was about 110,000 at the 1971 II Campeonato Mundial de Fútbol Femenil final in Mexico City. According to an AP writer, the 1971 tournament was planned as "something of a mixture between sports event and beauty contest." The writer quoted the tournament's own sponsor: "Women who play soccer are not muscular monstrosities, but generally pretty girls. We're combining the two passions of most men around the world: soccer and women. There will be beauty salons in the dressing rooms so the girls can present themselves for interviews and public ceremonies complete with false eyelashes, lipstick, and an attractive hairdo."

Imagine what the silly men who wrote and agreed with these sentences—if alive nearly thirty years later—would have thought when Brandi Chastain stepped up to the penalty spot in Pasadena, knowing that if she scored, the WNT would win its second World Cup. Striking with her left foot—not her dominant side—she buried the ball in the upper corner, past China's diving goalkeeper. In a spontaneous burst of emotion, Chastain ripped off her jersey, dropped to her knees in her sports bra, and clenched her fists.

Forty million Americans witnessed the event live. The image was instantly transmitted worldwide and chosen as the leading sports picture for the next morning's papers. It remains one of the most iconic sports moments of all time.* Three major magazines—*Newsweek*, *Sports Illustrated*, and *Time*—splashed it on their covers: "Girls Rule!" "Yes!" "What a Kick!" The event and its aftermath helped dismantle stereotypes—though not everywhere. A few years later, FIFA president Sepp Blatter revealed his crusty worldview when speaking about women's soccer: "Let the women

* The national media and the relatively rookie internet erupted in a chorus of opinions about *how* the act must have been planned by Nike to make millions in sports-bra orders; *why* ABC didn't focus on the American goalkeeper, Briana Scurry, a Black Minnesotan who had made an outstanding save moments earlier; and *when* would women, including female athletes, stop being used (or prevent themselves from being used) as sex objects. Ah, America, the melting pot, *er*, tossed salad. And the king (and now queen) of free speech.

play in more feminine clothes like they do in volleyball. They could, for example, have tighter shorts." The U.S. women have reached the summit four times now. But the battle to defeat sexism rattles on.

Back in MLS, it was slim pickings the first five years. Average attendance in 1996 hovered around 17,000, better than expected. D.C. United, with their humble Adidas uniforms, won the first league title—and the second. For 1997, attendance declined (alarmingly) by 16 percent, and questions arose about the league's financial model. Television coverage, while robust in its rookie year, was headed in the wrong direction. To gain exposure, MLS took on most of the production and broadcasting costs during its first three seasons, sharing advertising revenue with ESPN and ABC. By 1998, people were tuning out. Only a minimal amount of dirt had been moved in Columbus, Ohio, for the league's first soccer-specific stadium. Nobody else was kicking in a shovel. Most investor-operators were paying hefty rents to gridiron stadium owners, who had no qualms about charging high fees to the soccer people and pocketing the bulk of revenue from parking and concessions.

Troubles also formed on the legal front. In 1997, eight MLS players filed an antitrust lawsuit against the league, its investor-operators, and the USSF. Most of the claims fell under the Sherman Act, alleging, among other things, that the defendants had unlawfully created a market and colluded in restricting player wages and mobility. A class action was certified in 1998. Subsequent legal action resulted in a federal district and appellate court both finding in favor of MLS's single-entity structure. (Parts of the case, *Fraser v. Major League Soccer*, are still taught to law students.) Some claims survived and went to trial, where a jury returned a verdict in favor of the corporate defendants. For the first seven years of the league, the lawsuit dragged on behind the scenes. Plaintiffs appealed the whole way to the U.S. Supreme Court, which ultimately denied certification (legal-speak for the absolute end of a case). Legal fees cost both sides millions. Public opinions abound about the strategy of all the litigants (and their lawyers).

In any event, the evidence that came out in discovery and trial,* and subsequent negotiations, impacted labor relations between players and MLS, and shaped the future of player salaries and player movement for years to come.

The league entered year three with two additional teams, for a total of twelve, with seven teams featuring an American head coach. The Chicago Fire, an expansion team, beat D.C. United in the 1998 final at the Rose Bowl in front of 51,350 fans. The highest attendance that year was 56,404 for a midseason game between the MetroStars and Miami Fusion, another expansion team. The lowest figure was a dismal 4,130. In 1999, the Columbus Crew opened the U.S.'s first modern soccer-specific stadium, funded by a dropkick from Lamar Hunt worth $28.5 million. "One stadium in one city and one sold-out game don't make success," remarked Hunt, "but this stadium will be here for fifty years, even if I won't be."

The Columbus fans immediately rewarded the 1999 stadium endeavor with the highest attendance average in league history. Also that year, a whopping 73,123 spectators turned out for a July Fourth San Jose Clash meeting with D.C. United (at Stanford Stadium), attendance no doubt elevated by a doubleheader with the USWNT World Cup game and a glorious fireworks presentation. But the average crowd size league-wide continued to stumble downward during 1999–2000. Despite on-field excitement, the league faced falling attendance in many markets (four years in a row) and difficulty attracting a stable national TV audience. The owners continued to lose money. Two teams folded in 2002, shrinking the league back to ten.

Average attendance rose for 2001, and in 2002 it inched upward again, in sight of its rookie-year numbers. The MNT reached the quarterfinals of the 2002 World Cup (still its best-ever result in a modern World Cup). And, in May 2003, FIFA announced the U.S. would host the 2003 Women's World Cup, replacing China due to the SARS outbreak. Such were

---

* Court filings and witness statements revealed that the league had already lost $250 million, and the valuation of each founding franchise had already declined by more than half. The league was trying to keep these figures out of the press.

the currents in American soccer at its highest level: devotion and despair, opportunity and risk. Standing at the foyer of the new century, what was one to make of the future of elite men's soccer on U.S. soil? Outside the tent, it may not have been a tempest. But it was raining hard, the winds were howling, and no one knew how long the bad weather would last.

16

★★★★★

MLS QUADRUPLES DOWN

The owners make a series of bold, smart moves, while the National Team spreads (and contracts) its wings (2000–2007)

"I am Groot."

— Groot, *Guardians of the Galaxy*

One of the most impactful people in MLS history, Don Garber, from Queens, joined the league as commissioner in 1999, after cutting his leadership teeth with the international wing of the NFL. In the early 2000s, he guided the MLS through near bankruptcy and potential collapse. He led the charge to establish the league's commercial and investment arm, called Soccer United Marketing (SUM), which helped stabilize the league's finances by leveraging the sport's growing popularity in North America. SUM accomplished this by investing in ventures beyond MLS, including securing the U.S. broadcasting rights for the men's 2002 and 2006 World Cups and the women's 2003 World Cup. Over the next two decades, Garber oversaw the league's steady and ambitious rise.

But in late 2000, the forecast for the MLS looked bleak. As Don Garber and Mark Abbott tell the story, they were sitting in the living room of one of the investor-operators among a bevy of owners during a December

2000 meeting to decide the future of the young league. It was an existential moment for professional soccer in America.

The first option was to continue doing business as usual, which basically entailed kicking the ball in a singular direction down artificial fields, hoping for the best. The second option was outrageously bold at the time—"quadruple down, take some big risks," recalled Garber. The risky option required shuttering two teams (shrinking temporarily) and pledging to build many more soccer-specific stadiums and adjacent training facilities (for youth academies on up to the first team)—which everyone knew would eventually cost ownership groups and taxpayers billions of dollars, with the success of each endeavor hinging on a host of unknowable variables at the local level. The risky maneuver also involved investing, almost immediately, tens of millions of dollars into a new business venture focused on growing the commercial market around elite soccer broadcasting and marketing rights (*i.e.*, SUM). Some owners walked away. Three institutional owners—Philip Anschutz, Robert Kraft, and Lamar Hunt—committed to the new course.

Don Garber, like most of the Big Three sports commissioners over the past twenty-five years, has been a controversial figure among some pockets of the fan base, especially fans in Columbus, Ohio, who weathered a nasty relocation threat in 2017, and U.S. Open Cup* fans, who are still smarting over MLS's initial decision (December 2023) to abandon the more than 115-year-old competition. Today, about half the league participates in the Open Cup. Critics of Garber and MLS—who make good points, which are broached later in this book—rarely pause to understand the advanced mathematics of the entire American soccer landscape, where MLS is the keystone but not the only enterprise holding up the dome. In 2002, SUM (collectively owned by all the MLS team owners) started quietly gobbling up the rights to broadcast and market high-profile games that cut across the American soccer landscape. At first, SUM went after and attained the

* The U.S. Open Cup was renamed the Lamar Hunt Open Cup in 1999, a tribute to one of American soccer's longest and most generous benefactors. Most people still call it the Open Cup.

U.S. English-language broadcasting rights to the 2002 and 2006 World Cups. But when SUM got outbid for subsequent World Cups, SUM looked to secure the rights to broadcast and sponsor regional competitions.

Today, SUM owns the commercial rights to MLS, Leagues Cup, and other CONCACAF properties like the Gold Cup and Champions League. They also hold the rights to the Campeones Cup, an annual match between the MLS and Liga MX champions, and the broadcasting rights to the Mexican Men's and Women's national teams. SUM has been the little-known but powerful heart, pumping behind the scenes, keeping MLS alive and oxygenated. Without SUM, MLS would have probably died long ago. SUM, like just about everything else in the American soccer universe, has its critics. Detractors argue that SUM keeps MLS afloat as a monopoly, deflates the value of some USSF assets (and therefore diverts money away from American grassroots soccer), and exploits the Mexican football federation by extracting a large sum of money each year from its stateside fan base without giving back to the program or to the community.

In any event, SUM is very important but not solely responsible for the continued rise of MLS. No league at the pinnacle of the American soccer mountain can survive—or thrive—without the country's top players delivering victories, or at the very least showing steady improvement, on the international stage. Americans love winners. Nobody wanted to admit it, or to proclaim it loudly and publicly at the time, but the rise of MLS in the early 2000s to sustainability and profitability relied in large part on the rise and continued success of the members of the USMNT—who already had enough weight on their collective shoulders.

In late 1998, Bruce Arena took over from Steve Sampson as head coach of the National Team, bringing with him a track record of collegiate and professional success. Arena had led the University of Virginia to five national championships (including four in a row from 1991 to 1994), D.C. United's two MLS Cups (1996–1997), one U.S. Open Cup (1996), and the 1998 CONCACAF Champions Cup, becoming the first American coach and team to win the tournament. His players immediately added a bonus to Arena's record $2 million salary by defeating Germany twice, once in a friendly, the other in the Confederations Cup. The U.S. even dispatched mighty Argentina, 1–0, in a June 1999 friendly. The Yanks' 2002 World Cup first-round qualifying games got off to a rocky start, leaving the U.S. in the final match of an early qualification round needing a win to control their destiny. Away against Barbados, Clint Mathis, Earnie Stewart, Cobi Jones, and Ante Razov delivered in a 4–0 romp.

The U.S. entered the Hex on February 28, 2001, at Columbus Crew stadium in front of a sellout and mostly American crowd of 25,000, in cold weather so intemperate that the Mexican side didn't even venture onto the field for their usual pregame warm-up. The Yanks won *dos a cero* (Spanish for "two to zero") as the American taunt was largely coined that day—and would soon roll off the collective tongue every time the Yanks bested El Tri by a brace to zero. In the first half of their Hex schedule, the U.S. racked up four wins and a draw. But they then lost three games in a row, coming dangerously close to elimination. The U.S. needed a win over Jamaica in its ninth Hex match, which the Yanks achieved. Other results went their way that weekend, and the U.S. qualified, with a third-place finish guaranteed, regardless of the outcome of the tenth and final Hex fixture. Everyone breathed a sigh of relief.

The radiant mascots (yes, plural) for the 2002 World Cup, co-hosted by South Korea and Japan, appeared out of the ether, "symbolizing energy particles," looking and behaving like three gummies on gummies: Ato (yellow, the coach), Nik (blue player), and Kaz (purple player). Arena was more down to earth about his team's chances: "We're not going to win [the World Cup] because we're not a good enough team. I don't think anyone is going to be damaged by us saying that. I mean, how many countries have won it? If we can get a point in the first game, it will put the whole group [U.S., Portugal, South Korea, and Poland] in chaos." Indeed, the U.S.'s first result over Portugal split the group wide open—bringing smiles to the faces of the three World Cup mascots, since South Korea also benefited from the resulting chaos.

Arena's roster contained twelve players from MLS and eleven from Europe (six from Britain, five from the continent). Portugal entered the World Cup ranked fifth in the world, but didn't make it out of the group. The Yanks, of course, couldn't have known this, and prudently took the field expecting a mostly defensive battle. Imagine their surprise and delight when they stunned Portugal with three unanswered goals—scored by John O'Brien (a low-volley tap-in at the back post, off the goalie's weak clearance); Landon Donovan, only nineteen at the time, and the youngest on the roster (a cross that deflected into the goal off the back of a defender); and Brian McBride (a beautiful diving header). The rocket-fueled DaMarcus Beasley threatened defenders down the left flank all game. Portugal responded with a goal from Beto in the thirty-ninth minute and benefited from a Yankee own goal in the seventieth minute, narrowing the score to 3–2. Despite intense pressure, the U.S. held on to secure its first World Cup win on foreign soil in fifty-two years.

In their second group game, the U.S. faced host nation South Korea in a high-pressure atmosphere at Daegu Stadium. The Americans struck first with a twenty-fourth-minute goal from Clint Mathis. For most of the rest of the game, however, the U.S. was outplayed by the Taeguk Warriors (a reference to the Yin-and-Yang symbol of balance at the center of the South Korean flag). The final stats sheet was unbalanced, with the Warriors outshooting the U.S. 19–6 and earning seven corner kicks to the Yanks' none. Goalkeeper Brad Friedel delivered a stellar performance, including a penalty save. South Korea eventually equalized in the seventy-eighth minute, and nearly won late. But the match ended 1–1, setting the Americans up to advance if they could win or tie their third and final group match against Poland. But the Poles, who had already been eliminated, stunned the U.S. with two early goals and won 1–3.

It seemed like the U.S. had squandered their opportunity to advance. But South Korea defeated a nine-man Portugal squad 1–0, thanks to a fantastic goal by Park Ji-sung. In Dennis Bergkamp–like style, Park, at the back post, received a forty-yard pass in the air with his chest, and instead of immediately shooting it with his right foot, adjusted his weight and feet—letting a covering defender move past him—and then struck the ball (first time) with his left foot toward the near post and in, just beyond the hands of the diving goalie. It was one of the best goals of the tournament. The Taeguk Warriors advanced, knocked out Italy and Spain (two heavyweights), and finished the tournament in fourth place, a lesson in the triple benefits of hustling, never giving up, and hosting. Portugal's failure against South Korea permitted the U.S. to advance to the round of 16, to face their old foe, El Tri.

After absorbing early pressure from Mexico, the Yanks took the lead in the thirty-sixth minute with a goal from Brian McBride, followed by a second from Landon Donovan in the sixty-fifth minute, a gracefully headed ball while in full sprint. Mexico's frustrations boiled over, culminating in a red card for Rafael Márquez against the American speedster Cobi Jones, though Cobi, at the time, was barely moving, and merely jumping straight up to redirect the ball with his head. Despite some controversial moments, including a missed handball call when John O'Brien punched the ball clear of his own goal mouth with his right hand (in a reverse-Diego-Maradona-Hand-of-God moment), the U.S. held firm. Chants of "U-S-A! U-S-A!" segued to "Dos a cero! Dos a cero!" Arena praised his team's progress, though he acknowledged they were still chasing the world's elite. The world's elite had called the Yanks' tournament results (thus far) lucky, which is precisely what the Germans were in their next game—lucky not to get beat.

The U.S. faced Germany in a quarterfinal match, rarified air for the Americans, who had never made it that far in a modern tournament. The U.S. began the match confidently but failed to convert chances. And Germany took the lead in the thirty-ninth minute, off a free kick, with a header by Michael Ballack finding the back of the net. In the second half, the U.S. outshot Germany 11–6 but struggled to finish. Donovan was arguably the most dangerous player on either team in advanced positions. U.S. defender Tony Sanneh's work rate up and down the field was spectacular. In the forty-ninth minute, the Germans were the beneficiaries of a blatant no-call by the Scottish referee. Claudio Reyna delivered a corner kick that was flicked to U.S. defender Gregg Berhalter, who redirected the ball downward and toward goal. The German goalkeeper, Oliver Kahn, dove, swiped, and slightly tipped the ball with a finger. The ball spun up and was clearly about to cross the line and go into the goal—when in its path appeared the left arm of Germany's defender Torsten Frings, who was standing inside the post. Frings's arm, which was not within the natural silhouette of his body—indeed, the moment is a classic example of what the IFAB would later call making the body "unnaturally bigger"—prevented a certain goal. Kahn quickly gathered the ball in his hands. It was a penalty kick, and it was not called. The Yanks had come within an inch of a semifinal appearance.

"Football is a simple game," remarked the Englishman Gary Lineker, in the early 1990s. "Twenty-two men chase a ball for 90 minutes and at the end, the Germans always win." It was a gutsy performance by the Americans—who lost 0–1. Despite their elimination in the quarterfinal round, the U.S. team could hold their heads high for their 2002 World Cup campaign, which marked definitive progress on the international stage for over a decade. Claudio Reyna made the World Cup all-star team, the only modern Yank to win the award. And Cobi Jones, after five more appearances in the stars and stripes, set the MNT all-time caps record at 164, cementing his legacy and inspiring a new generation of fans. Germany advanced, won again, and contested the final, but lost to Brazil, led by the Golden Boot winner, Ronaldo Luís Nazário de Lima (famously R9). It was Brazil's fifth World Cup title.

With MLS's major lawsuit behind them, SUM up and running and generating money behind the scenes, and teams making inroads with fan bases, pro soccer on American soil started showing real signs of progress. In the final of the 2002 MLS Cup, the Los Angeles Galaxy, in a classic West meets East battle, beat the New England Revolution in front of a record 61,316 fans. The Galaxy had lost three previous finals, but its stiffer firmament replaced D.C. United as the brightest star in the MLS constellation—at least for a few years, winning the title again in 2005. In 2003, the Galaxy opened a state-of-the-art stadium (seating 27,000) and multiplex park in Carson,

California, developed by the Anschutz Entertainment Group, which had outspent Lamar Hunt's Columbus Crew stadium project by a multiple of five. LA fans quickly filled the seats, including forty-two luxury suites. By the end of the season, the Galaxy had set a new MLS average-attendance record of just under 22,000. The reception of MLS's second soccer-specific stadium—together with Columbus Crew's stadium, purring along in the middle of Ohio, which ranked third in attendance for 2003—underscored what MLS VIPs had been saying all along: Build soccer-specific stadiums, make them intimate, eschew gimmicks, and fans will reward the investments.

At pitch level, the competition continued to improve, at least for teams performing in the top half of the conference tables, whose coaches and sporting directors had figured out the complex rules governing salary caps, the college draft, and roster limits. In the parity-driven MLS, mastering the rules has always been the first step to maximizing talent on the roster. (Many present-day MLS teams still stumble at this step.) Rounding the new century, America's best players continued to take advantage of MLS's Project-40 program,* started in 1997 (renamed Generation Adidas in 2005), targeting underclassmen (sophomores and juniors) and permitting them to leave college early and sign professional MLS contracts. By entering Project-40, players gave up NCAA eligibility and MLS paid their salary (usually slightly above league minimum), and guaranteed scholarship money if they pursued a college degree within a certain period. These players didn't take up a senior roster spot, making them attractive to clubs. Some, like the shooting star Freddy Adu, opted not to go to college at all, entering the league directly through a Project-40 window.

Several players, like the MetroStars goalie, Tim Howard, graduated from Project-40, earned spots on their MLS first team, cut their teeth for a few years, and then caught the attention of foreign scouts. After his

* The "40" in Project-40 stood for the aspirational goal of young professional players appearing in forty competitive games per year, either with their designated MLS team or, if they couldn't make the gameday roster, on loan to a team that played in America's second division, then called the A-League.

standout 2002 season and strong MNT showings, Howard was nipping at the heels of MNT colleagues Brad Friedel and Kasey Keller. Howard soon drew interest from Manchester United's Sir Alex Ferguson. In mid-2003, MLS (still operating as a strict single-entity structure) accepted a record $4 million transfer fee from Manchester United, making Howard the Red Devils' first-choice keeper to replace Fabien Barthez. In January 2004, Clint Mathis was lured to Hannover 96, of the German Bundesliga (yes, 96 marks the club's 1896 founding—a reminder to us Yanks of the soccer history some nations enjoy). DaMarcus Beasley also moved that year to PSV Eindhoven, in the Dutch Eredivisie. MLS had finally become strong enough to springboard its best players across the pond.

For 2004, MLS nixed its two five-minute golden-goal overtimes at the end of regular season games that ended in a tie. Everyone in MLS had joined the football adults in the room who accept a tie after ninety minutes as an intrinsic part of regular season play. The first five years of the new millennium witnessed MLS making steady if not remarkable progress from the boardroom to the field.

On the MNT side, with Bruce Arena still in charge for a second World Cup cycle, the Yanks breezed through early qualification rounds for the 2006 World Cup and entered the Hex favored to place first, which they did (tied with Mexico on points with the same W–L–T record). In the middle, the U.S. beat Panama in the 2005 Gold Cup. Expectations for the 2006 World Cup in Germany were high. The U.S. team's quarterfinal appearance in 2002, together with CONCACAF qualification dominance, resulted in a FIFA ranking of fifth in the world—a ranking nobody took seriously. And yet a top-twenty ranking was plausible and notable for a country with a modern professional league only entering its tenth year.

The U.S. entered the 2006 World Cup in a difficult group, including the Czech Republic (not Czechoslovakia, which had dissolved in 1993), Italy, and Ghana. The Yanks opened June 12, 2006, with a heavy 0–3 defeat to the Czechs, managing just one legitimate shot on goal. Coach Arena criticized key players and singled out a relative newcomer as one of only a few who showed courage. Keeper Kasey Keller lamented the team's failure, complaining that peers “gave the game away,” while Claudio Reyna urged rapid improvement. Losing the first game at a World Cup often spelled doom.

The U.S. needed a win over pesky Italy—a relentless and oddly familiar adversary in World Cup and Olympic soccer tournaments over the past hundred years—to stay in control of its path out of the group. Italy went ahead in the twenty-second minute off Andrea Pirlo’s diving header from a free kick. Five minutes later, Bobby Convey’s back-post cross deflected off an Italian defender into his own net. A torrent of red cards ensued: Daniele De Rossi was sent off in the twenty-ninth minute for a foul on Brian McBride (an elbow reminiscent of the one that sidelined Tab Ramos in 1994). McBride left, received stitches beneath his left eye, confirmed his jaw and maxilla were intact, and returned. Pablo Mastroeni saw red right before halftime for a studs-up challenge on Pirlo. Eddie Pope was dismissed early in the second half after a second yellow.

Reduced to nine men, the U.S. still pushed against Italy’s ten—Beasley thought he scored in the sixty-sixth minute, only for an offside flag to rule it out. One of the best saves of the tournament involved Keller, standing his ground, acrobatically punching wide a Del Piero close-up volley. The save preserved a 1–1 draw. The point, coupled with Ghana’s upset win over the Czech Republic, gave the U.S. a chance to reach the knockout stage with a win over Ghana in their third and final group game, and an Italian victory over the Czech Republic.

But the Yanks couldn’t muster a victory, and fell to Ghana, the Black Stars, 1–2. After Ghana took an early lead, Clint Dempsey equalized in the forty-third minute with a stunning volley off a back-post pass from Beasley. It was the U.S.’s only goal in the tournament (the other score was an own goal credited to Italy). Just before halftime, an American defender, instead of clearing the ball, skied it straight up and lost the ensuing fifty-fifty head-ball. A Ghanaian winger headed it dangerously inside the U.S. box—where a nudge by the towering American Oguchi Onyewu sent the smaller Ghanian Razak Pimpong sprawling. The result: a penalty, which was converted by Ghana. The U.S. pressed in the second half, McBride hit the post, but the Yanks failed to score.

Despite Italy defeating the Czech Republic, the U.S. was eliminated, finishing last in their group for the second time in three consecutive cycles. They managed just four shots on goal, the fewest of any team. Arena was criticized for being too cautious. The Americans' overall performance was on par with Germany's lackluster World Cup mascot duo of a trouserless lion named *Goleo* (a blend of the German word for "goal" and the Latin word *Leo* for "lion") and his talking-football sidekick named *Pille* (German for "pill"). Whenever Pille opened his mouth to speak, he looked deflated (literally).

Italy won the tournament, defeating France in a final marked by Zinedine Zidane's infamous headbutt to Marco Materazzi in the 110th minute of extra time, earning a red card. The incident later inspired a book: Materazzi, aided by two journalists, penned *What I Actually Told Zidane* (2006), listing 249 possible insults, including the actual remark about Zidane's sister. Despite early elimination, U.S. TV audiences for the World Cup Final (16.9 million) surpassed the NBA Finals series average (12.9 million) and World Series games (15.8 million). Italy's captain, Fabio Cannavaro, won the World Cup's Silver Ball and the 2006 Ballon d'Or, becoming one of only three true defenders to win it.

Half of Arena's men returned to MLS where the weather was not all bad. In fact, it was about to get a whole lot better, at least for fans league-wide. The league was on the offensive. If anyone could bend their sight around the wall and look a few months into the future, they would see global superstar David Beckham, still playing for Real Madrid, and maybe a step past his prime at age thirty-one, about to ink a five-year deal with the LA Galaxy of MLS (signed on January 11, 2007, which took effect on July 11, 2007). Beckham's arrival brought about important league-wide rule changes, and ultimately boosted the league's global profile and commercial appeal.

But the gamble was steeped in risk and controversy from day one. And, for the first three and a half years of his Galaxy contract, David's contributions on the pitch were fantastically negligible.

17

★★★★★

MLS AND THE NATIONAL TEAM ENTER EXPEDITION AND ACCLIMATIZATION CYCLES

The Beckham Experiment revisited (2005–2015)

"The only easy day was yesterday."

— popular motto among U.S. Navy SEALs

The history of MLS over the past two decades is best told through the lens of the Beckham Experiment.* The hypotheses (there were many)

* The Beckham Experiment is a term used by the Americans involved in Beckham's wooing and playing phases, underscoring everyone's uncertainty about whether it would work, and if the league could continue to grow. It's also the title of a book by the late great American soccer writer Grant Wahl. He chronicles the LA Galaxy's signing of David Beckham—soccer player and global entertainment icon—and traces his playing days in MLS, which were constantly being interrupted by David's extended sojourns to Milan (AC Milan) and London (England's national team). Wahl's exposé is one of the best books to date on the inner workings of MLS, especially during its second decade of existence.

boiled down to several interrelated business questions—and the answers to those questions, known by about 2015, help explain the steady growth of the league up through the present day. Could the league's founding documents be amended to accommodate the price tag of a global superstar?

Yes. Just before the 2007 season, MLS introduced the Designated Player Rule—nicknamed "The Beckham Rule"—which remains in place today. It allows clubs to sign and pay up to three Designated Players (DPs), whose total compensation and acquisition costs exceed the team's individual maximum salary budget charge. These players can be domestic or international, though they are typically the latter. The bundle of rules* under the DP umbrella enables MLS teams and their investor-operators to compete for and sign, on their own dime, high-profile soccer players and entertainers, or even low-profile workhorses—within reason, as each DP is subject to league-wide oversight. DPs give teams the ability to flex their international muscles without causing an uncontrollable arms and foot race, like what the Cosmos and other bluebloods did back in the NASL days.

In practice, the soccer salaries of the true superstars in the DP category are often dwarfed by sponsorship deals worth many multiples of the club's DP expenditure. This helps explain the discrepancy between what an MLS team is paying a player, and the mega-millions often bandied about in the press (for example, $250 million for Beckham over five years, $150 million for Messi over two and a half years). Every team in the league is currently using some of their DP slots, though many of today's DPs are hardly household names. DPs are generally good for the league and usually improve

* MLS has a bundle of rules for just about everything—and they have only grown more complicated over time, as the single-entity structure has edged *toward* a quasi-franchisee model. In MLS, you can't really buy your way *out* of problems (which many coaches, sporting directors, and owners in the top European leagues have been trying to do for decades), nor *into* problems that endanger the league's economic model. Back in 2009, Grant Wahl called MLS the ultimate *Moneyball* league. Critics have argued that the institutionalized parity has curtailed the product on the field and hindered the growth of the league. The Designated Player Rule will continue to evolve as the league increases its salary cap and revises other league rules, shuffling toward traditional European-based business models and leagues (notwithstanding the lack of promotion-relegation).

the product on the field. Without them, the league would never be able to lure high-profile players from abroad such as, in chronological order, Beckham, Robbie Keane, Thierry Henry, Kaká, Zlatan Ibrahimović, and Messi, let alone sign numerous blue-collar DPs who are relatively unknown to all but hometown fans.

Could MLS attract a true global superstar? *Yes*, with DP money and endorsements. But even these enticements are not enough to acquire an all-time great in his prime, *yet*. Reasons why a superstar at the tail end of his playing career would want to come to MLS include: (i) Lucrative contracts and endorsements dwarfed nowadays only by the oil money propping up the Saudi Pro League, (ii) lifestyle and quality of life in the U.S. (where the entertainer can travel freely in public, often without being recognized, let alone hounded), (iii) reduced game-day pressures, and way less coverage and controversy in the media, (iv) legacy role as a league ambassador and chance to grow the game in the North American market (still considered a tremendous growth market), (v) extended playing career within world-class facilities and on excellent grass fields (notwithstanding the six remaining MLS artificial playing surfaces), (vi) luxurious accommodations away from the game, and (vii) post-retirement opportunities, like buying a portion of an MLS team. Beckham currently owns about a 10 percent share of Inter Miami, which his original LA Galaxy/MLS contract afforded at a discounted price. Messi has a similar provision in his Inter Miami contract, albeit at a nonsubsidized rate.

MLS naysayers have called MLS a retirement league, which is discordant. Players who come here to retire, on the pitch, don't last long, though there is some truth to the notion that superstars enjoy a slower pace on and off the pitch.

Could a global superstar immediately and markedly impact the gate and jersey sales at an individual club and provide a suitable return on investment (*yes*), and around the league (*mixed results*)? David Beckham and Messi proved they could flutter turnstiles wherever they appeared, with their signings resulting in a lasting rise in interest across the league. But most DPs around the league have had little to no lasting effect on the overall market. Take the trio of international stars Steven Gerrard, Frank Lampard, and Andrea Pirlo, circa 2015–2017. They boosted home-game attendance for a while, but didn't significantly move the gate away from home. In fact, their aging legs didn't do much on the field, either.

Which leads to the final question in the Beckham Experiment: Could a global superstar's presence on the pitch measurably improve the on-field performance of the entire team over a series of games and seasons? *Not unless his name was Messi, Thierry Henry, Landon Donovan, and several others*—a result that throws a decent amount of shade on the accusation that MLS is a retirement league.

With the results of the Beckham Experiment in, the researcher is left with a host of positive trends but an untidy ultimate conclusion. The league is the current embodiment of a series of soccer experiments on American soil that started about 150 years ago. Before a ball was kicked on an MLS pitch, pro soccer on American soil had already failed three times, bankrupting scores of investors and disappointing generations of fans. Major League Soccer has evolved tremendously from its founding thirty years ago, and its direction is trending mostly positive. Yet its future is largely being shaped by the business acumen of a small group of people. Is the MLS game beautiful? Is it ugly? At the extremes, neither camp is entirely right. Or wrong.

Three weeks after the 2006 World Cup ended, the USSF announced it would not renew Bruce Arena's contract. The Federation wanted, but could not secure, Jürgen Klinsmann, who desired unprecedented control over all U.S. National Team programs from youth to senior level. In December 2006, the USSF hired Bob Bradley, who had built a strong résumé in MLS with three different teams. Bradley's interim tag was removed six months later, and he led the U.S. to a 2007 Gold Cup title, beating Mexico 2–1, in the final after a dominant six-game run, outscoring opponents 13–3. The next month, the U.S. struggled as a guest nation in the Copa América, losing all three matches and being outscored 2–8. These two tournaments highlighted the

MNT's frustrating inconsistency against top teams in the Americas, which continues to this day.

The U.S. advanced through early 2010 World Cup qualifying games with a 7–1 record, their only loss away to Trinidad and Tobago. Entering the Hex with confidence, they beat Mexico, dos a cero, in Columbus, with both goals from Michael Bradley, the coach's son. The MNT then rallied from a 0–2 deficit to draw El Salvador 2–2, and beat Trinidad and Tobago 3–0, behind a Jozy Altidore hat trick—making him, at nineteen, the youngest Yank to do it. Landon Donovan assisted Altidore on all three goals. A 1–3 loss in Costa Rica followed, but the U.S. bounced back with a 2–1 win over Honduras, extending their seventeen-home-game unbeaten streak.

In the final Hex stretch, the U.S. lost 1–2 to Mexico at Estadio Azteca despite an early goal by the young phenom Charlie Davies. Then the U.S. responded with wins over El Salvador (2–1) and Trinidad and Tobago (1–0), before clinching a World Cup berth with a dramatic win away against Honduras (3–2). A draw at home against Costa Rica (2–2) secured an outright first-place finish—for the first time—in the Hex. Tragically, the night before the Costa Rica match, Davies was severely injured in a car crash in Washington, D.C. He was not the driver, but the incident ended his MNT career.

During the qualification campaign, Bradley gave opportunities to forty-three players, searching for the right combination. The U.S. performed well in the 2009 Confederations Cup, upsetting Spain, then ranked #1 in the world, before falling to Brazil in the final. In that year's Gold Cup, they defeated three CONCACAF opponents but were shut out by Mexico in the championship. Then the Yanks lost a bunch of friendlies, further clouding the team's form heading into 2010. Eight players from the 2006 World Cup squad made Bradley's final twenty-three-player roster for 2010. The squad featured just four MLS players, down from eleven in 2006 and 2002, and sixteen in 1998; the rest played in Europe.

Each cycle has its own story about how the group meshes—or pulls apart. Fault lines sometimes appear between domestic and European-based players, and more often between traditional American players and dual-nationalized players. The latter issue, when it arises, boils down to whether a player is suitably "American" and cares enough to perform well in a Yankee uniform, even if he's rarely stepped foot on American soil. When a team's performance dips, the fault lines rarely crater. Coaches and players protect locker-room privacy. Criticizing a teammate or coach publicly—or being too specific about a poor performance—is almost never wise. Nobody wants to jeopardize a future MNT call-up.

The only other American athletes who walk this line, albeit a simpler one, are USA Olympic basketball players. But there are big differences. All basketball Olympians come from the same league, and all international training events and tournaments are scheduled out of season. In contrast, American footballers are often asked to uproot themselves from their club teams at relatively short notice. The pros in Europe must often fly back and forth across the Atlantic, which is taxing. Further, nothing else in sports functions like FIFA International Windows.* The international national-team fixtures often crop up during the athletes' and their employers' regular season, where the athletes are making the vast majority of their money and building their future. Further, during these Windows, national team coaches face limited preparation time, travel demands, variable competition levels, squad rotation, and load management issues affecting individual athletes.† The basketball players in the NBA mostly avoid these complexities.

* As of 2026, there are five International Windows per year that are designated periods in the FIFA International Match Calendar when club teams must release players for national team duty. The Windows accommodate World Cup qualifiers, international friendlies, and regional tournaments—and are often tied to lucrative TV contracts.

† Load management is now an issue across all sports, but elite professional soccer players may have it the hardest. In top leagues worldwide, players often juggle multiple competitions simultaneously—domestic leagues, domestic cups, FIFA continental club championships (such as the UEFA Champions League), FIFA World Cup qualifiers, national team friendlies, and regional international tournaments. Modern footballers and their agents must navigate congested schedules, injury risks, recovery demands, mental fatigue, and relationships with both club and national team coaches—issues influenced by everyone from the head coach of the relevant teams to the relevant fan base (which could be from a city or an entire country). Some fans are quick to run this calculus and judge the outcome as if they were in the athletes' shoes.

Thankfully, the 2010 World Cup squad gelled, appeared to get along, and elevated one another's competitive edge. Donovan and Dempsey have stated how their rivalry, not always amicable, inspired each other's MNT performances. On the eve of the 2010 tournament, Donovan, at twenty-eight, was in his prime, coming off four years as the LA Galaxy's best player and one of the best in MLS, with MLS Best XI honors for 2008 (also Golden Boot), 2009 (also MVP), and 2010. Dempsey, at twenty-seven, was excelling with Fulham in the English Premier League and earning praise abroad.

Michael Bradley, the coach's son—earning every minute—was playing for Borussia Mönchengladbach and proved a tireless midfield presence. At age thirty-one, Tim Howard was still in his goalkeeping prime, having just completed four seasons as Everton's undisputed No. 1, rarely missing a minute of English Premier League (EPL) action. He played a key role in Everton's run to the 2008–2009 FA Cup Final, where the Toffees narrowly fell to Chelsea, 2–1. That year, Howard was named Everton's Player of the Season. He averaged ten clean sheets per year over his first four seasons, and consistently delivered outstanding performances. He was a gifted, transplanted Yankee goalkeeper, perhaps rivaled only by Brad Friedel, who himself was in the midst of a glorious seventeen-year career in the EPL (with five different clubs). Howard and Friedel earned respect—even from the British press, which had long viewed U.S. soccer skeptically. With the foreign media and fans, this American duo had done something as difficult as pulling off a panenka.*

The Americans arrived in South Africa for the 2010 World Cup to face, in group play, England, Slovenia, and Algeria. The Yanks brought loads of optimism that could not be drowned out by the loud and unremitting hum produced by tens of thousands of fans blowing their vuvuzelas (long, plastic horns, later outlawed by FIFA). Vuvuzelas originated from

* A *panenka* is a type of penalty kick where the kicker chips the ball toward the center of the goal, rather than shooting the ball forcibly toward one of the corners. In a slow arc, the ball leaves the kicker's foot and floats into the net—right where (hopefully) the goalkeeper was standing a moment before the kick. It is named after Antonín Panenka, a Czech player, who performed the audacious chip during the 1976 European Championship final.

traditional African instruments once used in rural areas to assemble people or announce events. The World Cup vuvuzelas blew for the entire month. The horns were so ubiquitous and energetic that almost nobody remembers the official World Cup mascot, Zakumi, a green and yellow anthropomorphized leopard.

The Yanks opened their South Africa account against England in a thrilling rematch of their 1950 encounter, which this time was watched (live) by 17.3 million people in North America (across ABC/Univision), making it, for the Americans, the most-watched opening round World Cup broadcast ever. Despite conceding an early goal in the fourth minute, the U.S. remained composed and found their rhythm. Nearing halftime, Clint Dempsey, after two decisive spin moves with the ball at his feet, took what looked to be an innocuous shot from outside the box that slipped off the gloves of England's goalkeeper and spun into the net. Dempsey became only the third U.S. player (with Landon Donovan and Brian McBride, and soon—hopefully!—Christian Pulisic and Timothy Weah) to score in two World Cups. The U.S. continued to fight, with standout performances from Tim Howard, who made crucial saves, and Jozy Altidore, whose powerful sprint down the left line and cut-in run and near-post shot nearly gave the U.S. the lead. The game ended in a tie. The front cover of the *New York Post* wryly boasted: "USA wins 1–1."

Against Slovenia, the U.S. again demonstrated their resilience in a thrilling 2–2 draw at Ellis Park, Johannesburg. After conceding two early goals, the U.S. mounted a spirited second-half comeback. Donovan led the charge, scoring a stunner in the forty-eighth minute—roofing the ball from about five yards out, at an extreme angle, at the end of a thirty-yard run. The U.S. continued to push forward. After a hallmark hustle sprint from the midfield, Michael Bradley scored a beautiful volley, in the eighty-second minute, right inside the box. A late left-footed volley at the back post by Maurice Edu off a Donovan free kick found the back of the net but was controversially disallowed. Upon review: Where is the foul committed by any of the U.S. players? The head referee and FIFA have never publicly addressed the incident. And it remains one of the most controversial decisions in World Cup history because the mistake was so blatant. The MNT's performance in the second half was gritty and gutsy. But they couldn't break the tie.

With two points from their first two group matches, the U.S. needed a win against Algeria in their final group game to guarantee advancement. Algeria needed a win to have any chance to advance. The U.S.-Algeria match remained scoreless for ninety minutes. The Yanks had numerous chances within the box to score. Algeria had their chances, too, but mostly from long range. It was a nervy, back-and-forth affair. But then a sequence of moves unfolded that remain etched in the memories of many American fans. In the first four minutes of stoppage time,* an Algerian forward at the back post headed the ball straight to Howard. It was an easy save.

Howard immediately double-palmed it downward for a bounce, and then whipped the ball downfield thirty yards or so to converge with a sprinting Donovan. At full tilt, Landon carried it across midfield and forward at least thirty more yards and then, just outside the eighteen-yard box, tapped it ahead to Jozy Altidore. Landon continued his run. A moment later, Altidore's square pass found the foot of Clint Dempsey, who, in full stride and a hair outside the six-yard box, one-timed a shot that ricocheted off the diving goalkeeper. The ball fell straight to Donovan, himself in full stride, whose right foot clinically redirected it into the back corner of the net. In real time, it unfolded over several glorious seconds—and it's worth a replay.

"The U.S. have numbers," observed the British play-by-play

* *Stoppage time* is the official FIFA phrases used for the amount of time the head referee adds to the end of each half (calculated by whole minutes) to compensate for stoppages of time for such things as injuries, substitutions, goal celebrations, throw-ins, disciplinary actions, and, nowadays, VAR checks. Fans and pundits also call it "added time" or "injury time." None of the terms are entirely accurate. In practice, the head referee relays the number of added minutes to the fourth official, who, at midfield, then displays that number on a portable electronic board that he holds above his head. Even after the board is shown, the head referee can add more time (or subtract time!), depending on further time lost during added time, or other issues that crop up. The head referee is the final decision-maker on time. And only his whistle ends the game.

commentator, as Landon bore down on the Algerian box. "The Algerians are stretched. Altidore squares it, Dempsey's missed it, Donovan has it! From hope there is glory! The United States are going through!" After scoring, Landon kept running toward the corner flag and dove headfirst into a chest slide. He was buried by his teammates. The American TV audience heard Ian Darke's iconic "Go, go USA!" and "You could not write a script like this!" To date, it remains the most high-stakes, down-to-the-wire moment in MNT history. The Yanks advanced as winners of their group for the first time.

In the round of 16, the U.S. faced the Black Stars again, their foe from the group stage a cycle earlier. Ghana struck early, off a darting long-distance run by Kevin-Prince Boateng. But in the sixty-second minute, Deuce (Dempsey's nickname) artfully nutmegged a defender at the edge of the box and then was brought down in the penalty area by a covering defender. Donovan banged the penalty kick in off the post to become the U.S.'s all-time World Cup leading goal scorer, with five. Former President Bill Clinton and Mick Jagger, sitting together, rose to their feet, and cheered; so did President Obama, from Canada, taking a break from a G20 Summit. So did another 14.9 million Americans watching on TV. The match went into two fifteen-minute periods of extra time,* where Asamoah Gyan's early goal sealed a 1–2 win for Ghana. Despite pressure from the U.S., the equalizer never came. And the Yanks bowed out. Ghana advanced to the quarterfinals, eventually falling to Uruguay.

Spain went on to win the tournament, over the Netherlands, on the

* *Extra time* is the official FIFA phrase for the two halves of fifteen minutes each (thirty minutes total) used to give both teams a chance to determine a winner on the field of play whenever a knockout match is tied after the regular ninety minutes. If the score is still tied after thirty minutes of extra time, the match goes to five rounds of penalty kicks from the penalty spot. If still tied after five rounds, the game goes to sudden-death penalty kicks. The change to two compulsory sessions of extra time started with the 2006 World Cup, and it followed the abolition by the IFAB in 2004 of the "golden goal," where any goal in extra time automatically ended the game, and the "silver goal," where the first goal didn't end the match immediately. Instead, the remaining time in the fifteen-minute session was played out, and if there was no tying goal, the match ended. FIFA used golden and silver goals for eleven years (1993–2004). They are relics of the past.

wings of a golden generation. The vuvuzelas were still going strong when Xavi Hernández, Cesc Fàbregas, Carles Puyol, Andrés Iniesta, Sergio Ramos, David Villa, Iker Casillas, Sergio Busquets, Gerard Piqué, and others ascended the dais and hoisted the World Cup trophy. The Spanish had outclassed the Dutch. They played a tiki-taka style the whole month that brought a smile to Johan Cruyff, the primary originator of Total Football, much of it in the heart of Barcelona—*and* a frown (such was Cruyff, ever the paradox and the contrarian), which was directed to his Dutch countrymen for playing an "ugly, vulgar" match marked by repeated fouls. The TV viewing audience in America for the Final was roughly twenty-six million people, another soccer record. This number considerably dwarfed the average viewers that year of the World Series (11.3 million) and the NBA Finals (18.1 million).

Between 2008 and 2015, the MLS underwent significant transformation and aggressive growth. The league expanded from fourteen to twenty teams, adding clubs rapidly: San Jose Earthquakes (2008), Seattle Sounders FC (2009), Philadelphia Union (2010), Portland Timbers (2011), Vancouver Whitecaps FC (2011), Montreal Impact (2012), New York City FC (2015), and Orlando City SC (2015). Investor-operators studied soccer-ready markets, built soccer-specific stadiums, and engaged passionate fan bases.

In one case, a group of fans from Philadelphia—without a soccer team—calling themselves the Sons of Ben (derived from Benjamin Franklin, one of the nation's Founding Fathers, who made Philly his adult home) engaged league officials by showing up to MLS events in *other* cities to make noise, chant, promise season-ticket sales, and generally hound league VIPs into awarding Philadelphia a franchise. It worked. Almost two years to the day after being awarded a team, and along the shores of the Delaware River, a stadium appeared where once there was a soggy waterfront. No one should underestimate the power of fans who love the beautiful game. Fan bases and franchises, marketers and ticket sales forces, had finally upped their game with the internet, and started working together to rally community involvement and enhance game-day experiences. The franchises and fans experienced many successes (and some growing pains), as outlined in Phil West's book *The United States of Soccer: MLS and the Rise of American Soccer Fandom*. Going on twenty years now, no one can reasonably dispute the claim that elite-level U.S. soccer fandom is on the rise, virtually everywhere. Proof is in the numbers.

The Seattle Sounders wrapped up their 2009 debut MLS season with a massive average crowd just shy of 31,000, a record for a pro soccer club in the modern era. Then the Sounders went on a six-year attendance tear. In 2015, Sounders home games averaged 44,247 fans, a figure bested only by the heyday of Pelé and the New York Cosmos in 1978–1979. Seattle's record stood for only two years. In 2017, expansion team Atlanta United drew an astounding average 45,881 fans per match, and then a glorious 53,000 in 2018, which still stands as the MLS record. In second place in 2015 was Orlando City FC with an average of nearly 33,000 fans, while New York City FC drew 29,000. No team in the NBA and NHL that year averaged more than 22,000 for the regular season.

On the field, the level of play continued to improve through better scouting, international acquisitions, Designated Players, and incentives regarding youth development. As to the latter, the Homegrown Player Rule, officially introduced in 2008, permitted MLS clubs to sign local players, almost always American or Canadian citizens, from their own development academies directly to the first team, bypassing traditional allocation methods like the MLS SuperDraft. Such signings had the added advantage of allowing much of the salary to not count against the salary cap. Homegrowns are "enormously important," observed Commissioner Garber. "Development academies are the future."

FC Dallas became a pioneer and immediately built out their youth academy. Since 2008, FC Dallas has signed a record forty-three Homegrown Players to its first team. In 2013, the Philadelphia Union received an enormous gift from minority owner Richie Graham, who founded and funded a private, fully accredited high school (YSC Academy) specifically designed for elite soccer players. Graham and the founding Head of School,

Dr. Nooha Ahmed-Lee, in concert with the Union, embedded it completely within the Union's soccer franchise, giving top talents the opportunity to pursue their dreams of becoming professional soccer players without sacrificing their education. To date, the Union has signed thirty players directly from its youth academy. Some MLS teams have followed Dallas and Philly's lead in establishing robust youth academies to provide quality coaching and a direct pathway to the professional level. Ah, finally, the pipeline! It's not perfect. But the path is real and has been improving each year. More about the pipeline in the final chapter.

Between 2011 and 2014, the LA Galaxy reestablished their dominance, capturing three MLS Cups in four seasons. David Beckham, healthier and more focused, played a key role in the first two championships, alongside longtime star Landon Donovan and new Designated Player Robbie Keane. America loves (and loves to hate) its sports dynasties. As of 2025, the MLS Cup (comparable, regarding playoff format, to the Super Bowl, though the soccer people are more generous to the mid-table teams*) tally stands at six for LA Galaxy, four for D.C. United, and three for the Columbus Crew. Every other club has won two, one, or none. Love it or hate it, parity is the name of the MLS game. The New York Red Bulls signed World Cup winner Thierry Henry in July 2010, while Orlando City SC signed Kaká, another World Cup winner, in July 2014. Both players played four seasons in MLS and scored a lot of goals. But neither won an MLS Cup.

Commercially, MLS continued along its path of steady growth. From 2010 to 2014, ESPN was the primary broadcaster of regular season games and the MLS Cup. But in August 2011, MLS signed a three-year media rights agreement with NBC Sports Group that included forty-five MLS games and four MNT contests televised live across NBC and NBC Sports Network. In 2014, MLS inked a landmark eight-year deal with ESPN, Fox Sports, and Univision Deportes, which increased MLS rights fees, and eyeballs, significantly. True: Viewership numbers have been uneven and occasionally

* Currently, in the thirty-team MLS, eighteen teams make the playoffs. In the thirty-two-team NFL, fourteen teams do.

low, particularly for small-market games and late-season matches with no playoff implications (and no relegation-promotion excitement). Critics, including the aging anti-soccer lobby, love citing the poor ratings out of context. Going into MLS's third decade, fans enjoyed improved experiences at stadiums, while television viewership continued climbing. The league also benefited from enhanced media deals and increased sponsorship from major companies such as Adidas and Herbalife.

By 2015, the storm had subsided and the skies opened up. The league had successfully put down ropes on the mountain and carved crampon lanes along the steep sections. The summit—which could be characterized as a profitable and entertaining domestic pro league, and international esteem for the National Team (one prodigious step up from respect)—was in sight.

But mountains, as the climbers' adage goes, have a way of dealing with overconfidence.

18

★★★★★

THE NATIONAL TEAM FACES SUMMIT STORMS

And returns to base camp (2010–2018)

"Failure is only the opportunity to begin again more intelligently."

— Henry Ford

After a heartbreaking loss to Ghana in the 2010 World Cup round of 16 (knockout stage), the MNT, still under coach Bob Bradley, aimed to bounce back during the 2011 CONCACAF Gold Cup. Despite early optimism and a strong start, leading 2–0 in the final against Mexico, the U.S. collapsed, losing 2–4. The defeat, including their first-ever loss to Panama earlier in the group stage, marked a low point for the team and led to Bradley's dismissal. In July 2011, Jürgen Klinsmann, former German national team player (1990 World Cup winner) and former German national team coach from 2004 to 2006 (2006 World Cup third-place finish)—the apple of the USSF's eye for about five years—was hired as head coach.

Klinsmann had already fully embraced American life by marrying an American woman in 1995 and settling in Newport Beach, California, about three hundred yards from the Pacific Ocean. His house was also conveniently located near one of the main National Team training facilities located in Torrance, California (about a fifty-minute commute for Jürgen by car). The sandy-haired German quickly blended into American life. He had been driving his two children, Jonathan and Laila, to school and soccer practice nearly every day. The Federation had high hopes that Klinsmann would transform the MNT through an exciting, attacking style of play, and lead the Yanks through qualification and competition at the 2014 World Cup in Brazil. Jürgen was the first foreign coach to take the helm since Bora Milutinović's campaign during the early 1990s.

Klinsmann had grand goals for the Federation and the MNT. And his appointment and public statements during his first several years underscored the friction between two long-standing attitudes and beliefs about who should lead the National Team. In one camp are people who believe the MNT should be led by American coaches rather than foreign ones. (In many leading soccer countries, this debate is less prominent, as fans are typically more welcoming of foreign coaching talent—though this sentiment likely reflects a different historical connection to the game.) The American contingent argues that American coaches better understand the unique challenges, culture, and development pathways of soccer in the U.S., and the peculiar milieu of MLS. This group feels that relying on foreign coaches undermines domestic talent and slows the growth of a distinct American soccer identity.

While not expressed publicly, this group's ethos is likely rooted in a reaction to the very origins of soccer on U.S. soil. During its formative years, the sport was primarily being run by immigrants—beginning with the AFA in the late 1800s and continuing until around 1920, when the USSF (operating then as the USFA) finally took full control. The legacy of foreign influence persisted in the NASL, dominated by non-American players and coaches. Today, this camp views with skepticism foreign talent assuming command—not only of the MNT, but of the broader soccer development program down to the youth level. This skepticism resurfaced when Jürgen, less than two years after being hired as head coach of the MNT, requested and was granted the role of USSF technical director, overseeing the development philosophy for all U.S. men's National Teams. It was clear Klinsmann wanted to grow and change the game—but on his terms.

The other camp believes international coaches bring valuable experience, tactical sophistication, and a global perspective that can elevate the team's performance. They argue foreign coaches often come from more competitive soccer cultures and can instill a winning mentality, better game management, advanced tactical strategies, and possess experience managing elite professional footballers. This camp sees international expertise as essential for helping the U.S. compete at the highest level, especially in World Cup contexts.

People from both camps frequently disagree on sub-issues, but one sparks the most debate. A growing number of people are fond of MLS or at least support it while acknowledging its limitations. These people recognize that MLS has come a long way, and while it's not on par with the top European leagues, it's decent and occasionally outstanding—we're still growing. Others, a shrinking group, eschew MLS and pay it little attention. At the extreme are people who loathe MLS, seeing it as a symbol of how bad U.S. soccer is or has become. They believe America's pay-to-play model and the MLS's frozen table (no promotion-relegation) kill good soccer and that everything about soccer is better in Europe—we stink, and there's nothing we can do about it short of blowing up the system and starting again.

Curiously, a portion of the American soccer community harbors a deep-rooted self-loathing. There are still too many Americans who would rather watch (on TV) two teams at the lower end of the English Premier League table battle it out on a wet field in mid-April than attend a live professional soccer game on a beautiful day in their own backyard under an MLS or USL banner. I see this attitude expressed by some of my own student-athletes in my job as an English teacher at YSC Academy, the academic school embedded completely within the Philadelphia Union franchise.

I occasionally come across teens who complain incessantly about Major League Soccer and the MNT, even though the boys are part and parcel of the very pipeline leading to the promised land. The negativity is not innocuous. I worry that when they don't make it to the professional level (which most won't, as a statistical fact), they will shrug their shoulders because they think, *MLS sucks*. The negative sentiment and messaging—often inherited from their parents—is inimical to the very student-athletes they are striving to become.*

A major fault line between the MLS-likers and MLS-haters often forms at the great quandary of American soccer excellence and development at its highest level. When an American player becomes so good in MLS and makes the jump to one of the top European leagues, what happens if he experiences a prolonged decline in form or reaches what appears to be a ceiling on the other side of the pond? Is it better to stay in Europe and train with players and coaches in better leagues and not get a lot of playing time? Or to return to (or stay in) the U.S. and get more consistent playing time on a team within MLS? There are no easy answers for athletes, their

* From my perspective as a former coach and current English teacher of elite athletes, there is at least one possible solution to this knee-jerk defense mechanism and negativity. It is for the boys to see their soccer journey as one chapter in a much broader story called the Hero's Journey, first articulated by the American professor and mythologist Joseph Campbell. By the time the boys enter my class, they have already answered the "call to adventure" by moving from the "ordinary world" of their respective high schools to the Philadelphia Union Youth Academy and its embedded high school. During their upper school years, they will face many "tests, enemies, and allies"—which include the perpetual battle for playing time (minutes), stronger teammates or opponents, jealousy, exhaustion, burnout, red cards, distractions, frustrations, injuries—and plenty of annoying homework. The boys' goal, for now, is to prepare for college while simultaneously approaching the "inmost cave" to "kill the dragon," which is a metaphor for making it to the professional level. Most will fail somewhere along the way to that specific goal. And their journey will shift to other worthwhile endeavors. That's the way it works for most young aspiring professional athletes in just about all sports. But the vast majority of really good athletes who don't make it to the NFL, NBA, MLB, or NHL (*i.e.*, "the Show") don't turn around and bad-mouth the league and the players who did make it. No, they support the top professional league. So, too, should our student-athletes and their parents. Why is it that too many soccer people fail to realize that the reward for trying and failing is not failure but a deeper understanding of the game, teamwork, hard work, persistence, fun, and joy? The list of valuable lessons learned along the way is significant, and lasting. The message should be: Support the student-athletes and their journeys (wherever they lead)—and support the Show!

agents, and all of us fans. Like many hot-button topics in American soccer, the answer is: It depends.

Klinsmann's appointment stirred emotions and controversies across both camps, which was healthy. But Jürgen positioned himself right off the bat as a guru ready to take on all barriers holding back U.S. soccer. It soon became clear he didn't much like anything about the U.S. system, including Major League Soccer of the 2011 era: "We have to change the mentality of the country. We have to make soccer a priority." Making soccer a priority meant getting the best players out of America: "I want to see American players go abroad and play in the best leagues in the world." He also criticized European-based players returning to the States: "With Clint [Dempsey's] move back [to the Seattle Sounders, from Tottenham Hotspur of the English Premier League] and Michael [Bradley's] move back [to Toronto FC, from AS Roma of the Italian Serie A], it's going to be very difficult for them to keep that same level that they experienced at the places where they were." His hot takes, even if there was a lot of truth to them, were not the best way to start building a team for the 2014 World Cup. And such strong opinions, and how he expressed them, would dog Klinsmann during his entire time with the MNT.

The German-American's tenure began poorly, with just one win in his first six games. Further, the U-23 team, within Klinsmann's orbit but not yet under his direct oversight, failed to qualify for the 2012 Olympics.* But the

* Men's Olympic soccer is primarily an Under-23 tournament and it takes place in alternating years with the FIFA World Cup, ensuring a major global football competition occurs every two years. As of 2026, each men's Olympic team may include up to three overage players to add leadership and talent. Qualification for the tournament is determined through regional competitions, such as the CONCACAF U-20 Championship for North America. The Olympics are not on FIFA's Official Calendar. Therefore, clubs are not required to release players. In contrast, the World Cup is owned and sponsored by FIFA, and clubs cannot unilaterally refuse to release players. The injury scenario necessitates private discussions between the club, the athlete, and his agent, which gives some leverage to the clubs. But clubs must tread carefully. Just about every player genuinely desires to play for his country in an Olympics and a World Cup. Even multinationals who are eligible to play for several countries—including those for which they may have only tenuous ties—covet such appearances. The Olympic and World Cup stages elevate all players' profiles and can and do boost their "brands."

senior MNT quickly turned things around, winning five straight matches, including its first-ever victory over Italy in a friendly in Genoa. The glow of Klinsmann at the wheel helped the team gain global recognition, fueled by strong performances from Tim Howard, Clint Dempsey, Michael Bradley, Jozy Altidore, DaMarcus Beasley, and later contributions from Omar Gonzalez, Kyle Beckerman, Fabian Johnson, Jermaine Jones, DeAndre Yedlin, John Brooks, Matt Besler, and Alejandro Bedoya.

As the third round of CONCACAF World Cup Qualifying began, the MNT struggled unexpectedly against weaker opponents like Jamaica, Guatemala, and Antigua and Barbuda, raising concerns about Klinsmann's leadership and constant lineup changes. Although a landmark win over Mexico in a friendly at Estadio Azteca in August 2012 (the only Yankee victory to date at El Tri's fortress) briefly silenced critics, it didn't carry over into qualification matches. The team's advancement to the Hex was only secured through a last-minute goal by Eddie Johnson during a hard-fought win over Guatemala. After all the hype of Jürgen's hiring and the changes afoot on the technical side, the MNT squeaked into the final qualification round by the skin of their cleats.

Before the start of the Hex in February 2012—and a little over two years before the start of the 2014 World Cup in Brazil—Landon Donovan announced a break from soccer, citing physical and mental exhaustion, dealing a psychological blow to the MNT. In a 2014 interview, Donovan acknowledged his four-month break from soccer was due to depression, rather than just burnout or exhaustion. He stated that the time away helped him gain better self-awareness and habits to improve his emotional well-being. Donovan emphasized the importance of mental health and the need for athletes to address issues in a safe place. Landon's candidness and openness were pioneering and paved the way for future athletes, over six years later, like Kevin Love (NBA), Simone Biles (gymnast), and Naomi Osaka (tennis player), who began speaking publicly about mental wellness in high-pressure sports and the importance of stepping away when necessary.

Klinsmann never directly commented on Donovan's sabbatical, but

Jürgen's decisions to come would underscore his discontent with how Donovan was conducting himself—indeed, discontent was the theme of an investigative article published in March 2013 citing several players (anonymously) questioning Klinsmann's leadership, game preparation, and tactics. The report highlighted deep divisions within the team, leaving morale at an all-time low.

After an unfortunate loss to Honduras in the MNT's opening Hex game, and other struggles, the Americans rallied impressively during the rest of their Hex matches. They secured a gritty win over Costa Rica in blizzard-like conditions, just outside of Denver, in a March 22, 2013, game coined the *Snow Clasico*, and earned a rare draw against El Tri at Estadio Azteca. This turnaround sparked a strong run, including wins over Germany (friendly), and excellent Hex wins over Jamaica, Panama, and Honduras, and a dominant 2013 Gold Cup performance by a squad absent several top European-based players, but highlighted by Donovan's return and Golden Ball award.

With continued success, the MNT completed a remarkable comeback, including a key win over Mexico (dos a cero) in Columbus to clinch qualification at the uncontested top of the Hex for the second straight cycle, setting a twelve-game win streak, the second-longest in team history. It was the USA's seventh consecutive World Cup qualification berth. And yet one celebrated Yank, Landon Donovan, would not be traveling with the MNT to Brazil. Klinsmann had unexpectedly left him off the final roster. It was a decision that was hard to square in light of Donovan's contributions to the MNT for over a decade and then-current form, which had remained (after his sabbatical) consistently high for over a year for his club and the MNT.

Like many hot-button issues in the American soccer community, there are at least two camps. Some argue that Klinsmann's decision was driven by personal feelings toward Donovan, a stab at MLS, or both, and was impossible to square with the data. For 2013, Donovan's eight goals and eight assists for the MNT essentially tied his 2007 personal best of nine goals and four assists. Further, his eight goals and seven assists for the LA

Galaxy in his first seventeen matches back after his hiatus helped propel the club to the playoffs and Donovan to the 2013 MLS All-Star Team. Klinsmann's comments the day of his decision didn't particularly help: "The media thinks [Landon] is untouchable. The media thinks he should be in Brazil based on what he did . . . but that is not how it works. I have to choose the twenty-three best players based on what I see today."

In the other camp are people, including some professional athletes, who view the specific timing of Donovan's mid-career break as evidence of his diminished commitment and competitive drive at the highest level, aggravated by the fact that he had effectively walked away from the Galaxy and the MNT during several important and difficult Hex games. This camp is quick to rope in observations about Donovan's career in Europe, which was marked by unfulfilled potential. Despite his talent, he struggled to establish himself at major clubs like Bayer Leverkusen and Bayern Munich, and later at Everton. After each stint in Europe, he returned to the more comfortable environment of MLS. Overall, Donovan never fully adapted to the European game or proved himself as a consistent force at the highest club-level abroad.

In any event, Jürgen's 2014 final World Cup roster included ten MLS players and thirteen European-based pros. The Cup kicked off in Brazil, among a soccer-mad population with serious undercurrents of people unhappy that public coffers had been drained to build and renovate stadiums. Reports of corruption surfaced. Over $11.6 billion was spent on stadiums and infrastructure (including venues that would return to disuse as soon as the World Cup lights were turned off), while millions lacked quality health care, education, and housing. Many argued the money should have gone to basic public services. Curiously, Brazil's local FIFA organizing committee unveiled a World Cup mascot—an armadillo (blue armor, yellow skin) called *Fuleco* (a blend of the Portuguese words for "football" and "ecology")—intended to champion biodiversity and conservation. But Fuleco spent most of the Cup dancing, engaging in crowd antics, and urging fans to clean up after themselves.

The U.S. was drawn into arguably the toughest group (Group of Death) and faced Ghana (which had knocked out the MNT in the two preceding cycles), Portugal (with Cristiano Ronaldo, CR7, at age twenty-nine, at the peak of his power, straddling consecutive Ballon d'Or trophies for 2013 and 2014), and Germany (the tournament favorite and ultimate winner).

In their opening game, the Yanks beat Ghana's Black Stars, 2–1. Clint Dempsey, at the end of a brilliant solo run, scored just twenty-nine seconds in—the fifth-fastest goal in World Cup history. The rest of the contest was marked by intense physical play, key injuries to Jozy Altidore and Matt Besler, and good chances for both teams. After Ghana equalized in the eighty-second minute, John Brooks's eighty-sixth-minute downward-header (off a corner kick) bounced in front of the keeper and zipped into the net. The victory, watched by nearly sixteen million Americans, stirred national excitement and gave the Yanks momentum going into the game against Portugal and CR7. The staccato call-and-response chant, "I BELIEVE THAT WE WILL WIN!"—first coined in 1998 and adopted by various sports teams in the early 2000s—gained spondaic momentum and became a rallying cry for the MNT during this particular tournament. These days, though, it's seldom heard on matchday, surviving mostly as a nostalgic refrain.

In their second group match, the Yanks came within seconds of defeating Portugal and automatically securing a round-of-16 spot. After an early defensive mistake led to a goal by Nani, the U.S. fought back with goals from Jermaine Jones (a lovely long-range curling shot just inside the back post) and Clint Dempsey (a ricochet off his chest, just inside the six-yard box), taking a 2–1 lead. However, in the ninety-fifth minute, CR7—up to that point having a pedestrian game—delivered a perfect cross to the back post to Silvestre Varela, who redirected it into the net, resulting in a 2–2 draw.

Despite the disappointment, the U.S. could still advance with a win or a draw against Die Mannschaft, Jürgen's old team, in their final group game. Portugal, on the other hand, was on the brink of elimination after two poor performances. Germany controlled much of the possession and attack against the U.S., but lacked finishing quality. The Germans, unsurprisingly, were patient and relentless. Eventually, a batted-ball clearance by Tim Howard fell to Thomas Müller just outside the eighteen-yard box. Müller struck it first-time. The ball "threaded the eye of the needle" through a bevy of defenders and into the inside netting of the far post. Thirty-five minutes remained, but the Yanks could not score. The game ended 0–1. Germany advanced, top of the group. Tim Howard made several excellent saves, earning man of the match honors. And to everyone's delight, the U.S. still went through on goal difference over Portugal to face Belgium in the knockout stage.

The Red Devils dictated the tempo from the opening whistle with composed possession and determined attacks. Only Tim Howard's remarkable performance—sixteen saves, the most by any goalkeeper in a World Cup match since 1966—kept the U.S. in the game. It was likely the best goalkeeping display by an American in a World Cup game since Frank Borghi's historic 1950 triumph over England. A missed opportunity at the back post by the American Chris Wondolowski, right before the end of regulation, could have won the game. Belgium was led by their own golden generation, including Vincent Kompany, Kevin De Bruyne, Thibaut Courtois, Eden Hazard, Jan Vertonghen, Thomas Vermaelen, Toby Alderweireld, and Romelu Lukaku.

The Yanks somehow got the game into extra time. But De Bruyne and Lukaku finally picked Howard's lock, going up 0–2. The U.S. pulled one back late in the first period of extra time with a goal from dual-national Julian Green. Final score: 1–2. But truth be told, the Red Devils had outclassed the Americans. The Devils demonstrated that while the U.S. had continued to impress with athleticism and technical progress, there was still a gulf between them and the top teams in the world, especially in coordinated and composed tactical movements on and off the ball. And yet—the Yanks had almost won.

Meanwhile, Germany's World Cup knockout run was marked by dominant performances, tactical discipline, and historic moments. They began by edging past Algeria 2–1 in extra time, then defeated France 1–0 in the quarterfinals. In the semifinals, they stunned the world by demolishing host nation Brazil 7–1, scoring five goals in the first thirty minutes in one of the most lopsided knockout matches in World Cup history. Fuleco the armadillo was nowhere to be seen. The Final against Argentina and Messi was a tense, hard-fought battle that went into extra time, where Mario Götze scored the decisive goal in the 113th minute to secure Germany's fourth World Cup title and their first since reunification. The victory also marked the first time a European team won the World Cup in the Americas. Messi would have to wait until 2022 to lead Argentina to its second World Cup title.

Despite the Yanks' ouster in the round of 16 for the second straight cycle, the 2014 World Cup highlighted the resilience and spirit of the U.S. team. Fans across the country, inspired by the team's persistence, showed an unprecedented level of engagement with soccer, reflected in record-setting viewership and widespread watch parties. The MNT's performances sparked a surge in soccer's popularity in America, especially among younger generations, marking a cultural shift that dovetailed with the steady rise of MLS. Among knowledgeable fans and critics, however, the word was still out on Klinsmann. He had managed to get the U.S. to its second consecutive World Cup knockout round. But his team had only narrowly made the Hex to begin with, and at the World Cup the U.S. had needed help from Portugal to beat Ghana—but not by too many goals—for the Yanks to even meet a Red Devil.

In the next major international tournament, the 2015 CONCACAF Gold Cup, the U.S. finished a disappointing fourth, its worst result since 2000. The Yanks opened with wins over Honduras (2–1) and Haiti (1–0), but then drew with Panama (1–1). In the quarterfinals, they routed Cuba (6–0). However, the team faltered in the semifinals, losing to Jamaica (1–2)—their first failure to reach the final since 2003. In the third-place match, the U.S. again faced Panama, and lost 2–3 in penalties. Despite the team's struggles, Clint Dempsey won the Golden Boot with seven goals, and Brad Guzan took home the Golden Glove.

Two worrying trends had been revealed during the Gold Cup performances. The first issue centered on the idea that MLS, by providing playing opportunities and development platforms, had helped elevate the quality of players from the U.S. as well as *other* CONCACAF nations, and thus contributed to the narrowing of the competitive gap in the region. As MLS stood at the doorstep of its third decade, the 2015 Gold Cup was perhaps the first genuine example of how regional competitions had become more formidable for the MNT. The other narrative was the continuation of the Jürgen Klinsmann story. From 2015 to 2016, Klinsmann's tenure was marked by inconsistency and growing criticism. In 2016, the U.S. U-23 team failed to qualify for the Olympics, again—the young Yanks missing out on two Olympic cycles in a row for the first time in half a century. And the MNT continued to deliver erratic performances.

A month after the Gold Cup, the MNT made a deep run in the 2016 Copa América Centenario, where they fell to Argentina (0–4) in a lopsided semifinal game. Colombia then beat the Yanks 0–1 in the third-place match. Argentina advanced but lost to Chile in the final, which precipitated the retirement (briefly) of Messi from international play. A writer from the London-based *Guardian* described: "The defeat continued Argentina's 23-year trophyless run and Messi's own personal misery now extends to four lost finals with the national side—at the 2014 World Cup against Germany and at three Copa Américas, in 2007, 2015, and 2016." The usually poised and tight-lipped Messi was crushed. In the changing room after the game, he openly expressed sadness, regret, and international retirement scenarios, all this coming two days after he openly criticized the Argentine soccer federation as "a disaster." Only a player of Messi's stature could shoot an arrow to the head of his own federation. On the American side, the Yanks on the MNT and larger player pool had to be more circumspect. But many were angry, too.

In 2016, Klinsmann was well into his fifth year as head coach and continued to show a strong preference—critics called it an infatuation—for recruiting and fielding players with German-American heritage. Many of these players were born and raised in Germany but were eligible to play for the U.S. through an American parent, often a father who had served there with the U.S. military. Jürgen claimed his efforts were rooted in a strategic effort to boost the technical quality and international pedigree of the MNT. His selections sparked debate about National Team culture, loyalty, and development priorities, which continue to this day.

Some of the players Klinsmann supported and turned into key MNT players turned out to be unmitigated success stories. Take Jermaine Jones, born in Frankfurt, Germany, who was developed in German youth academies and then top clubs like Eintracht Frankfurt, Bayer Leverkusen, and Schalke 04. Initially playing for Germany, he switched to the MNT in 2009 after FIFA's eligibility rules were revised to permit dual-nationals who had played only friendlies to change their allegiance. Former head coach Bob Bradley had identified him. Under Klinsmann, Jones blossomed into a core player in the 2014 World Cup and went on to play in the MLS for three different teams. He was a tenacious and fearless midfielder. Virtually every time Jones put on a jersey for the MNT, he played his heart out. The same could not be said for some of Jürgen's other recruits, like Timothy Chandler, who, when he put on the stars and stripes, looked as if he had been saddled with a sedative. The dual-national debate exists across many football federations, so the issue is not unique to America. The only point of agreement for most people is to take each selection on a case-by-case (wait-and-see) basis.

In early CONCACAF qualifying for the 2018 World Cup, and still under Klinsmann, the U.S. faced Trinidad and Tobago (T&T), Guatemala, and Saint Vincent. After a strong 6–1 opener over T&T, a shocking 0–2 loss to Guatemala raised concerns. The U.S. rebounded with a 4–0 win over Saint Vincent, and topped the group to reach the Hex. Clint Dempsey, however, was sidelined by a serious health issue described as an irregular heartbeat, forcing him to miss the first two Hex matches and four months of the MLS season. His absence from the MNT caused an emotional blow. On November 11, 2016, in their first Hex match, the U.S. lost 1–2 to Mexico in Columbus, Ohio, which had long been a Yankee stronghold. The loss marked the end of a fifteen-year streak where the MNT had never lost a home game to Mexico. That night, half of Klinsmann's starting field players were dual nationals from Germany.

Just four days later, on November 15, 2016, away to Costa Rica, Jürgen started the game with the same field players. They were crushed 0–4 by the Ticos in one of the worst losses in U.S. World Cup qualifying history. The second loss in a row left the Yanks at the bottom of the Hex and off to their worst final-qualification round ever. Klinsmann was fired six days later. Even though the MNT would not play another Hex game for four months, the day after Jürgen's ousting, the USSF rehired Bruce Arena (who had helmed the MNT from 1998 to 2006) to rescue the qualifying campaign. Curiously, a *New York Times* piece from November 15—the day of the Costa Rican debacle—quoted USSF president Sunil Gulati saying he hadn't spoken with Arena about the MNT job "in recent weeks." This was likely false, as described by Bruce Arena in his book *What's Wrong with US?: A Coach's Blunt Take on the State of American Soccer After a Lifetime on the Touchline*.

In any event, Arena's initial impact was positive. He stabilized the team with several good results, including a 6–0 demolition of Honduras at home, a 1–1 draw at Panama, a 2–0 victory over T&T at home, and a rare 1–1 tie against Mexico away. However, the campaign took a bad turn with a 0–2 loss to Costa Rica at home at Red Bull Arena (now Sports Illustrated Stadium), approximately ten miles from the heart of NYC—in front of a hostile crowd that was predictable and easily preventable. The decision to host the U.S.–Costa Rica game at Red Bull Arena was another unwise U.S. Soccer Federation decision in light of the incontrovertible fact that the margin for error for the MNT was *remarkably thin* (after losing their first two Hex games). Further, the Federation had nearly ten months to figure out where to host the return leg against Costa Rica—which everyone knew would be a tremendously difficult match.*

Four days later, a 1–1 tie with Honduras on the road turned worry into panic in some circles and sparked accusations in others. Less than a week later, Alexi Lalas, serving as a pundit on a live Fox Soccer broadcast, chided the team: "Are you going to continue to be a bunch of soft, underperforming, tattooed millionaires?" After issuing a series of invectives against specific players and Bruce Arena, he prophetically concluded: "You are a soccer generation that has been given everything. You are a soccer generation that is on the verge of squandering everything."

With only two games left for each team in the Hex, there was just a single point separating third from fifth place—the tightest the table had been between those three positions since the qualifying format was adopted for the 1998 World Cup. The U.S. then thrashed Panama 4–0 at home. Which meant that all the Yanks had to do was fly down to Trinidad and Tobago (at the bottom of the Hex) and win or tie the game, on October 10, 2017, to qualify for the 2018 World Cup in Russia. Even with an unthinkable loss, there were still a remarkable number of W–L–D combinations involving the other four teams in the Hex (playing their two games simultaneously) that would permit the MNT to punch its ticket to Russia the following summer. For instance, even with a *fourth-place* finish in the Hex, the U.S. could still qualify after a run-off match against the fifth-place finisher from the Asian Football Confederation.

---

* Three days before the match, a Grant Wahl *Sports Illustrated* article quoted Sunil Gulati, then President of the USSF, who acknowledged that the foreign-crowd issue was considered and dismissed. Not surprisingly, Red Bull Arena sold out for the important Hex clash, with "a massive Costa Rican presence." Some who were at the match recalled anecdotally that close to three-fourths of the fans were backing the Ticos. It was not the right time to bring this particular game to the outskirts of Manhattan. The author of this book, together with generations of MNT fans, want to remind the Federation that the goal is to do everything within our collective power and within the rules to win every game that really matters. This requires placing soccer decisions ahead of financial decisions when it comes to the MNT. The Federation and U.S. fans must be forever unified on this goal. And fans must do their part by showing up in greater numbers every time the MNT plays on U.S. soil.

The day before the match in T&T—within a tiny stadium in Couva, about an hour south of Port of Spain—"the running track ringing the field was so inundated with water that had the heavy rain continued [into game day] it might have been necessary to issue the substitutes with snorkels." T&T's federation teased the U.S. before the match by posting images of the 2013 Snow Clasico in Denver. (As all soccer people know: Both teams perform on the same pitch, regardless of its conditions.) On that soggy pitch, the U.S. started slowly and did not recover. And the unthinkable happened. The U.S. lost 1–2 to T&T. And the other Hex matches on the same day went the absolute worst way from the Yanks' perspective, creating a perfect storm.* At the close of the final whistles of the three games playing out simultaneously, the U.S. finished a dismal fifth out of six teams in the Hex—and had failed to qualify for the World Cup for the first time since 1986.

Only minutes after the loss, ESPN's Taylor Twellman famously launched into an impassioned on-air rant criticizing the entire U.S. soccer system, repeatedly asking, "Are you kidding me? We can't beat Trinidad on a field that's too wet and too heavy? What are we doing! WHAT ARE WE DOING!" During the post-game press conference, Coach Arena bluntly admitted, in a calm, almost (some would argue) dismissive tone: "We didn't qualify for the World Cup. We have no excuses. We failed today." Several days later, Arena resigned. Less than two months later, the USSF President, Sunil Gulati, announced that he would not seek reelection. The loss haunts the players to this day.

The result triggered nationwide criticism of U.S. soccer. Traditional media and the internet lit up with guns going off in all directions, with targets from the very top to the very bottom. The Federation, for years, knew

* Notably, all four goal scorers in the other two Hex games that played out simultaneously (Mexico vs. Honduras, and Panama vs. Costa Rica)—whose goals materially blocked the Americans' chance to advance on points even with their loss to T&T—were either current MLS players (three) or had just retired from MLS (one). It was abundantly clear that MLS had provided and would continue to provide opportunities for players in other CONCACAF countries to get better. And that the talent gap among the top five or so national teams in the region had diminished. This trend is not likely to reverse.

about Jürgen Klinsmann's propensity to skate on thin ice and stubbornly alienate certain constituents. And the USSF had mounds of data on Bruce Arena's approach to the MNT, including his apparent lack of creativity and tactical inflexibility. The Federation itself was no Einstein, and suffered repeatedly from mental errors and infighting and poor performances, and too often played the role of Judas to the very team it was supposed to serve. The players weren't good enough either.

Bullets continued to fly. The entire U.S. development system was not just flawed, but rotten to the core, from the ubiquitous pay-to-play system, to the incongruent college soccer network, to the lack of an integrated promotion-relegation pyramid in MLS and across the country. Youth coaches and club administrators care more about winning games, making money, and promoting big, fast, strong kids (over those with technical and tactical ability)—and those who can afford that season's fee—than focusing on genuine long-term player development. The best foreign players rise from the lower classes. There's not enough money in the pro system. The best athletes in the U.S. don't play soccer. Suburban parents with their big SUVs and fancy TVs will never produce world-class players. Latinos are underrepresented. There are too many participation trophies. Too many games and tournaments. Not enough training time. Too few truly gifted coaches. Too much standing around. Too little scouting. Not enough unstructured play. Nobody cares about MLS. Nobody cares about soccer, except maybe once every four years. Not enough vision, culture, leadership. NFL is king.

Behind all the hand-wringing and good points in some of the more nuanced and cogent arguments, it was almost easy to forget about the emergence of *a player* and the *presence of an American player development system* (albeit imperfect) already up and running behind the scenes. Christian Pulisic, at nineteen years old, had emerged during the losing Hex campaign as the U.S.'s most dangerous and creative force. He scored five goals and assisted on four others in the Hex, directly contributing to more than half of the team's output. During the same time, he had made twenty-nine appearances for Borussia Dortmund in the German Bundesliga, scoring three goals and providing several assists. He was even speaking to the

German press in rudimentary German and waving respectfully to approximately 25,000 members of the Yellow Wall (that is, the fans in the towering south stand at Dortmund's stadium, one of the most intimidating supporters' sections in all of world football). The Yellow Wall knows their football—and they saw a lot of talent in Christian, a spunky kid who spent the majority of his childhood in Hershey, Pennsylvania.*

Behind all the walls and roadblocks in America set up to slow the development of youth soccer players, which had grown entrenched over the decades, was a young ecosystem of elite soccer academies—the MLS academies *and* a nationwide community of independent superclubs—which, in 2017, were in place, but not yet ready to bear significant fruit. More about them at the tail end of the next chapter and in the final chapter. If only America could get its act together, topple walls and remove frictions, and bring the USSF, MNT, MLS, USL, and all the pre-professional academies and independent youth superclubs, *all of them*, into a much more thoughtful and systematic development model, *maybe, just maybe*, America could produce three players of Pulisic's quality. Then five, then eleven. And eventually move the needle from good to great.

* Christian Pulisic shares his soccer journey from the time he was a toddler through 2025 in a nine-part docuseries titled *PULISIC*, produced in partnership with CBS Sports and Emmy-winning senior creative director Pete Radovich. The first episode premiered on December 9, 2024, as a Paramount+ Original. The docuseries is also available to stream on Prime Video and Apple TV.

19

★★★★★

THE 2018 AND 2022 WORLD CUPS, MLS MATURES, AND PREPARATIONS FOR THE 2026 WORLD CUP

Additional summit preparations (2018–2025)

"I don't want to be the next Michael Jordan.
I only want to be Kobe Bryant."

— Kobe Bryant

After the MNT, under old USSF leadership and coach Bruce Arena, crashed out of 2018 World Cup qualifying, the Yanks entered a period of self-evaluation that led to some major changes within the USSF and youth development. Meanwhile, the World Cup went on without them, in Russia (2018), then with them, in Qatar (2022). The latter tournament many believe was originally destined for the U.S.

The football fraudsters from Russia and Qatar have plenty of all-stars from FIFA Team Infamy to thank—*i.e.*, people who took bribes during the

2010 venue-vetting and final voting sessions regarding which countries would host the 2018 and 2022 World Cups. The fraud occurred under the ever-languid eyes of Sepp Blatter. Once awarded hosting responsibilities, both countries seized the opportunity to transform the tournaments into sweeping public relations campaigns—blatant sportswashing events.*

A book about the history of U.S. soccer would be remiss to omit commentary about a corpulent Yank known in FIFA circles as "Mr. Ten Percent." Back in 1990, Chuck Blazer slipped an outrageous provision into his original contract as CONCACAF's General Secretary (1990 to 2011), entitling him to a one-tenth cut of all future media deals. For over two decades, Blazer broadly interpreted and vigorously applied this provision, with impunity. Blazer, together with his slithy Trinidadian compatriot Jack Warner, CONCACAF president (1990 to 2011), used their FIFA power and connections to bilk the soccer world out of millions of dollars.

During the FIFA gravy train, Blazer maintained CONCACAF's main office and two private apartments in NYC's Trump Tower. Blazer, according to friends, was often content to roll out of bed and conduct FIFA business in his underwear instead of taking the elevator to the office. The only eyewitnesses to the crimes piling up were Chuck's cats, which lounged in their own adjacent apartment. Never was an expansive view of Central Park—and an accommodating maid for all the torpid occupants—less appreciated. FIFA, of course, picked up virtually all the bills. The Blazer-Warner suction machine purred along for nearly two decades until the FBI started digging and scratching, eventually catching Blazer for income tax evasion. It's hard to imagine a more pathetic and morally corrupt duo in world football.

Despite the avalanche of mid-2010 football scandals, guilty pleas, and extradition battles (the U.S. claiming jurisdiction because U.S. banks were

* Sportswashing is a *portmanteau* (French for a blending of two or more words) of the word "sports" and the latter part of "whitewashing," which originally meant covering or disguising flaws with white paint. Coined in 2015 to describe Azerbaijan's use of the European Games to distract from human rights issues, sportswashing became a popular term leading up to the 2018 World Cup in Russia. No global occasion delivers more bang for the sportswashing buck than hosting a World Cup, making it the ultimate instrument for revising a nation's image on the world stage.

used to facilitate fraudulent payments), the 2018 World Cup in Russia continued as planned. President Vladimir Putin claimed that the tournament helped break down "many stereotypes about Russia," which "is a hospitable country and friendly." The official 2018 World Cup mascot, *Zabivaka* (Russian for "the one who scores")—a brown wolf in matching red shorts and sports goggles—concurred. Curiously, a FIFA website called Zabivaka "a fair player" who "values his team members and respects his opponents." All this occurred about the same time the International Olympic Committee (IOC) and World Anti-Doping Agency began proceedings to ban Russian athletes amid revelations of a brazen, state-sponsored doping program.*

In Russia, France rolled through the tournament and was eventually crowned champion after defeating Croatia 4–2 in the Final. The match featured standout performances from France's young phenom Kylian Mbappé, who won the Best Young Player award, and Croatia's Luka Modrić, who, at thirty-two, earned the Golden Ball as the tournament's best player. It was Les Blues' second World Cup title, after their 1998 triumph, and Croatia's first Final. Defending champion Germany suffered a shocking early exit in the group stage, while England reached the semifinals for the first time since 1990, with Harry Kane earning the Golden Boot for his six goals.

The Yanks, of course, never made it to Russia. Recall it took the USSF one day to replace Jürgen Klinsmann with Bruce Arena in the midst of the failing Hex campaign for the 2018 World Cup. Eleven months later, the U.S. lost to Trinidad and Tobago in soggy Couva. Arena resigned several days later. But it took the USSF fourteen months (a strange and unjustifiable delay) to hire former American MNT player and MLS veteran (as a player and coach) Gregg Berhalter, fresh from an MLS playoffs loss at the helm

* The fraud involved Russia's own federal police cutting holes in athletes' walls to pass urine back and forth. Agents also impersonated plumbing contractors to gain access to laboratory testing facilities under the IOC's direction and control, and used microscopic tools to swap "dirty" urine for "clean" urine.

of the Columbus Crew. Known for meticulous preparation, Berhalter had kept detailed journals on tactics and personal growth since his playing days in top leagues across the Netherlands, England, and Germany, several years with the LA Galaxy, and his five-year tenure as head coach of the Crew. His Columbus teams, though lacking star power, gained respect for being well organized and consistently outperforming the odds.

Under Berhalter, the MNT navigated CONCACAF's new "Octagonal" qualifying format—eight teams, fourteen matches—earning a 2022 World Cup spot by finishing third behind Canada and Mexico. The roster was notably young, with an average age of just under twenty-four, with European-based players like Christian Pulisic, Tyler Adams, Weston McKennie, Yunus Musah, Tim Weah, and Antonee Robinson forming the core, alongside MLS pros such as Matt Turner, Walker Zimmerman, Kellyn Acosta, Shaq Moore, and DeAndre Yedlin.

If Qatar—a small, mostly desert peninsula jutting east into the Persian Gulf like a sore thumb—sounded like a bizarre place to host a World Cup, that's because it was. Qatar had no history of professional football, virtually no suitable infrastructure, and no natural grass due to extreme heat. Their bid to host included not only names of stadiums that hadn't been built, but the names of cities that didn't exist. That didn't seem to bother members of Team Infamy—or the hereditary monarchy of Qatar. Oil money, together with hundreds of thousands of migrant laborers recruited from South Asia, over twelve years, built stadiums and cities out of the desert under exploitative conditions. Newspaper reports and accounts from migrant workers claim over five thousand laborers died in the desert.

The grass for all pitches had been flown in from Adel, Georgia, on wide-body cargo jets and installed within ultra-air-conditioned, modern, surreal stadiums, rising out of the desert like pyramids. It's amazing what hard work, cheap labor (bordering on indentured servitude), human ingenuity, and money can do. The World Cup mascot for 2022 was an anthropomorphic keffiyeh, a popular men's white headdress, named *La'eeb* (Arabic for "super-skilled player"). He floated in the air, like a sheet, and had eyes, lips, and an open mouth. He looked conspicuously like a ghost—Casper's ultra-thin brother—perfectly symbolizing a joyful character that loves to help everyone. Or representing the dead.

In the group stage, the MNT faced Wales, England, and Iran. The Yanks kicked off against Wales (and Gareth Bale) at Ahmad bin Ali Stadium. It was a tale of two halves. Wales ceded possession in the first half, absorbing pressure. Josh Sargent nearly scored in the ninth minute, but his header hit the post. In the thirty-sixth minute, Christian Pulisic sprinted past midfield with the ball and passed to Tim Weah, who had slipped behind the center-back. Weah scored with a deft first touch with the outside of his boot. Wales pressed in the second half, nearly scoring on two headers and an open shot. The U.S. had chances, too. But Walker Zimmerman, in the eightieth minute, fouled Bale with a sloppy challenge from behind. Bale converted the penalty. The game ended 1–1.

In their second group match against the Three Lions, Berhalter's squad outplayed Gareth Southgate's eleven in the first half and exchanged salvos in the second. Weston McKennie and Christian Pulisic led a strong U.S. effort, with Pulisic hitting the crossbar and McKennie advancing into scoring positions at least three times. The game ended 0–0. *The Guardian* acknowledged that "the USA were the better team." Some of England's international stars—Bukayo Saka, Declan Rice, Harry Kane, and Jude Bellingham—delivered lackluster performances. The Brits must admit their team, on the day, looked no better than the Yanks. Indeed, the Three Lions have never beaten the U.S. at a World Cup competition. The tally still tilts our way: one victory, no defeats, and a pair of draws. The result left the MNT in control of their fate. A win over Iran would secure progression.

In a high-stakes, emotionally charged match with lively chanting on both sides, the U.S. outplayed Iran in most areas. Christian Pulisic scored the only goal in the thirty-seventh minute with a fearless side-footed volley from close range off a Sergiño Dest cross. Pulisic collided with the goalie in the process, injuring Pulisic's pelvis, and was removed at halftime for hospital evaluation. Iran had several second-half chances but couldn't score. After the game, Iran's players appeared devastated, carrying the weight of political turmoil and civil rights protests back home ("Woman, Life,

Freedom"). Several MNT players consoled members of the Iranian team in a show of good sportsmanship. Despite the loss, Iran earned respect for their determination. Coach Carlos Queiroz praised their spirit but admitted the U.S. was sharper, describing their organization and speed as overwhelming.

The United States entered the knockout cauldron against the Netherlands with confidence. In the second minute, a back-post chance by Pulisic almost put the U.S. ahead. Despite outperforming the Dutch in some statistical categories, the Americans' attacking inefficiency and defensive positioning were repeatedly exposed. In the ninth minute, the Netherlands dismantled the Americans' press with a twenty-pass sequence that eventually found Memphis Depay, wide open, just inside the eighteen-yard box. Depay's clean first-time strike careened past the gloves of Matt Turner. The Americans, who hadn't conceded from open play previously, found themselves trailing and tactically outmatched. The midfield trio of Tyler Adams, Weston McKennie, and Yunus Musah, typically a strength, faltered under extreme pressure and fatigue. Daley Blind's goal before halftime, nearly a copy of Depay's earlier strike, set the game nearly out of reach, at 0–2.

In the seventy-fifth minute, however, a low driven pass into the box from Pulisic was somehow scuffed by Haji Wright. The ball popped up and looped oddly across the goal mouth and spun into the inside back-post netting. With fifteen minutes remaining, and at 1–2, the Yanks had a punter's chance. But less than five minutes later, a wide-open Denzel Dumfries, positioned at the back post, crisply volleyed a cross out of the air and into the Americans' net, sealing a 1–3 victory for the Dutch. Berhalter called it "a game of moments," where brief lapses proved decisive against elite opposition. The U.S. fielded the third-youngest lineup in Qatar, giving valuable experience to a core group of players likely available for the 2026 World Cup.

The tournament rolled on. Argentina, led by the illimitable Lionel Messi, and France, led by explosive Kylian Mbappé—both superstars at opposite ends of their careers—advanced through the knockout rounds to meet in the Final. The match drew nearly twenty-seven million viewers across North America, a record. In his twenty-sixth World Cup match, Messi led Argentina during a dazzling battle that defied belief. Argentina led twice, France equalized twice, and after two extra time periods, it went to penalties. Messi had already scored twice, and calmly converted his penalty, while Dibu Martínez's heroics and Gonzalo Montiel's final kick sealed the win. Argentina, hungry for a title since Maradona's 1986 triumph, finally had its Messi-inspired grand prize.

The night belonged to Messi. The win brought a World Cup journey marked by heartbreak to a joyous resolution—though not closure, as Messi will probably play for La Albiceleste in the 2026 tournament. Members of the Argentinian squad had already assembled on the far side of the stage and waited for Messi, last to mount the steps, to receive the World Cup trophy. The jubilant Messi was greeted by the Emir of Qatar, who placed a semi-transparent robe called a *bisht*—a traditional Arab garment—over Messi's shoulders, which he did not remove for the rest of the ceremony. The Emir's act was a gesture of honor *and* the icky pinnacle of sportswashing. Messi respectfully took the trophy, caressed it, kissed it, held it like his child, and then delivered it to his teammates. Messi's performance throughout the tournament was masterful—seven goals, key assists, and a sense of destiny fulfilled. With this final masterpiece, Messi not only won the World Cup, but cemented his name as the greatest of all time.

The MNT in Qatar included twenty players born or raised primarily in the United States. Most of them were developed through various components of the USSF's Development Academy (DA) system, which began operations in 2007. The DA is a notable and lasting achievement of our Federation, which studied other countries' programs and then created a structured nationwide player development program for elite youth players to fit our unique soccer history and geography. For thirteen years, the DA provided high-level environments across U-12 to U-19 age groups, emphasizing quality training, coaching education, and meaningful competition to develop college players, pre-professionals, and national-team-caliber players. The USSF also contributed to cost-cutting measures for players and their parents—even if affordability was then, and remains, a very big problem. The plan, from the start, included the MLS academies as well as over a hundred independent clubs around the U.S.

Over time, the elite teams in the DA were overtaken by the growing influence of MLS and their youth academies. In April 2020, the USSF formally shut down its DA system (citing, oddly, economic woes brought about by COVID-19), and ceded control of the elite of the elite (during the teen years) to the MLS academies and their MLS NEXT model. That nationwide program, as of 2026, includes two divisions, 273 clubs, and over 2,000 teams. Major League Soccer has tweaked the program each year. Today, each *club* that participates must provide at least one full scholarship per season, fully covering participation costs. Hopefully this requirement will quickly grow to include each *team* that wishes to compete. Under-13 matches have shifted from two 35-minute halves to three 25-minute periods, and every player must play at least one uninterrupted period (notwithstanding an injury). Players in U-14 matches may reenter the game after being substituted. Starting in October 2025, and continuing annually, MLS NEXT will host a free Talent ID Weekend across thirteen markets for aspiring U-13 and U-14 players (inside or outside MLS NEXT). These initiatives will keep evolving.

The thirty MLS academy teams compete in the same regional leagues as the top-tier, independent "superclubs"—many of which employ excellent coaches and regularly produce Division I players and professional players. Some even outperform MLS academy teams. It's no secret that MLS academies seek to poach players. The non-MLS-academy club can be compensated under the MLS NEXT Development Grant Program when their eligible players progress through the professional player pathway. MLS academies are free.

A book could be devoted to the USSF-DA-MLS-NEXT story. Today, MLS academies are the primary driving force of U.S. youth development during the teen years. The current system, and its success, is tied to the future of MLS. While these dramatic changes have critics, even the MLS naysayers and American soccer curmudgeons (the *grumpudgeons*—my word) must concede it makes the most sense under the circumstances. All thirty MLS academies already have a base camp and a pipeline to each professional team in the league.

The player development system in the U.S. will probably never look like systems in other soccer nations. No other country has three time zones, a locked league at the top of its soccer pyramid, and a massive college soccer network that awards scholarships, and will continue to award them. The latter will continue to promote pay-to-play models no matter what MLS and the USSF do around the edges.

From 2015 to 2025, MLS experienced a steady and strategic rise, marked by expansion, investment, and increasing global relevance. One of the most visible aspects of this growth was rapid club and geographic expansion. In 2015, MLS had twenty teams. By 2025, it had grown to thirty, on par with the NFL (thirty-two teams), NBA (thirty), MLB (thirty), and NHL (thirty-two). Many of the new clubs hit the ground running, often with modern, soccer-specific stadiums. Aggressive marketing strategies quickly generated large and passionate fan bases. The growth was matched by a sharp rise in expansion franchise fees, which climbed from around $10 million in the league's early years to over $300 million by the early 2020s. In May 2023, the investor-operators of San Diego FC paid a staggering $500 million—demonstrating strong investor confidence in MLS's projected profitability models.

MLS invested heavily in infrastructure, with nearly every club moving into or planning a soccer-specific stadium and building training centers and academies. Teams shifted from relying on drafts and internal trades to signing young international talent through Designated Player slots and promoting Homegrown Players. Once seen as a retirement league for aging European stars, MLS has gained respect as a developer and seller of elite talent. What was once a trickle of players moving to Europe is now a narrow but steady stream, with rising transfer fees placing MLS in the Americas just behind Brazil's Série A and Argentina's Primera División.

Media contracts have improved, injecting serious money into MLS. On June 14, 2022, Apple and MLS announced a ten-year, $2.5 billion broadcasting deal. Apple holds global streaming rights to all MLS and Leagues Cup matches plus select MLS NEXT Pro and MLS NEXT games, featuring many top U.S. youth prospects. All first-team matches are produced in 1080p with Dolby 5.1 audio. For American viewers, the 2025 "MLS Season Pass" costs $99 per year ($79 for Apple TV subscribers). While criticized for putting most games behind a paywall, it remains the only deal worldwide giving full streaming access to a country's top league, its main developmental league, and some academy games. Apple also partners with traditional networks, and more accessible broadcasts are expected.

Another major step was the revamped Leagues Cup in 2023, a midseason tournament integrating MLS and Liga MX. MLS teams quickly became competitive with Mexican clubs, boosting the league's regional credibility and popularity with Latino fans. The four finalists for the 2024 and 2025 Leagues Cup were all MLS clubs. This would have been unheard of ten years ago.

But, of course, the biggest boost in public interest came with the announcement and then the arrival of Lionel Messi—the greatest footballer to ever lace up boots—to Inter Miami CF. Messi officially signed a two-and-a-half-year contract with the MLS club on July 15, 2023, committing through the 2025 season. He later extended that deal, securing his place with the club through the end of the 2028 season. "After winning the World Cup [in 2022] and not being able to return to Barcelona," Messi reflected, "it was my turn to go to the league of the United States to live football in another way." David Beckham, part-owner of Inter Miami, boasted: "We always knew that bringing Leo to America, not just to Miami, was our gift to America and the MLS. We bought him to inspire the next generation of soccer players in America."

Messi made his debut for Inter Miami on July 21, 2023, in a Leagues Cup match against Cruz Azul, coming off the bench in the fifty-fourth minute. In the ninety-fourth minute of stoppage time, Messi scored a dramatic free kick from about twenty-five yards out that has happened so many times that the soccer world has almost come to take it for granted. Off of Messi's boot, the ball rose up and over the wall—and then dipped slightly, right into the top corner of the net. The goal secured a 2–1 victory and ended the team's eleven-game losing streak.

Messi's arrival had an immediate and profound impact on both Inter Miami and MLS. His presence instantly elevated Miami's performance on the field, resulting in the club's first-ever trophy, the 2023 Leagues Cup. The following year, Messi led Miami in assists and goals (OK, he tied his Uruguayan friend Luis Suárez for goals, but Messi's were better!). He also materially helped the team clinch the Supporters' Shield (*i.e.*, the league's annual trophy to the team with the most regular season points), setting a league record for the most points in a single season. Messi also became the fastest player in league history to reach forty goals—and as soon as the ink was dry on that sentence, it was obsolete. Messi has surely set another record.

Immediately upon his arrival, ticket prices soared, merchandise sales broke records, the club's valuation skyrocketed, and turnstiles in stadiums all across North America fluttered with forces fast enough to make even David Beckham's head spin. Messi's move to MLS heightened the league's global profile and attracted new fans, domestically and internationally, and new talent. Messi's MLS presence soon resulted in the arrival of reinforcements and global superstars in their own right: Sergio Busquets, Jordi Alba, and Luis Suárez.

Ten years ago, nobody in the American soccer community, except in their dreams, could have imagined these particular FC Barcelona players reassembling in South Miami to don pink jerseys with a pair of herons on the team's crest. On December 6, 2025, Inter Miami defeated the Vancouver Whitecaps to claim the club's first MLS Cup. It took Messi about two and a half years to reach the American pinnacle, roughly the amount of time it took Pelé and the Cosmos to reach the NASL summit.

The Messi Effect has already delivered major financial and cultural gains. In his first year, MLS generated $665 million in sponsorship revenue, up 13 percent from 2023 and 44 percent from 2022. Inter Miami owner Jorge Mas called Messi's signing a historic turning point for U.S. soccer. Messi turned down a $400-million-per-year Saudi offer to join MLS—reportedly to win titles, prepare for the 2026 World Cup, grow the league, and inspire young players. His contract includes a future part-ownership option of Inter Miami, which would keep Messi involved with the growth of soccer in America. His impact already extends far beyond the pitch, and his American story isn't finished.

After the USMNT's 2022 World Cup loss to the Netherlands, Gregg Berhalter was expected to return as head coach and prepare for the 2026 tournament, which the U.S., Mexico, and Canada had already qualified for as hosts. So, it was back to the lab again for Berhalter. Instead, a series of unnerving events derailed those plans. Gio Reyna, son of ex–MNT player Claudio Reyna, saw limited minutes in Qatar and reacted poorly when told of his reduced role. After apologizing to his teammates and improving his behavior, the matter seemed settled. No one could have predicted that a locker room kerfuffle in the Qatari desert would evolve to a story with marathon-class legs.

But days after the U.S. exited the tournament, Berhalter unwisely told an "off-the-record" story at a NYC leadership conference about nearly sending a player home—widely assumed to be Gio. Soon after, Gio's mother unwisely contacted U.S. Soccer officials, alleging Berhalter had assaulted Berhalter's now-wife, Rosalind, back in 1992, when the three were in college at the University of North Carolina. An independent investigation confirmed a single incident, committed by Berhalter, and no subsequent issues; and, as to the Reynas, found no violations of law, USSF policy, or SafeSport rules. Berhalter, who had been put on ice for a few months to let the investigation play out, was rehired in June 2023. But his return to the helm was short-lived.

Less than a year into his second stint as MNT head coach, the Yanks exited early from the 2022 Copa América, played on the U.S. soil (to help the U.S. prepare for the mechanics of hosting most of the games in the 2026 World Cup). After a 2–0 win over Bolivia, the Americans lost 1–2 to Panama—playing most of the match with ten men after Tim Weah's red card—and then lost 1–2 to Uruguay, becoming the first host nation ever to miss the knockout round. Berhalter was let go ten days later. With the 2026 World Cup approaching, the USSF sought a coach to fix problems exposed in Copa América, which included discipline issues, defensive lapses, and a lack of creativity in the final third.

On September 10, 2024, the Federation hired Argentinian Mauricio Pochettino, known for tactical flexibility, defensive organization, and developing young talent. His résumé included leading Tottenham to the 2019 Champions League final, PSG to the 2020 Ligue 1 title, and Chelsea to a 2023–2024 top-six Premier League finish. Pochettino's first year in charge brought mixed results. The U.S. beat Jamaica in the 2025 Nations League quarters but lost to Panama and Canada, ending a three-title streak. About half the likely 2026 World Cup starters skipped the 2025 Gold Cup (the last major tournament before the World Cup), angering fans and irritating Pochettino. Still, the young U.S. team reached the final but fell 1–2 to Mexico. Pochettino praised his roster, called for tougher, more committed players *and* fans, and criticized inconsistent CONCACAF officiating—particularly the way the U.S. is treated by referees.

With all MNT group-stage games on home soil in Los Angeles and Seattle, the 2026 World Cup will be a rare chance for a deep run. Most professional soccer players the world over never get to play a World Cup match in their own country. Can the Yanks advance out of their group? If so, can they win their first game in the expanded thirty-two-team knockout round? Can they reach the round of 16, which they've done five times (1994, 2002, 2010, 2014, 2022)? Can they make the quarterfinals, achieved only once in a modern World Cup (2002)? Can they reach the semifinals? And since we're Americans: Can—or when will—we ever win a World Cup? The next and final chapter lays out a possible map to the summit.

20

★★★★★

TOTAL IMMERSION

Ingredients for success (2026 and beyond)

"Mentally it's pretty tough. But once you get used to it, it becomes routine. I would say it almost becomes an addiction."

— **Ninth-grade YSC Academy student discussing his intertwined soccer training and school experiences with a TV reporter**

It may seem strange to start the last chapter talking about current NBA stars, but hear me out.* The NBA's 2025 MVP, Shai Gilgeous-Alexander, grew up in Canada, and didn't move to the States until the cusp of his seventeenth birthday. Basketball in Canada arguably ranks third in interest and popularity behind ice hockey and soccer. That didn't stop SGA. Runner-up MVP Nikola Jokić grew up in Serbia and didn't move to the States until he

* The opinions in this last chapter stem from private conversations with over twenty people across five professional franchises, including MLS owners, sporting directors, first- and second-team coaches, youth academy directors, and youth coaches. I also spoke with about a dozen current MLS players, and former (i) professional players (including two World Cup participants), (ii) high-ranking former USSF officials, and (iii) former youth National Team coaches. I conducted these conversations off the record, and invited them to share freely. This is not *the* map—it is a map. And it focuses less on the base of the mountain and more on the upper peaks.

was twenty. Serbia's most popular sport by a comfortable margin is soccer. Didn't stop the Joker. Also didn't stop Luka Dončić (Slovenia), Giannis Antetokounmpo (Greece), or Victor Wembanyama (France).

The flood of foreign NBA stars—and it is a flood—has proven the incontrovertible fact that it is possible to become a world-class athlete despite growing up in a country where your team sport is not the most popular. How did these athletes do it? They did it by totally immersing themselves in their chosen sport, together with that sport's social trappings, within a network of dedicated, caring adults. These gifted athletes never had to feel that their sport and dreams were less-than, unimportant, or unattainable. I call this concept Total Immersion (TI). Before we get into the specifics of TI for elite American soccer players, let's dispense with some myths and misunderstandings about the current soccer landscape in the U.S.—and reset the conversation.

Does the *current* USMNT lack athletes and athleticism? *No*. Nobody is outsprinting, outjumping, or outrunning us. Let's go to the other end of the pipeline. Does the U.S. youth soccer system in its early development stage (U-6 to U-12, what the USSF calls Zone 1) lack athletic boys? *No, not really*. Attend any major youth tournament and look solely at the athleticism (not the soccer!). We have athletes. And, no, we don't need LeBron James, Tyreek Hill, and Aaron Judge playing soccer. We just need a lot of young people of all colors and socioeconomic backgrounds assembling at the base. True, in Zone 1, we need more diversity in all senses of the word. But we already have a sufficient number of athletic boys playing soccer.

Does the U.S. lack infrastructure for elite young soccer players? *No*. All the MLS academy teams and virtually all the independent superclubs have really good, and, in many cases, extraordinary, facilities. A growing number of American youth sports complexes rival the facilities of the best soccer academies in the world (notwithstanding the annoying field hockey and lacrosse lines on many of the pitches).

Are there enough options in the U.S. for elite soccer players whose families exert an extraordinary amount of money, time, and energy pursuing soccer, and still don't turn pro? *Yes.* It's called college. The U.S. currently boasts over two hundred colleges and universities that sponsor NCAA Division I soccer teams (not to mention Division II, III, and the NAIA-member schools). Many Division I schools offer athletic soccer scholarships. Even without scholarship funds, coaches often go out of their way to help deserving athletes navigate the admissions process and find alternative financial aid. America has the best schools in the world. And top soccer talent helps unlock the college admissions gate. It's the stuff that dreams are made of for the poor kid from Brazil or Croatia who isn't quite good enough to make the local pro team. No other country offers this unique system that links athletics with the opportunity to earn a college degree.*

As noted, MLS already has a fully operational academy system up and running (which lassoes many superclubs into its MLS NEXT program across the country), all with pipelines to the pro teams. The MLS Homegrown Player Rule lets clubs sign their academy players directly to the first team, bypassing the college SuperDraft, provided the player has spent at least one year in the club's youth system and lives in the club's territory. The signing clubs receive salary cap benefits and now keep virtually *all*

* Readers may recall my earlier critique of the college system as the lone path for elite soccer development, which was terribly constrained by NCAA rules that disadvantage soccer athletes. Some important dynamics have changed. Today, the best young Americans will turn pro (MLS) in their teens and probably won't enter college directly out of high school or at all. That's the way it's done in the rest of the world. Many MLS clubs also offer homegrown players a flexible "College Tuition Program" stipend, which pays for or reduces the cost of college. Players can use this benefit during or after their playing days. With very few exceptions, this benefit is not available anywhere else in the world. Those high-schoolers who aren't good enough (yet)—but who are still chasing the soccer dream—can matriculate to college, play soccer, and, if they develop and impress, may get drafted by an MLS club. Beginning with the 2025–2026 academic year, NCAA Division I schools will move from offering 9.9 full-equivalent scholarships to allowing up to twenty-eight *full* scholarships. In June 2025, the USSF created the NextGen College Soccer Committee to better integrate college soccer into the wider soccer system. A key proposal is expanding the season from fall-only to year-round, easing match congestion and aligning with pro calendars. All of this is good news for elite American soccer athletes. *Great news* for Division I athletes would be if the NCAA, with the full support of the USSF, would limit the number of full scholarships awarded to international students to three per team.

homegrown player transfer fees from sales to non-MLS *and* MLS clubs. The latter is a massive change and it will promote investment in youth development.* True: It's unclear to the general public whether some (many?) current MLS ownership groups genuinely care about their youth academies. The feeling is that the academies don't offer a suitable return on investment (ROI). This sentiment, if it gathers steam, is a real problem for the American player development model.

Some owners would rather spend several million dollars on a Latin American or Eastern European player under the Designated Player (DP) Rule—riding him for a few years—than invest the time, money, and effort needed to strengthen their own youth academy. And when only 30 percent or so of the MLS academies are genuinely operating at full capacity, it's hardly fair to criticize the current ROI *league*-wide. (I will come back to this issue in a moment.) In any event, our entire soccer ecosystem—even with the pay-to-play model ruling the roost and sucking the oxygen out of most conversations about soccer development in this country—is more than sufficient to propel elite soccer players to the professional level. Why isn't it working better or faster? Three primary reasons.

First, the base of the pyramid does not have enough qualified coaches and enough grassroots soccer programs making serious inroads into underserved populations, such as Latino and Black populations. Therefore, we are missing out on some very good athletes, statistically speaking. This issue has been true for many years and is the theme of many articles and books, including, more recently, George Dohrmann's *Switching Fields: Inside the Fight to Remake Men's Soccer in the United States*. We need to assemble better athletes and coaches at the base of the mountain.

Second, the good coaches that the U.S. does have, both domestic and international, too often focus on winning games during the formative

* Internal MLS sales and transfers of players, including homegrown players, is incredibly complicated and rapidly changing.

years. This happens even though we've known for years that the priority should be placed upon building a "learning environment" on the pitch that emphasizes skill development, problem-solving abilities, Total Football competencies, and grit. Better coaches are the cradle of everything. We can, and often do, blame the USSF and the pay-to-play model for this situation—even though lots of blame should also be placed upon the large number of relatively oblivious parents at youth matches yelling from the sidelines about goals and victories. But the coaches and the clubs (the employers) need to do better, too.

And the coaches and clubs could be helped immensely by the USSF, which has too often made coaching and credentialing courses too expensive, too elite, and painfully inaccessible. Currently, the Federation's Pro License costs in excess of $10,000, requires ten months of coursework, and is more selective than getting into Harvard. The other USSF coaching tiers have many of the same obstacles. This is ridiculously silly. The USSF's primary duties are to run the U.S. National Teams and be a credentialing agency. So why doesn't the Federation partner with every MLS club and their corresponding academy (that's where most of the men's National Team players come from, at least for a portion of their careers) and USL top-tier franchises? And why not accelerate learning and credentialing—especially national coaching licenses A, B, C, and D—at the existing nodes across the country? Who is training and supercharging the Sherpas?

Third, most of the elite of the elite youth academies in America (the MLS academies and the best independent superclubs) still haven't figured out how to situate their academies within *a larger holistic learning environment that emphasizes soccer within a Total Immersion environment.* Thus, even the best academies in the nation are still only scratching the surface of their potential. It is to this TI environment that this chapter turns. And this book concludes.

★ ★ ★

Most of the top American soccer academies focus solely on the sport itself. But to truly move the needle, elite academies need to adopt a more holistic approach to player development. This means creating and supporting a model that integrates social and academic components within a strong academic school. The latter is crucial both because it's the right thing to do and because it keeps the college pathway open if the professional route doesn't work out. The school could either be located on-site and operated by the MLS franchise, or be a soccer cohort within *an already existing* independent school (often the more affordable option). Such an environment should work as both a place and as a process, supporting student-athletes on and off the field.

In this setting, soccer training, development, and academics are seamlessly woven into the daily routine. Most importantly, the social cues throughout the school environment *must* reinforce soccer and the dream it represents—approaching the natural cultural climate found within communities and schools across soccer-obsessed nations. No U.S. school has a monopoly on how to do this well. And we already have several good models.

Take two soccer schools, one real, one imagined. The Philadelphia Union's campus includes YSC Academy (School), an independent, accredited school that partners with the club to provide education for its academy players. The School has been completely embedded within the MLS franchise for over a decade. It is club-neutral, though most of its students populate the Union's academy teams.* My kid is a young teen and currently

* Allow me to shill just this once: YSC Academy provides a rigorous education designed for elite student-athletes. Here is how the current Head of School, Dr. Nooha Ahmed-Lee, articulates the School's atmosphere: "What really sets YSC Academy apart is the way we blend elite soccer training with academic excellence and emotional growth. We built our program based on how young people learn best—based on the science and research of adolescent brain development. Our goal is to help students build flexibility in their thinking, emotional maturity, and resilience. Coaches and teachers work closely together, forming strong relationships that give student-athletes confidence, a sense of ownership, and a clear sense of who they are and who they can become. And that drives excellence on and off the field." The School is open to any player (boy or girl) through its virtual education program called YSC Advantage. Advantage offers a similar rigorous academic solution for student-athletes anywhere in the world. YSC Advantage teachers, like their compatriots in the School building, are highly qualified and accustomed to adjusting the curriculum and pace to support student-athletes with the demands of travel, training, and competition.

a student at the School (where I also teach English). He loves the place. When I'm fiddling with my morning coffee, he is already badgering me, complaining about running late for morning training.

We jump in the car and head to campus. During our fifty-minute commute, he knocks out some homework and scrolls through his social feeds, often packed with clips of older peers—soccer moves, team victories, National Team call-ups, teens in his school closing in on pro contracts—alongside highlights of Mo Salah, Ryan Gravenberch, and Alexis Mac Allister (Liverpool is his favorite club). Lamine Yamal probably sneaks in there, too.

Nearing our destination, we come upon the Commodore Barry Bridge that crosses the Delaware River. But we don't take the bridge. Instead, we edge onto an off-ramp, and for a few glorious seconds—like a joyous coaster rounding a curve high in the air—we catch an expansive view of the entire campus: the training fields, Subaru Park stadium, WSFS Sportplex, and the academic building. It's a rare footprint that reflects a deep alignment between school and sport. Way off in the distance, the bridge and the river keep going. I always say the same thing every morning, tapping my son on the knee for emphasis: "Looks like *optimism*!" Lately, my remark has become an annoyance to him, a sign that puberty is kicking in.

I drop him off at the training facility, and he walks past the fence next to the pristine grass field where the first-team players are already training. Some of the pros are only a few years older than my son. For the young pros beyond the fence, MLS is quite an achievement. Yet the very best of them are already setting their agents' sights on Europe, just as top Latin American players do. But we are getting ahead of ourselves and the ball again (for the last time). Some of the pros still have homework to finish—yes, a high school degree is required at YSC Academy, even for the pros. My son is grinning, still buzzing from watching those same pros play under the lights the previous weekend. "Doop! Doop! Doop!" (*i.e.*, the universal crowd chant after a goal is scored for the Union). On his way to meet his coach, he passes student-athletes from other age groups, all in identical gear with the same crest, honing their skills within view of Subaru Park stadium on one side, and his School on the other. All this occurs before 9 AM.

After morning training, he showers at the Sportplex and heads to the academic building, a five-minute walk. Around 10:45 AM, he grabs a snack before starting his first class. His schedule includes five classes—English, Math, History, Science, and Spanish—which run until 3:15 PM. There's no band, chorus, or art. The curriculum is intentionally streamlined to support the boys' athletic commitments while maintaining academic rigor and purpose. The classes are taught by highly skilled teachers. They are experts in academics, not soccer (though huge fans!). And they focus on intellectual and social growth while supporting overall development as young student-athletes.

The teachers have become very good at adapting to soccer needs (and lingo). OK, you'll be out next week for a U-16 National Team camp? Let's create a plan for your homework and some accommodations (upon your return) so you can perform at your best. Good luck. OK, the whole team (basically the whole grade) will be out next month for a two-week trip to Spain? Here's your curated homework schedule, organized by teacher, and aligned with the peaks and valleys of your training and game schedule (what the athletic people call periodization). OK, you're injured? No worries—soccer isn't quite as important as preparing for college. There are multiple paths to get where you want to go. Here's more homework.

The boys know the odds of signing a professional contract are slim. Yet compared to most youth players, their chances are strong. Over the past decade, more than 15 percent of YSC Academy students have signed pro contracts before their high school graduation, while the others go on to college—most of them on an athletic scholarship. Some turn pro after college. Over a third of YSC Academy alumni have turned professional before their twenty-second birthday. It's a win-win.

On any given school day, about eighty boys crisscross the campus, talking, laughing, playing Teqball (in the courtyard), sharing videos—

usually soccer clips—eating, doing homework (hopefully not with the aid of ChatGPT or Photomath), and bantering with teachers, coaches, and each other. They attend extra math sessions, review game footage with coaches, sit in on nutrition talks with the first team's nutritionist, meet visiting college coaches for panel discussions, and hear from YSC Academy alumni—who are eager to return to campus and talk about careers after competitive play. Each week features a different speaker. The School buzzes like a traditional single-sex independent school—a vibrant hive of teens. But it is unmistakably unique.

The main hallway is lined with scores of college pennants representing the places graduates have matriculated and graduated. In a conference room off the hall hang the jerseys of YSC graduates capped by the senior USMNT—seven as of 2025. The students named it the Jersey Room. For a while it displayed the jerseys of *all* the graduates who turned pro. But now there are too many pros (thirty and counting) and not enough wall space. Around 4 PM, my son walks to afternoon training with his peers—none of them ever feeling, let alone noticing, that soccer ranks fourth or fifth in popularity among the general public.

On weekend home games, my son's youth team is watched by about six Union coaches and a couple of teachers. Every other weekend, it's back to the stadium lights to see the first team play, where he sees maybe a fifth of his high school peers in the stands, including a few lucky enough to score box seats (the soccer Academy and School have their own boxes—they're connected by sliding panel doors!—and tickets for the game are pretty easy for the boys to score, either from Union VIPs or the pros on the first team). Rinse. Wash. Repeat. For four years or more. The only missing piece is the immediacy of young women. But the Union's model can't be perfect (though a coeducational component is in the works!). That's the secret sauce behind how Mauricio Pochettino selected six YSC Academy graduates for the senior USMNT Gold Cup roster during the summer of 2025, and how the School's graduates have earned over one hundred caps over the past five years—a darn good ROI for one MLS team.*

Now, pause and consider that other, *imagined* school, where they have the best soccer coaches in America by a drop-kick mile. But after ninety minutes of training each day, the boys go home, eat dinner, go to sleep, get up, and go to their normal high school. Their academic day doesn't have to be imagined. It's much like the school you went to, where soccer was a second-class citizen. Or worse, invisible.

There's no time machine. But I wonder why the bigwigs at the USSF, back in early 2020—before it killed its baby, the Development Academy (DA), and essentially abdicated all responsibility for elite youth soccer development to somebody else (without providing any clarity about the future)—didn't call Commissioner Don Garber and the bigwigs in MLS. That call could have gone to the heart of the current American owners with very deep pockets—such as Arthur Blank, Stan Kroenke, Robert Kraft, Philip Anschutz, Lamar Hunt's family, Carl Lindner III (there are too many American owners to name). And the voice on the line could've said something like this:

"Look, we love what you guys have done with the soccer-specific stadiums across the U.S. But we really need your help now on the human side of elite youth development.

"And before we turn the DA over to the MLS people, which we believe is the right thing to do at this point in time, we would like a financial commitment from all of you that has legs. Yeah, we know MLS has a bunch of owners who don't care about American athletes or American soccer youth development. But you do; we Americans do. We want to win the World Cup. Before we do the turnover thing, we also need an independent board of

* On October 4, 2025, the Philadelphia Union won their second Community Shield (for the best regular-season record)—and the 2025 Community Shield, incredibly, was accomplished with more homegrown players on their game-day rosters, playing more minutes, than any other MLS team.

oversight for all the MLS academies, with metrics, targets, and quality controls (regular audits), and a cadre of independent employees—including a bevy of credentialing people, scouts, and coaches within or related to each franchise but focused solely on youth development in Zone 1—who will look outward and into local underserved communities that no single MLS academy has the resources for. Yes, all this will cost money. But it will be *a lot cheaper* than the stadiums. Yes, we also know it will be a hassle getting all the owners to toe the line. But we can do this together. And, in the long run, it will make all of you a lot of money.

"Now, let's go make this big announcement to the American fans."

Appendix

★★★★★

ANCIENT ORIGINS

Almost any game with a round ball is a good game (circa 3500 BCE–1000 CE)

"The gods don't hand out all their gifts at once."
— Homer's *The Odyssey*

Balls have been used in sport for thousands of years. We just don't know how far back the games go, especially for kicking games. The first mention in any written language of a ball game comes from the oldest known literary work, the *Epic of Gilgamesh*, with parts of the story some four thousand years old. Most of the *Epic* was discovered on fragmented tablets in the ruins of a library in the Tigris–Euphrates River area of modern Iraq, once the center of Mesopotamian civilizations (Sumerians, Assyrians, and Babylonians). The *Epic* tracks the adventures of the first documented dynamic duo: the brutish king Gilgamesh, two-thirds god and one-third man, who is oppressing his people, and Gilgamesh's companion Enkidu, a wild man sent by the gods to tame Gilgamesh. But the king will not be tamed.

In one of the later stories, Gilgamesh is playing ball with the young men of his city—while riding atop some of the men, like ponies—when his ball and mallet fall to the bottom of the underworld: "O my ball, which I have not enjoyed to the full!" cries Gilgamesh. "O my mallet, with which I have not had my fill of play!" Enkidu ventures to the underworld to retrieve the king's lost sports gear, but gets trapped there, never to return. The king, down his favorite companion, is left to confront his impotence and mortality. Could the game above be an early form of polo?

Across the Mediterranean Sea, and around three thousand years ago, the Greeks started playing *episkyros*, a kicking and throwing game with a centerline, two teams of about a dozen people each, and hazy rules. The Greeks also played *phaininda*, a rugby-like game with clearer characteristics. In one of the first written accounts of gameplay, the poet Athenaeus chronicles a phaininda sequence: "He seized the ball and passed it to a teammate while dodging another and laughing. He pushed it out of the way of another. Another fellow player he raised to his feet. All the while the crowd resounded with shouts of 'Out of bounds,' 'Too far,' 'Right beside him,' 'Over his head,' 'On the ground,' 'Up in the air,' 'Too short,' and 'Pass it back in the scrum.'" A game report, finally: a ball, some strategy, and a vocal audience.

On an Athenian marble monument some 2,400 years old, a young man balances on his thigh what appears to be a perfectly round size five ball. It's unclear whether he is engaging in a solo training exercise or is part of a team. Greek balls were various sizes. The smallest were made of linen and hair, wrapped in string. Larger ones were packed with feathers. The Greeks eventually made balls out of pigs' bladders, blew air into them (calling them "bags of wind"), and covered them in patches of leather that look astonishingly like modern soccer balls.

Ball-playing appears twice in *The Odyssey*. Odysseus washes ashore on the island of the Phoenicians. There, on the bank of an inlet stream, near dead and naked, he is roused by a beautiful princess, Nausicaa, and her lovely maidens who are "all anointed with oil" (according to the Robert Fitzgerald translation most of us were supposed to have read back in high school). An errant ball they are playing with rolls to Odysseus, who is awakened by the giggling maidens, which is precisely how most modern male sports fans wish to be awakened after battling the elements (in our dreams). Odysseus is invited to a grand feast. After enjoying food, libations, and entertainment featuring ball-juggling (with the hands), he recounts his many adventures—stories told and retold for centuries—with Odysseus the center of attention. Which is precisely how most modern male sports fans wish to be treated after a post-game meal (in our dreams).

From the Greeks' episkyros and phaininda, the Romans developed *harpastum*, all three activities more akin to rugby than to soccer. Galen of Pergamon—physician, surgeon, and perhaps the world's first medical scholar—wrote a book in about 180 CE called *On Exercises with a Small Ball* where he described the benefits of harpastum: "When the players line up on opposite sides and exert themselves to keep the man in the middle from getting the ball, then it is a violent exercise with many neck holds mixed in with wrestling holds . . . The combination of running forwards and backwards and jumping sideways is no small exercise for the legs."

Galen was a polymath. He was a personal physician to three Roman emperors, performed all kinds of surgeries, studied diseases and body systems, lectured on the connection between mind and body, and commented on the soul. He knew gladiators coming and going. He coached them to avoid fatal injuries in the ring, treated those that survived, and dissected the bodies of those dumped near the Colosseum or tossed into the Tiber River. Twenty scribes managed his manuscripts. His work in anatomy, physiology, and neurology shaped Western thought for over a thousand years. (Consider this output, dear reader, when your spouse or loved one asks you to vacate the couch after a weekend of gorging yourself on soccer games.) But was the activity described in his little exercise book the forebear of soccer?

The Chinese do not believe so. We have it by two unreliable sources (the central Chinese government and FIFA) that China is the birthplace of football. At the 2004 Beijing Football Expo, and on the cusp of the 2006 World Cup in Germany, then-FIFA president Sepp Blatter (a windbag of the highest order) announced that football originated in Zibo, China, and derived from an activity called *cuju* (Chinese letters for "kick-ball"). Ten years and $22 million later, the Linzi Football Museum opened in Zibu and confirmed that China is the birthplace of football.

Among mostly crude exhibits of pre-football activity is the granddaddy of grovel: an entire room dedicated to all the past FIFA presidents. A portrait of Sepp Blatter, surrounded by candles and crystal dragons, occupies a table along a wall—even though Blatter stepped down in June 2015, a week after Swiss authorities, at the behest of the FBI, arrested a gang of FIFA officials and accused them of fraudulently funneling millions of dollars (through U.S. banks) to other FIFA representatives (think: World Cups awarded to Russia and Qatar under Blatter's watch). Seven years of investigations ensued, during which time a FIFA ethics panel (ahem) issued Sepp two consecutive six-year bans from football. In 2022, a Swiss court exonerated him for fraud. Blatter has repeatedly maintained his innocence with haughty smirks and dismissive waves of his hand, which best sums up FIFA's approach to doing business since its inception in 1904.

FIFA's 2024 website presents a decent historical account of cuju, the ancient Chinese game at the center of the soccer-origin debate. Historians say cuju is at least 2,500 years old, and underwent tremendous changes over the millennia. Military training manuals during the Warring States Period (475–221 BCE) illustrate kicking and running activities with a ball. Cuju advanced out of its military cradle during the Han Dynasty (220 BCE–220 CE) to involve demonstrations at royal courts and continued for centuries, eventually captivating all walks of life during the Song Dynasty (960–1280 CE). As the centuries wore on, the game evolved away from opposing goals and toward a single target, either a pole or a vertical hoop. The latter required the ball to be passed back and forth through a hole about the size of a hula hoop, turned on its side, held aloft by latticework. The objective was for the ball to never touch the ground. The first ruler in the Ming Dynasty in the late 1300s banned cuju because it was a distraction from work and military training. Violators had a foot removed. Within a generation, the game disappeared.

At least one version of ancient cuju looked remarkably like modern football. In about 100 CE, the Han poet Li You described a game involving a round ball, two teams, a referee, and—voilà!—six goals on either end of a playing field: "A round ball and a square wall, / Just like the Yin and Yang. / Crescent-shaped goals are opposite each other, / Each side has six in equal number." It's not hard to imagine ancient Chinese players dribbling, passing, and changing directions, as they attack one goal, then one of the other five. Such strategies would have required the conscious use of space and movements on and off the ball—tactics not repeated in earnest by ball-playing kickers elsewhere in the world until the latter part of the nineteenth century.

People will debate this point, just as some will contest the claim that China exported cuju along the Silk Routes (land and sea), which probably inspired various Asian and Oceanic ball games. Some 1,500 years ago, a highly ritualistic and collaborative juggling game, called *kemari*, appeared in Japan. Kemari was played within a square area about the size of a standard two-car garage, often with four different planted trees (pine, willow, maple, and cherry) in each corner, which served as literal boundaries. Royal courts used all pine trees, whose branches were meticulously pruned and maintained over many years—like giant bonsai. The boughs eventually conformed to the shape of the court. Six to eight players assembled to demonstrate their skill with the ball (hollow, deerskin, about eight inches in diameter) by performing a series of predetermined moves. Sometimes the collaborators purposely kicked the ball off the branches of the trees.

For hundreds of years, kemari was mostly for the nobility. Participants wore stiff, colorful kimonos with long sleeves, an erect angular hat, and duck shoes about the size of, well, ducks. It was a stylized and cheerful affair, with no winners. According to the English writer David Goldblatt, "A day's kemari was best ended by a single high kick from the most senior player who gracefully caught the ball in the folds of his kimono." Kemari survived the long line of emperors, their dynasties, and imperial courts. The activity was even taken up by the samurai warrior class, after 1200 CE, who used the sport to maintain relations with their employers, the aristocracy. By the 1700s, kemari had spread to towns and villages across the island, where formal schools were founded, licenses issued, fees collected, and local as well as regional tournaments organized—resembling modern martial arts schools. But kemari did not survive the industrialization and Westernization that swept through Japan in the latter part of the nineteenth century.

Other collaborative juggling games developed along the Silk Routes, like *chinlone* (itself some 1,500 years old) in Burma, and *sepak raga* (perhaps 500 years old), native to islands southeast of China. Chinlone usually involved six people, with one person in the middle called the pivot (who determined where the ball went next), and the others walking fluidly in a counterclockwise fashion. The soft thwack of the handwoven rattan ball has made a rhythmic melody down through the ages. A couple of hundred miles southeast of Burma, in Malaysia and Indonesia, and in adjacent archipelagos, sepak raga (another collaborative juggling game) braved centuries of refinement and even made it to the 1950s when two teams and a net were added, spurring a competitive new game called *sepak takraw*. Gameplay of takraw approximates soccer-volleyball, with various combative maneuvers along a five-foot-high net. A successful "roll spike," for instance, is a modified bicycle kick (with a full sideways twist of the torso in midair) that sends the ball zipping downward, while the kicker somehow lands on his takeoff foot. You have to see it to believe it. There has been an annual takraw world championship for the last four decades.

Farther south, in Australia, indigenous people have been playing *marngrook* for hundreds of years. White European settlers started arriving in the late 1700s and began their cruel march across indigenous lands. Eyewitnesses described a game involving fifty to a hundred people, over large fields, using round balls often made from a kangaroo scrotum and wrapped in possum skin ("somewhat elastic but firm and strong"). Game rules varied. An 1870 report recounts: "Each side endeavors to keep possession of the ball, which is tossed a short distance by hand, then kicked in any direction. The side which kicks it oftenest and furthest gains the game. The person who sends it the highest is considered the best player and has the honor of burying it in the ground till required the next day." To non-Aussies, marngrook probably looks a lot like an early form of the professional game played today called Australian Rules Football. Maybe it was; maybe it wasn't. A debate in Australia persists to this day about whether marngrook died out completely, or survived the settlers and co-inspired (with English proto-rugby activities) the form and spirit of Australia's most popular contemporary sport.

Northeast of Australia and across the Pacific Ocean, in what is today known as Mexico and Central America, the earliest known Mesoamerican civilizations started playing a rubber ball game of mythic importance, with artifacts and evidence of courts dating as far back as 1600 BCE. It is perhaps the oldest team game in the world to primarily use parts of the body other than hands and arms. For the next three thousand unbroken years or so, the Olmecs and their descendants (the Toltec, Mayan, and Aztec civilizations) played the game in large stone courts, over 1,500 of which have been found as far north as Arizona and as far south as the upper-Amazon region of South America. Hundreds of figurines have been found across nearly five thousand miles. The figurines show players attired with protective gear such as helmets, wrist and thigh pads, and thick U-shaped belts (leather, wooden, stone) called yokes. The opening at the "U" allowed players to slip into the yokes at the hip, with buckles or fasteners at one side. The yokes served as protectors for the waist, hips, and groin area (the world's first sports cups!). Many figurines possess balls at their hips and feet. The sport has received only modest attention from football historians the world over.

Perhaps the most notable feature of the game were the round rubber balls, solid (or mostly solid), about eight inches in diameter, and fabricated from the unique rubber trees and morning glory flowers in the region. The Spanish, who started establishing settlements in the early 1500s, were mystified by the bounce of the balls (rubber was unknown in Europe). Gameplay probably involved a dueling two-team (no hands or forearms) bouncing game where the object was to keep a ball moving back and forth across a centerline—without touching the ground in a team's backcourt or coming to a complete stop in the frontcourt—using only hips, shins, knees, thighs, shoulders, legs, and buttocks (no kidding). Bigger, more elaborate courts were shaped like a giant capital letter "I," with a long stone alleyway and gently sloped embankments on either side, shaped like aqueducts, that helped keep the ball in play.

The largest ball court discovered to date resides in Yucatan, Mexico, within the Chichén Itzá site. The playing venue (which could be ceremonial) measures an astounding 514 feet long and 118 feet wide (about one and a half times longer than a maximum FIFA pitch today, and half as wide). The Chichén Itzá court features two vertical stone rings mounted high on the side walls at midcourt. With openings barely wider than the ball, these rings resemble basketball rims in their downward, breakaway position—bonus goals for very skilled players. "A man, throwing the ball by hand at close range, could not put it in once in one hundred tries, nor in two hundred." Hitting the ball through one of the rings ended the game. The virtuoso was then honored by spectators who offered him their best wares and goods, treating him like a deity for the day.

The game was vital to the people, and perhaps a life-or-death matter. A large stone panel atop the enormous Chichén Itzá court portrays a decapitated player, suggesting human sacrifices probably occurred. On the relief, serpents spring from the neck, while blood flows down and into the ground, forming cacao plants (new life). Similar images are repeated on murals in other regions. Grand notions of the games' connection to everyday life and belief system take a central role in a series of myths that eventually became known as the *Popol Vuh* ("Book of the People"). The stories in the *Popol Vuh*, considered sacred, were passed down orally for generations until they were recorded in a book in about 1525 CE, then translated by a Spanish friar in 1701.

The *90-in-30/RedZone* version of the ball-playing portion of the myth goes like this: Two mortal hero twins became so good at the rubber ball game and made so much noise they disturbed the gods in the underworld below. The gods opened a portal and sucked the twins into the underworld where they challenged the men to a rubber ball game. The gods cheated and won. And then decapitated the twins. Their heads were placed upon the spiked branches of a calabash tree, where they lingered until one of the heads spat upon the hand of a passing goddess, impregnating her. She gave birth to twin demigod boys. The other gods banished the trio to the upper world.

The demigod boys grew up and became great ballplayers who made even more racket than their ancestors, setting up a cosmic rematch. This time the twins won. The gods rewarded the twins by allowing them to resurrect their father and uncle—who themselves were transformed into immortals, becoming the sun and the moon. Historians claim that the myth and the game were central to the life of the people, symbolic of seasonal harvest cycles (life, death, rebirth), and underscored the community's understanding of the cosmos. The myth was the game. The game was the myth. Or perhaps, as the centuries wore on, the ballplayers played and the spectators watched, mostly for fun, the line between the sacred and secular lost to the jungles of time.

No one knows who first kicked a round object across the surface of the earth, smiled, and then called to one of his mates. But in just about every region of the world, wherever people gathered, ball-playing ensued. Any game with a round ball anywhere on earth was probably a good game. But none of the games (with the possible exception of the multiple-goal form of cuju) looked anything like modern soccer. Football would have to wait for a small band of schoolboys, graduates of some of the finest schools in England, to gather in a London pub, in 1863, to codify the rules and set the world on the path to modern football.

NOTES

Every history book is built on other books. And this is especially so with this book, which gets assists from many diligent soccer writers who too often found themselves benched by the mainstream press. In this book I've tried to tell (and, in many cases, retell) the American soccer story. In doing so, I relied on the work of some writers so heavily that they deserve special recognition.

The American author David Wangerin and his DNA are all over these pages. I looked to his triumph, *Soccer in a Football World: The Story of America's Forgotten Game*, almost as a skeletal frame for my book. If I retraced his steps too closely at times, I apologize. His moves were just too damn good.

For the early chapters about pre-football in America, American birth, and initial spread of the beautiful game (late 1800s to 1920), I received some great passes from Ed Farnsworth and his articles on the evolution of football in Philadelphia, and from Brian Bunk in his *From Football to Soccer: The Early History of the Beautiful Game in the United States*. And from several writers of the compelling pieces collected in *Soccer Frontiers: The Global Game in the United States, 1863–1913*, edited by Chris Bolsmann and George Kioussis.

For the English story about mob football, codification of the Laws of the Game, and initial spread around the British Isles, I looked to Englishman David Goldblatt and his 1,100-page *The Ball Is Round: A Global History of Soccer*. Americans have their own tireless archivist in David Litterer, whose delightfully detailed compendiums are hosted online by the Society for American Soccer History (SASH) as the "American Soccer History Archives."

For my chapters on the first iteration of the American Soccer League (1921–1931), I relied on Colin Jose's meticulous tome *American Soccer League: The Golden Years of the American Soccer League*. For the NASL chapters, I tried to keep up with the razzmatazz of Ian Plenderleith in his *Rock 'n' Roll Soccer: The Short Life and Fast Times of the American Soccer League*.

Hal Phillips's *Generation Zero: Founding Fathers, Hidden Histories & the Making of Soccer in America*, Phil West's *The United States of Soccer: MLS and the Rise of American Soccer Fandom*, and Beau Dure's *Long-Range Goals: The Success Story of Major League Soccer* helped bridge the gap from the NASL to MLS, and inspired my chapters on the Yanks' rise from irrelevance to respectability, both home and abroad.

For many of the later chapters in this book, where I ping balls back and forth between the USSF, USMNT, and MLS (all those blunders and assists and occasional outstanding victories), I often looked to the coaching and general management of Ed Farnsworth and Roger Allaway. This duo has been covering American soccer's vibes and victories, flubs and fluxes, for decades. In addition to their independent publications, their work for SASH is Herculean.

And I can't forget the audaciously humble Grant Wahl and his remarkable exposé on MLS (circa 2005–2012) in *The Beckham Experiment: How the World's Most Famous Athlete Tried to Conquer America*, his many soccer articles for *Sports Illustrated* over the years, and then his podcasts. Wahl knew how to attack a story, high-press an interviewee, and elegantly move the ball out of the back. He often showed us something new, or got us thinking, about the sport we love. And not much more can be asked of a sportswriter.

In the notes that follow, phrases that do not have quotation marks pinpoint the source for an area of my book where I leaned heavily on the specific work of others. Phrases within quotation marks refer to larger content that is being quoted verbatim from the named source. If somebody sees a mistake or an omission, let me know. If I get back in the game in a subsequent edition, I'll happily fix it.

CHAPTER 1

9: **Evidence of ball-playing going back at least 4,500 years:** Wertmann et. al. 2020.

10: **Native Greenlanders confronting Englishman John Davis (and quotes):** Bunk 2021:11–12.

10: **Native Americans playing pre-football (and quotes):** Bunk 2021:15–18.

11: **Greenlanders, pre-football, and Northern Lights:** Bunk 2021:26–27.

11: **Lenape Native Americans playing a game "in the true aboriginal style":** Bunk 2021:19–20.

11: **"fresh, green breast of the new world":** Fitzgerald 2004:171–172.

12: **"a bloody and murthering practice":** Stubbes 1877:187 and Farnsworth "Philadelphia Part 2" 2020.

12: **William Penn and his contemporaries getting into the anti-football act (and quote):** Farnsworth "Philadelphia Part 2" 2020.

14: **Harvard's "Bloody Monday" contests and text of mock poem:** Bunk 2014 and 2021:41–43.

14: **"Ballown":** Bunk 2021:46–47 and Smith 2015.

14: **"Old Division Football":** Meacham 2006.

14: **"you must only kick":** Bunk 2021:47.

15: **"Foot-ball fightum" and text of gravesite mock-eulogy:** Bunk 2014.

15: **"it made me think of home":** Patch 1862.

15: **"we expect to have a Regimental game of foot-ball":** Messinger 1862.

15: **Nathan Hale description (and quote):** "The Last Days" 2007 and "The Revolutionary War Spy" 2025.

16: **"It was a magnificent sight":** Crawford 2013:38–39.

16: **Harper's Weekly prints of Civil War soldiers engaged in pre-football activity:** Bunk 2021:65–66 (figs. 3.2–3.5 and commentary).

16: **Photograph of Civil War Union soldiers from New York's Thirteenth Heavy Artillery Division playing pre-football:** Bunk 2021:63–65 (figs. 3.2 and 3.3 and commentary).

16: **"for the amusement of the troops":** Bunk 2021:63.

CHAPTER 2

19: **"born of modernity":** Goldblatt 2008:18.

21: **Scholarly joke about Romans bringing *harpastum* to the British Isles:** Butterfield and McCormick 2021 and Gardner 1996:2.

21: **William Fitzstephen's description of a "famous game of ball" (and block quote):** Magoun 1929:34.

22: **Henry's fatal "misadventure" and proclamation concerning "the striking of great foot-balls in the fields of the public" (and block quote):** Magoun 1929:35–36 and Goldblatt 2008:17.

23: **"who should chulle [bandy about] a football":** Holt 1884:47.

23: **"Sometimes their necks are broken, sometimes their backs":** Stubbes 1877:184.

23: "vain game of no value": Magoun 1929:38.

23: "24 bonny boys . . . playing at the ba'": Sir Hugh (see nursery ryhme variants).

23: "rolleth under foot as dooth a ball": Chaucer 2003:line 2614.

24: "propel a huge ball . . . with their feet" (and block quote): Walvin 1994:13 and Goldblatt 2008:17.

24: Fines for playing pre-football on English roadways: Highway Act 1835 and Goldblatt 2008:23.

25: Student revolts and disruptions to the school environment: Turner 2015:54–59 and Goldblatt 2008:24.

26: "we were ready to fight everybody": Turner 2015:56.

26: "It was a system of anarchy [students] tempered by despotism [masters]": Gaylord 1994.

27: The school you went to determined the version of the game you played: Goldblatt 2008:24–25 and Holt 1989:77.

27: Two types of pre-football activities existed, influenced by the shape of campus grounds: Goldblatt 2008:25, 29.

27: "The ball games . . . were a big problem": Gardner 1996:5.

27: "more fit for farm boys and labourours than for young gentlemen": Anderson 1981:54.

27: "The central dilemma . . . [was] how to take control" (and block quote): Goldblatt 2008:26.

28: "Muscular Christianity" inspiring games on campus: Goldblatt 2008:27.

29: Trio of students at the Rugby School (and all quotes): Graham 2001:28–30.

29: "how the Eton man howled at the Rugby man for handling the ball": Alcock 1898:3.

30: Pamphlet called "The Rules of Foot-Ball: The Winter Game" (and all quotes): Thring 1863. See also Goldblatt 2008:30.

30: The game before the game involved deciding on the rules: Goldblatt 2008:30–31.

30: "I will be bound to bring over a lot of Frenchmen": Goldblatt 2008:31.

30: "If we have hacking": Goldblatt 2008:31.

31: "To kick a player on the shins purposefully": Winner 2013:34

31: Text of original Laws of the Game (and block quote): Bodleian Library 2006:41, 51–57.

31: "retain[ed] the hacking and carrying practices": Goldblatt 2008:32.

32: Lexical derivation of the term "soccer": Perrigo 2018, citing Stefan Szymanski and his 2014 academic paper.

33: "no longer confounded customs officers" and "Tell me how you play": Galeano 2013:32, 243.

CHAPTER 3

35: Earliest officially documented collegiate soccer game in North America: Wangerin 2008:20, Smith 2015, and Farnsworth "Philadelphia Part 4" 2020 (though Farnsworth may argue that the activity was soccer-like or proto-soccer).

36: Description of 1869 Rutgers–Princeton contests (and quotes): Kelly 2019:8, 10.

36: November 18, 1869, Thanksgiving Day game between two Philadelphia cricket clubs: Farnsworth "Philadelphia Part 4" 2020.

38: Failed attempt in New York to found America's first "intercollegiate football association": Farnsworth "Philadelphia Part 5" 2020.

38: "From that moment on, [gridiron] football never looked back": Wangerin 2008:21.

39: "taste which prefers Harvard's rough and tumble scrimmages" and "resulted in giving [Princeton] the appearance of a hospital for disabled veterans": "The Changing Shape of American Football" 2016.

39: "a uniform system of rules" and twenty-eight years passed before another intercollegiate soccer match took place: Wangerin 2008:21–22.

39: "America's strong desire to assert its cultural independence [would] have prevented" soccer from reaching "heights similar to those it had attained elsewhere," leaving it "subjected to countless modifications": Wangerin 2008:22.

40: "it would not have lasted very long in the colleges": Gardner 1996:243–244.

40: Annual photographs of Princeton's "soccer" team and athletic balls during the 1860s and 1870s: "The Changing Shape of American Football" 2016.

41: Oneida Football Club and post hoc "commemorative endeavors": Marston and Cronin 2021:23–37.

42: Immigrant explosion in America 1860 to 1914: Taylor 2011:645–654.

42: Soccer-loving immigrants found their way to textile mills (and related factories), shipyards, steel mills: Wangerin 2008:27–30 and Apostolov 2021: 47–48.

CHAPTER 4

43: Outside of the U.K., the U.S. was the second nation after Canada to form a football association, following the English FA while Canada followed the Scottish FA—until harmony prevailed across the British Isles: Farnsworth "Noxious Scottish Weed" 2022 and Allaway 2023.

44: Fall River teams and Spindle City: Allaway 2005, Wangerin 2008:56, and Farnsworth "Fall River and Pawtucket Soccer" 2022.

45: U.S. vs. Canada: "Canadians the Victors" 1885:7.

46: Circulation war, and gridiron college games rapidly gaining "a significance well beyond the competing schools and their localities": Wangerin 2008:22.

48: The short and very unhappy life of the ALPF and the AAPF, and "baseball managers as 'coaches'": Wangerin 2008:31–33, Farnsworth 2015 and "After the Collapse" 2020, Bunk 2021:6–8, and Allaway 2015.

CHAPTER 5

53: AFA Cup and birth of AAFA (which quickly changed its name to the USFA, in 1913): Wangerin 2008:32–34, McCabe 2015, and Allaway 2023.

55: "aims to make soccer the national pastime of the winter in this country": Wangerin 2008:33.

56: Some venerable teams in the Northeast were eager to switch: Allaway 2023.

56: "No sport will ever succeed here which is directed [from] across the water": Wangerin 2011:39.

57: Increasing irrelevance of the AFA Cup and disappearance of the cup trophy: Wangerin 2008:43.

57: "salaries of professional soccer players . . . ranging from $3,000 to $6,000": Wangerin 2008:47.

58: Cahill's three American tours abroad, and "returned weighted down with medals": Wangerin 2008:42–43 and 2011:65–66 (the quote), 152–154. See also Farnsworth "first USA international tour" 2015 and Lang 2023.

CHAPTER 6

59: Many teams disbanded, and only baseballs outnumbered soccer balls for our troops: Bunk 2021:166, 177.

60: Major American businesses sponsor soccer teams: Markovits and Hellerman 2001:109, Wangerin 2008:37–38, and Bunk 2021:195.

61: Charles Goodyear's rubber ball: Kilpatrick 2021:67–68.

61: Fore River FC, shipbuilders, and entertaining Quincy residents: Apostolov 2021:48–49.

62: The Ben Millers beating Fore River and setting records (and nifty advertising), and the St. Louis soccer scene in the early twentieth century: Wangerin 2008:41–42 and Lange 2011.

63: Story of Thomas "Bullets" Cahill: Wangerin 2011:58–88 (chapter titled "Bullets") and McCabe 2024 (podcast).

64: "anxious to impress upon [newcomers] the wonders of soccer," and rookie ASL requirements and schedule: Wangerin 2008:49–51 (all quotes), Bunk 2021:195, Jose 1998, and Creel 2022.

65: Everyone lost money in the first year of the ASL, Bethlehem Steel's geographic yo-yo, and "every American boy" will be playing soccer "from the time he is able to toddle": Wangerin 2008:51–52 and 2011:49, 72.

67: "the first soccer-specific facility of any consequence," "We need permanent fields and stands," and first several years of ASL: Wangerin 2008:53–57.

67: "The torch was passed": Wangerin 2008:56–57.

CHAPTER 7

70: Stoneham as "serial philanderer, quasi-bigamist": Lamb:2017.

71: ASL withdrawing from Challenge Cup, one-year U.S. Professional Cup, start of Lewis Cup: Wangerin 2008:60–62.

72: Top teams in ASL in mid-1920s rivaled any teams in the world: Wangerin 2011:77.

72: Snagging Scottish international winger, convinced others to join, "Booked

my passage," and "hundreds of players crossed the Atlantic": Jose 1998:7 and Allaway 2022.

73: **"scores of crack footballers," U.S. Immigration ruling regarding "artists," and "respect each other's registrations and suspensions":** Curran 2018:317–318.

73: **"The American Menace":** Jose 1998:2–8 and Allaway 2022.

74: **"promising United States players have been permitted to lie idle":** Wangerin 2011:78.

75: **The magnificent story of Archie Stark:** Wangerin 2008:58–60 (all quotes) and Allaway "The record-setting Archie Stark" 2022.

77: **Archie Stark scores five goals in a November 8, 2025 USMNT game against Canada:** Vidmer, "Stark's Five Goals," November 9, 1925, 16.

77: **"I started soccer in America, and here is where I'll stay":** Wangerin 2008:63.

77: **Hakoah Vienna summer tours (and quotes):** Wangerin 2008:64–65.

CHAPTER 8

79: **Stoneham and the ensuing Soccer War:** Wangerin 2008:72–77.

80: **The ASL playing by its own rules:** Wangerin: 62–63, 67–68.

80: **$1,000 fine, "outlaw league," formation of EPSL:** Wangerin 73–74. See also "Regret league action" 1928.

80: **Bethlehem Steel joins EPSL (and all quotes):** "Regret league action" 1928.

81: **Cahill and unnerving and backstabbing events:** Wangerin 2011:73–77.

81: **Soccer war (and all quotes):** "Regret league action" 1928, Wangerin 2008:73–77, Goldblatt 2008:98–99, and Allaway "What Was the Soccer War?" 2022.

82: **"both factions stridently predicted victory and blamed each other":** Wangerin 2008:74–75.

82: **Game in front of an astounding 21,583 fans (in a standing-room only affair):** Wangerin 2008:75.

82: **"wearing off the surplus avoirdupois picked up during the summer":** "A Swing Along Athletic Row" 1929.

83: **"a statistic keenly felt in the soccer enclaves" and Sam Mark "turning his back on the game altogether":** Wangerin 2008:77, 79.

84: **"a major force":** Garratt 2015.

85: **"he continued to pay opera singers to sing at parties" (and all quotes):** Whelan 2022.

85: **"field delegate" and "I have given everything":** Wangerin 2011:83–84, 87.

CHAPTER 9

87: **"rear of the headquarters":** "FIFA Marks" 2003.

88: **"not see the advantages of such a Federation":** "A History of the FA" (undated).

88: **English role in FIFA deemed vital for an international organization claiming to represent the interests of a world game:** Allen 2024.

88: **"it was like cutting water with a knife":** "The Mystery of Robert Guérin" 2022.

89: **"with a more liberal attitude to amateurism":** Wangerin 2008:88.

91: **Elmer Schroeder:** Farnsworth "The life—and murder" 2022 and Wangerin 2008: 89–90.

91: **Dent McSkimming, "the dean of soccer writers":** Wangerin 2008:112 and Fatsis 2014.

91: **"our puny, half-baked outfit was doomed in advance":** Wangerin 2008:90.

92: **"a universal language":** Lichfield 2006.

93: **"the sort of immigrant turf":** Wangerin 2011:88.

93: **USFA (later, the USSF) perpetually teetering on economic and intellectual bankruptcy:** Wangerin 2011:81 ("dysfunctional"), 85 ("no money," "its own worst enemy"), 88 ("fractious and petulant cosmos"). See also Gardner 1996:244 ("internal squabbling, an activity that has since become almost the trademark of soccer in the United States").

93: **"in the biting cold":** Wangerin 2011:85.

CHAPTER 10

97: **"wet, sticky pitch":** Wangerin 2008:94.

97: **"shot-putters":** Holroyd 2015.

98: **Patenaude's hat trick:** Wangerin 2008:94 and Williams 2015.

98: **"Cool as cucumbers":** Wangerin 2008:95.

99: **"kick in the face so hard," "talented athletes who play a smooth game," and "the error of his ways":** Farnsworth "The US at the 1930 World Cup" 2014.

100: **"right where those careers had started":** Farnsworth: "The US at the 1930 World Cup" 2014 and Wangerin 2008:96.

101: **"amateurs in the pejorative sense of the word":** Gardner 1996:245.

101: **"perception of the game as separate from American sports culture" and "no soccer in the United States":** Markovits and Hellerman 2001:109, Preface at 10.

102: **American soccer casting a wide participatory ethnic tent from the beginning:** Wangerin 2008:58 (Tefik Abdullah), 64 (Hakoahs), 74 (Hakoah All-Stars and New York Hispano). See also Farnsworth and Bunk 2022, examining the earliest accounts of Black soccer players in the U.S., including positive references to integrated teams in contemporary newspapers dating back as far as 1894.

103: **"American kids who grew up in soccer-loving New England neighborhoods":** Farnsworth email correspondence, November 2025.

104: **"Gonsalves would win a place and be a star in any team in the world":** Wangerin 2008:92.

105: **Bert Patenaude, the hat-trick hero, and his grandson, Professor Patenaude III:** Barboza 2010.

CHAPTER 11

107: **"Depression had eroded much of the bedrock on which the game existed":** Wangerin 2008:96.

108: **"show the universe what is the true fascist ideal of the sport":** A History of Sports" 2024.

110: "If they can die for Italy, they can play for Italy!": Glanville 2004.
110: "their right arms outstretched": Galeano 2013:69.
110: Oppressive fascist atmosphere of the 1934 World Cup, and "In the name and in the presence of the Duce": Gordon and London 2005:41–64.
111: Another trophy, a fascist behemoth: The Football History Boys "1934 World Cup" YouTube video at timestamp 9:20.
113: "part-timers who played in their off hours" and "the size of the Americans' defeat": Farnsworth "The US and the 1950 World Cup" 2014, citing Tony Cirino from his book U.S. Soccer vs. the World (1983), and John Thompson's article in the London-based Daily Mirror.
115: "A band of no-hopers drawn from many lands": Longman 2009.
115: "We ain't got a chance against your boys": Leptich 1986.
115: "Joe Gaetjens either purposely got a piece of the ball and directed it left, or it was a ricochet": Raskin 2022, including several wonderful photographs, not of the goal, but of the players on both teams involved in the historic game. See also Harris 2019 and Wangerin 2018:112–114.
116: Attendance swelling three or four times the original 10,000 as the game unfolds: Wangerin 2008:114.
116: "Colomb wouldn't hesitate to knock a guy on his rear": Schaerlaeckens 2010.
117: "We didn't think we could win": Neal 2003.
117: "We were going in as complete underdogs": Townsend 2019.
118: "In less than a few hours, [you] will be hailed as champions by millions of compatriots!": Bellos 2014.
119: Americans turn up in five-figure numbers to watch foreign touring teams: Gardner 1996:247–248.

CHAPTER 12

122: Full text of ransom note, and "this cup will go into the melting pot": Sjödin 2021.
122: "a sacrilege that would never have been committed in Brazil": Zenou 2022.
123: Three separate investment groups, then two, then one, then limping into the Sixties: Wangerin 2008:122–144 and Gardner 1996:248–250.
123: "a soccer ball and a billiard ball": Wangerin: 2008:126.
125: "They nearly ruined the whole thing before it got off the ground": Plenderleith 2015:17, quoting Paul Gardner from a personal interview.
125: "I didn't know I was in San Jose until I read it on me jersey": Plenderleith 2015:61.
126: "tearing the sheet into small bits and burying them in the nearest snowdrift": Plenderleith 2015:188.
126: Beat Manchester City twice during the summer of 1968: Plenderleith 2015:9, 27 and Wangerin 2008:142.
127: "The North American Soccer League will be the world's No. 1 soccer league": Anderson 1977:34–36.

128: "bacchanalian celebration": Plenderleith 2015:115.

129: San Diego Chicken soccer antics (and quote): Plenderleith 2015:127.

129: Cavalry charges up the wings, ducks behind the goals, firecrackers going off: Plenderleith 2015:127.

129: "The Yanks, as usual, tend to overdo it": Plenderleith 2015:66.

129: "she wanted to know was how long I'd been a superstar. I said 'about three days'": Plenderleith 2015:68.

129: "there weren't too many people who knew you made a mistake": Plenderleith 2015:63–64.

130: "overpaid and under-worked": Plenderleith 2015:72.

130: "I wouldn't even consider going to a soccer match in England": Plenderleith 2015:58.

130: "English football is a gray game played on a gray day before gray people": Plenderleith 2015:127.

130: "I found a country that not only celebrated its stars, but enjoyed them too": Plenderleith 2015: Foreword at xii.

130: "Who's looking out for the Americans in the NASL?": Plenderleith 2015:76–77.

130: "You don't start with pro soccer and wind up with eight-year-olds playing soccer": Wangerin 2008:143.

CHAPTER 13

135: All quotes about hard surfaces, ridiculous heat, bucket of ice: Plenderleith 2015:74, 168, 173.

137: "I spent a lot of money on booze, birds [women], and fast cars. The rest I just squandered": "Best" 2005.

137: Ahmad Rashad quip: Wangerin 2008:175.

138: "in a few years who's going to come and see old stars like me play?": "A Modified American Plan" 1980.

139: "It needs something new and fresh. Elephants! Pageants! The Village People!": "A Modified American Plan" 1980.

140: "They're a sinking ship right now, and I refuse to go down with them": Wangerin 2008:216.

140: "When are we ever going to play a home game?" Wangerin 2008:226.

141: "no way to prepare for international matches": Holroyd "The Year in American Soccer—1973."

141: "you're out of the final," "interest of the sport," and "weirdo idea" of rules: Plenderleith 2015:182–183.

142: Johan Cruyff's journey and Total Football concepts (and all quotes): Winner 2000 and Kuper 2022:30–105.

CHAPTER 14

151: "carry any credibility as a host": Wangerin 2008:229.

151: tectonic plate had begun to move: Wangerin 2008:230.

152: “what country the game is being played in”: Wangerin 2008:231.

153: “We had to qualify” (and all quotes from players regarding World Cup 1994): “The Billion Dollar Goal” 2023.

153: “shot heard around the world”: French 2014.

154: “galumphing side of corn-fed college boys”: Wangerin 2008:235.

155: “That team changed everything”: “The Billion Dollar Goal” 2023.

156: “United States closer to . . . worldwide preeminence”: Wangerin 2008:241.

156: “a minivan and two kids who play on Saturday”: Wangerin 2008:241.

157: “anti-soccer lobby”: Curtis 2018, referencing Franklin Foer’s book *How Soccer Explains the World* 2004.

157: “FIFA shall not bring the World Cup to New York” and “haggling over a few centimeters”: Wangerin 2008:248–249, quoting FIFA then-secretary Sepp Blatter.

158: “The pitch is perfect” and “a miracle”: Harvey 1994.

160: “Yanks 2, Planks 0”: “Up in Arms” 1993.

160: Bora Milutinović, the nutty professor (and his quotes): Longman 1994 and Evans 2022.

161: World Cup Draw: ASB 2020. See timestamp 32:30 for the entrance of Robin Williams.

162: “choose to watch a good soccer match”: Wangerin 2008:257.

162: “took endless delight in corralling the American-in-the street”: Wangerin 2008:253–254.

163: “more live coverage”: Wangerin 2008:256.

165: “fleet-footed Earnie Stewart”: Wangerin 2008:259.

166: “the man who died standing”: Baggio 2021.

167: “The evangelists could be identified”: Personal interview with Sheldon Phillips, Senior Director, Club Welfare and Compliance for the Philadelphia Union, and former member of the Washington, D.C., World Cup 1994 Organizing Committee for RFK Stadium.

CHAPTER 15

170: “I ran into Rothenberg’s office and said, ‘I’ll do it,’” and “I knew he loved soccer . . . incipient project”: Silverman 2022.

170: Jim Paglia’s cockamamie idea about a game “placed into zones marked with chevrons” that Rothenburg eventually determined had “no substance behind it”: Dure 2010:4–8.

171: “you are buying a share of this limited liability company”: Silverman 2022.

172: The USL plans to operate three elite divisions by 2027, with some sort of promotion-relegation: Becherano 2025.

175: Game ensued only after a giant white MLS logo was repainted in green: Dure 2010:1.

176: “I’m not crying because Argentina lost”: Carlisle and McIntyre 2016, quoting Eric Wynalda.

178: Wynalda's description and forgiveness regarding Harkes's affair: CBS Sports 2024, Wynalda speaking.

179: "They stunk. And they hated their coach": Wangerin 2008:287, quoting an Associated Press writer.

180: "something of a mixture between sports event and beauty contest" (and all quotes): "Soccer Goes Sexy" 1971.

180: "Let's get women to play in more feminine garb": "Women Give Blatter" 2004.

181: Slim pickings in MLS first five years: Hopkins 2010:100–120 and Dure 2010:71–89, 129–131.

181: Antitrust lawsuit: Dure 2010:91–115.

182: "One stadium in one city": Wangerin 2008:302.

CHAPTER 16

185: Soccer United Marketing (SUM): Hopkins 2010:155–163, 165–168, 211–213 and Dure 2010:133–136, 194–195.

186: "quadruple down, take some big risks": Tenorio 2024.

188: "Dos a cero" chant and context: "What Is 'Dos a Cero'"? 2025.

188: "we're not a good enough team": Wangerin 2008:319.

191: "at the end, the Germans always win": Finnis 2018.

CHAPTER 17

207: Passionate Philadelphia-based soccer fans: Sons of Ben 2016.

208: Rise of MLS fandom: West 2016.

208: "Development academies are the future": Sharrett 2013 and Tenorio 2019.

CHAPTER 18

211: Jürgen Klinsmann story (and all quotes): Borden 2016 and Grove 2014.

216: Landon Donovan's pioneering comments and candidness regarding mental health and elite athletes: "Landon Donovan's Other Legacy" 2014.

218: "The media thinks [Landon] is untouchable": Bennett 2014.

222: "The defeat continued Argentina's twenty-three-year trophyless run": Hytner 2016.

222: "a disaster": "Lionel Messi calls" 2016.

224: Gulati hadn't spoken with Arena about the MNT job: Borden 2016.

224: Hosting second leg of U.S.-Costa Rica in NYC area (and Arena's quotes): Wahl 2017.

226: Snorkels: Dart 2017.

CHAPTER 19

229: FIFA, fraud, and awarding World Cups to Russia and Qatar. Panja and Draper 2020.

231: Putin quotes: "Putin says" 2018.

231: Zabivaka the "fair player": "Wolf chosen" 2016.
232: Thousands die in the Qatari desert: Walter and Ford 2022.
233: "the USA were the better team": Hytner 2022.
238: "to live football in another way": "Soccer Shocker" 2023.
238: "our gift to America": Gorostieta and Roche 2023.
240: Berhalter-Reyna legal report: U.S. Soccer 2023.

CHAPTER 20

248: Total Immersion the Philly way: YSC Academy: https://yscacademy.com/ and YSC Advantage: https://yscadvantage.com/.

APPENDIX: ANCIENT ORIGINS

255: The parade of ancient ball games around the world (and all quotes): FIFA Museum (Virtual Exhibit) "Origins: Pre-Histories of Football." See also Goldblatt 2008:4–18.

BIBLIOGRAPHY

All hypertext links below were accurate as of January 1, 2026.

Alcock, Charles William. "Association Football: No. 1—Its Origin." *The Sportsman* (London), no. 8851, January 8, 1898, 3.

Allen, William, and Calum Roche. "Why do England, Scotland, Wales & Northern Ireland play as separate teams if they belong to UK?" AS.com. June 14, 2024. https://en.as.com/soccer/why-do-england-scotland-wales-northern-ireland-play-as-separate-teams-if-they-belong-to-uk-n-3/.

Allaway, Roger. "The American Football Association." Society of American Soccer History (website). November 8, 2023. https://www.ussoccerhistory.org/the-american-football-association/.

______. "The 'American Menace.'" Society of American Soccer History (website). December 21, 2022. https://www.ussoccerhistory.org/the-american-menace/.

______. *Rangers, Rovers and Spindles: Soccer, Immigration and Textiles in New England and New Jersey*. Haworth, NJ: St. Johann Press, 2005.

______. "The record-setting Archie Stark." Society of American Soccer History (website). November 16, 2022. https://www.ussoccerhistory.org/the-record-setting-archie-stark/.

______. "A stumbling start for U.S. pro soccer." Society of American Soccer History (website). December 2, 2015. https://www.ussoccerhistory.org/a-stumbling-start-for-u-s-pro-soccer/.

______. "U.S. vs. Canada in Kearny, 1885 and 1886." Society of American Soccer History (website). June 18, 2025. https://www.ussoccerhistory.org/u-s-vs-canada-in-kearny-1885-and-1886/.

______. "What was the Soccer War?" Society of American Soccer History (website). October 5, 2022. https://www.ussoccerhistory.org/what-was-the-soccer-war/.

Anderson, Dave. "Nothing but Blue Skies Does Woosnam See." *Sports Illustrated*. May 30, 1977, 34–36. https://vault.si.com/vault/1977/05/30/nothing-but-blue-skies-does-woosnam-see.

Anderson, Nancy. *The Sporting Life: Victorian Sports and Games*. Edited by James Mangan. London: Routledge, 1981.

Apostolov, Steven. "Soccer, Ethnicity, and Shipbuilding in Industrial Quincy, Massachusetts, During the Early Twentieth Century." In *Soccer Frontiers: The Global Game in the United States, 1863–1913*, edited by Chris Bolsmann and George N. Kioussis, 46–64. Knoxville: University of Tennessee Press, 2021.

"Archie Stark." Society of American Soccer History (website). Undated. https://www.ussoccerhistory.org/national-soccer-hall-of-fame-biographies/national-soccer-hall-of-fame-player-biographies/archie-stark/.

ASB. "USA '94 | FIFA World Cup Draw | EUROSPORT." YouTube video, 48:21. Posted December 27, 2020. https://www.youtube.com/watch?v=WxX2tQNiv6w&t=2244s.

Baggio: The Divine Ponytail. Directed by Letizia Lamartire. Netflix, 2021. Streaming video.

Barboza, Scott. "Credit for Patenaude long overdue." ESPN.com. June 10, 2010. https://www.espn.com/boston/columns/story?id=5370416.

Becherano, Lizzy. "USL announces plans to start new league that would rival MLS." ESPN.com. February 13, 2025. https://www.espn.com/football/story/_/id/43827636/usl-announces-plans-new-league-rival-mls.

Bellos, Alex. "Rebuilding Brazil from the ruins of 1950." ESPN.com. May 21, 2014. https://www.espn.com/soccer/story/_/id/37362165/rebuilding-brazil-ruins-1950.

Bennett, Roger. "The inside story of Jurgen Klinsmann's decision to cut Landon Donovan." ESPN.com. May 23, 2014. https://www.espn.com/soccer/story/_/id/37338703/the-story-klinsmann-decision-cut-donovan.

"Best: Decline of the Golden Boy." BBC News online. June 14, 2005. http://news.bbc.co.uk/2/hi/uk_news/4090840.stm.

The Billion Dollar Goal. Directed by Anthony J. Cortese and Pete Radovich. Paramount+, December 11, 2023. Streaming video.

Bodleian Library. *The Rules of Association Football, 1863*. Prepared for publication with a foreword by Sir Bobby Charlton and an introduction by Melvyn Bragg. Oxford: Bodleian Library, 2006.

Borden, Sam. "Costa Rica Pummels the U.S. and Puts World Cup Qualifying in Doubt." *New York Times*. November 15, 2016. https://www.nytimes.com/2016/11/16/sports/soccer/usmnt-costa-rica-world-cup-qualifying.html.

______. "Jurgen Klinsmann Promised a Lot for U.S. Soccer. But Did He Deliver?" *New York Times*. November 21, 2016. https://www.nytimes.com/2016/11/21/sports/soccer/jurgen-klinsmann-united-states-promises.html.

Bunk, Brian D. "The First Football Funeral and the Origins of the College Sport." We're History (website). November 13, 2014. https://werehistory.org/first-football-funeral/.

______. *From Football to Soccer: The Early History of the Beautiful Game in the United States.* Urbana: University of Illinois Press, 2021.

______. "Who scored the first professional goals in US soccer history?" Society of American Soccer History (website). November 23, 2022. https://www.ussoccerhistory.org/who-scored-the-first-professional-goals-in-us-soccer-history/.

Butler, Dylan. "Inside the process that led to the hiring of Gregg Berhalter as USMNT coach." MLS.com. December 4, 2018. https://www.mlssoccer.com/news/inside-process-led-hiring-gregg-berhalter-usmnt-coach.

Butterfield, David and Gavin McCormick. "Greeks, Romans, Monks, and Murder: The Chaotic History of Football in Britain." Antigone Journal (website). May 2021. https://antigonejournal.com/2021/05/greeks-romans-history-football/.

"Canadians the Victors." *New York Times*. November 29, 1885. https://timesmachine.nytimes.com/timesmachine/1885/11/29/103642445.html?pageNumber=7.

Carlisle, Jeff and Doug McIntyre. "The 1995 U.S. Copa América team tells its story: from pay disputes to glory." ESPN.com. May 30, 2016. https://www.espn.com/soccer/story/_/id/37448985/the-1995-us-copa-america-team-tells-remarkable-tale.

CBS Sports. "S2023 E25: Eric Wynalda." *Kickin'It*. June 11, 2024. Video, streaming on Paramount+. https://www.paramountplus.com/shows/video/uQUc_VRLXHDORyQusW42qENTLwP_WxeQ.

"The Changing Shape of American Football at the College of New Jersey (Princeton)." Princeton University Archives housed in Seeley G. Mudd Manuscript Library. February 2016. https://universityarchives.princeton.edu/2016/02/the-changing-shape-of-american-football-at-the-college-of-new-jersey-princeton/#:~:text=On%20November%202%2C%201876%2C%20Princeton's,a%20hospital%20for%20disabled%20veterans%E2%80%A6%E2%80%9D.

Chaucer, Geoffrey. "The Knight's Tale" in *The Canterbury Tales*. Translated by Nevill Coghill. London: Penguin Classics, 2003.

Crawford, Scott A. *A History of Soccer in Louisiana: 1858–2013*. New York: CreateSpace Independent Publishing Platform, 2013.

Creel, Daniel. "The American Soccer League, 1921–1934." Society of American Soccer History (website). April 27, 2022. https://www.ussoccerhistory.org/overview-the-american-soccer-league-1921-1934/.

Curran, Connor. "Unscrupulous Adventurers Who Are Domiciled in 'the Land of the Almighty Dollar'? The Migration of Irish-Born Soccer Players to the American Soccer League, 1921–31." *Journal of Sport History* 45, no. 3 (Fall 2018).

Curtis, Brian. "The Death of the American Soccer Troll." *The Ringer*, July 6, 2018. https://www.theringer.com/soccer/2018/7/6/17539860/american-soccer-troll-death.

Dart, Tom. "Woeful USA fail to make 2018 World Cup after loss to Trinidad & Tobago." *The Guardian*. October 10, 2017. https://www.theguardian.com/football/2017/oct/10/usa-trinidad-and-tobago-world-cup-2018-qualifier-soccer.

Dure, Beau. *Long-Range Goals: The Success Story of Major League Soccer*. Washington, D.C.: Potomac Books, 2010.

Evans, Chris. "World Cup '94: How Bora Milutinovic shaped an inexperienced USA team." BBC Sport. September 28, 2022. https://www.bbc.com/sport/football/62994127.

Farnsworth, Ed. "After the collapse: ALPF vs. ALPF in Baltimore and Fall River, 1894–1896." Society of American Soccer History (website). April 27, 2020. https://www.ussoccerhistory.org/after-the-collapse-alpf-vs-alpf-in-baltimore-and-fall-river-1894-96/.

______. "The life—and murder—of the first American-born president of U.S. Soccer." Society of American Soccer History (website). September 16, 2020. https://www.ussoccerhistory.org/the-life-and-murder-of-the-first-american-born-president-of-u-s-soccer/.

______. "'The Noxious Scottish Weed': Early North American soccer and the Laws of the Game." Society of American Soccer History (website). March 31, 2022. https://www.ussoccerhistory.org/the-noxious-scottish-weed-early-north-american-soccer-and-the-laws-of-the-game/.

______. "The origins of soccer in Philadelphia, Part 2: Colonial football." Society of American Soccer History (website). March 3, 2020. https://www.ussoccerhistory.org/the-origins-of-soccer-in-philadelphia-part-2-colonial-football/.

______. "The origins of soccer in Philadelphia, Part 3: 19th century football before codification." Society of American Soccer History (website). March 12, 2020. https://www.ussoccerhistory.org/the-origins-of-soccer-in-philadelphia-part-3-19th-century-football-before-codification/.

______. "The origins of soccer in Philadelphia, Part 4: The first account of soccer-style football after codification?" Society of American Soccer History (website). April 10, 2020. https://www.ussoccerhistory.org/the-origins-of-soccer-in-philadelphia-part-4-the-first-account-of-soccer-style-football-after-codification/.

______. "The origins of soccer in Philadelphia, part 5: Local college-based football after the 1863 Laws of the Game." Society of American Soccer History (website). April 16, 2020. https://www.ussoccerhistory.org/the-origins-of-soccer-in-philadelphia-part-5-local-college-based-football-after-the-1863-laws-of-the-game/.

______. "Philadelphia and the other first professional soccer league in the U.S." Society of American Soccer History (website). October 21, 2015. https://www.ussoccerhistory.org/philadelphia-and-the-other-first-professional-soccer-league-in-the-u-s/.

______. "Philly and the first USA international tour." Society of American Soccer History (website). May 8, 2015. https://www.ussoccerhistory.org/philly-and-the-first-usa-international-tour/.

______. "The rise and fall: Fall River and Pawtucket soccer, 1883–1896." Society of American Soccer History (website). February 1, 2022. https://www.ussoccerhistory.org/the-rise-and-fall-of-organized-soccer-in-fall-river-and-pawtucket-1883-1896/.

______. "The US at the 1930 World Cup." Society of American Soccer History (website). March 19, 2014. https://phillysoccerpage.net/2014/03/19/the-us-at-the-1930-world-cup/.

______. "The US and the 1950 World Cup." Society of American Soccer History (website). April 4, 2014. https://phillysoccerpage.net/2014/04/04/the-us-and-the-1950-world-cup/.

Farnsworth, Ed and Brian D. Bunk. "Gentlemen of Color: Oliver and Fred Watson, the earliest known African American soccer players in the United States." December 8, 2020. https://www.ussoccerhistory.org/gentlemen-of-color-oliver-and-fred-watson-the-earliest-known-african-american-soccer-players-in-the-united-states/.

Fatsis, Stefan. "Who Was Dent McSkimming?" Slate.com. July 2, 2014. https://slate.com/culture/2014/07/dent-mcskimming-the-truth-behind-the-legend-of-the-lone-american-reporter-at-the-1950-world-cup.html.

"FIFA Marks 99th Birthday by Announcing Centennial Launch Date." FIFA.com (press release). May 21, 2003. https://www.sportcal.com/pressreleases/fifa-marks-99th-birthday-by-announcing-centennial-launch-date/#:~:text=FIFA%20was%20founded%20in%20the%20rear%20of,in%20Paris%20on%2021%20May%201904%20by.

FIFA Museum. "Origins: Pre-Histories of Football." Virtual Exhibit. https://www.fifamuseum.com/en/exhibitions-and-events/exhibitions/editorials-and-virtuals-exhibitions/origins-pre-histories-of-football.

Finnis, Alex. "Gary Lineker has updated his most famous quote after Germany's late win over Sweden." inews.co.uk. June 24, 2018. https://inews.co.uk/sport/football/world-cup/gary-lineker-germans-football-quote-168757.

Fitzgerald, F. Scott. *The Great Gatsby*. Penguin Classics Deluxe Edition. Introduction by Min Jin Lee; edited with notes by Philip McGowan. New York: Penguin Publishing Group, 2021.

The Football History Boys. "1934 World Cup | Coppa Del Duce." YouTube video. 10:55. Undated. https://www.youtube.com/watch?v=fTRFEzELw6A.

French, Scott. "The Shot Heard 'Round the World: 25 years later, Paul Caligiuri recalls goal that changed US soccer forever." MLS.com. November 19, 2014. https://www.mlssoccer.com/news/shot-heard-round-world-25-years-later-paul-caligiuri-recalls-goal-changed-us-soc.

Galeano, Eduardo. *Soccer in Sun and Shadow*. Updated edition. Translated by Mark Fried. New York: Bold Type Books/Nation Books, 2013.

Gardner, Paul. *The Simplest Game: The Intelligent Fan's Guide to the World of Soccer*. 3rd ed. New York: Macmillan USA, 1996.

Garratt, Rob and Steve Treder. "Horace Stoneham." Society for American Baseball Research (website). 2015. https://sabr.org/bioproj/person/horace-stoneham/.

Gaylord, Alan. "This Passion for books" in Dartmouth College Library Bulletin. April 1994. https://www.dartmouth.edu/library/Library_Bulletin/Apr1994/Gaylord.html.

Glanville, Brian. "Luck or Judgment? Managerial Choices at Euro 2004 Raise Eyebrows." *Sports Illustrated*. July 5, 2004. http://web.archive.org/web/20110604050359/http://sportsillustrated.cnn.com/2004/soccer/07/05/glanville.ws/index.html.

Goldblatt, David. *The Ball Is Round: A Global History of Soccer*. New York: Riverhead Books, 2008.

Gordon, Robert S. C. and John London. "Italy 1934: Football and Fascism." In National Identity and Global Sporting Events: Culture, Politics and Spectacle in the Olympics and the Football World Cup, edited by Alan Tomlinson and Christopher Young, 41–64. Albany: State University of New York Press, 2005.

Gorostieta, Diego and Calum Roche. "David Beckham: 'Messi is a gift for the United States and the MLS.'" EN.AS.com. November 16, 2023. https://en.as.com/soccer/david-beckham-messi-is-a-gift-for-the-united-states-and-the-mls-n/.

Grove, Daryl. "Two Interpretations of Don Garber's Angry Response to Jürgen Klinsmann." PasteMagazine.com. October 15, 2014. https://www.pastemagazine.com/soccer/two-ways-of-looking-at-don-garbers-response-to-jur.

Harris, Daniel. "Remembering U.S. Soccer's Greatest, Most Improbable Triumph." The Ringer. January 14, 2019. https://www.theringer.com/2019/01/14/soccer/usa-england-1950-world-cup.

Harvey, Randy. "WORLD CUP '94: Playing Host to the Most: Venues for the World Cup Games Are Counting on Good Soccer and Booming Business." *Los Angeles Times*. May 15, 1994. https://www.latimes.com/archives/la-xpm-1994-05-15-sp-58077-story.html?utm_.

Highway Act 1835. LXXII Penalty on Persons committing Nuisances by . . . play[ing] at Football." https://www.legislation.gov.uk/ukpga/Will4/5-6/50/section/LXXII/enacted.

"A History of Sports & Dictators, Part 2: The Rise of Fascism." Human Right Foundation (website). August 9, 2024. https://hrf.org/latest/a-history-of-sports-dictators-part-2-the-rise-of-fascism/.

"The History of the FA." FA.com. Undated. https://www.thefa.com/about-football-association/who-we-are/history#:~:text=The%20first%20World%20Cup%20was,channel%20open%20for%20future%20negotiation.

Holroyd, Steve. "Meet the Babe Ruth of American Soccer." Society of American Soccer History (website). May 4, 2015. https://www.ussoccerhistory.org/meet-the-babe-ruth-of-american-soccer/.

______. "The Year in American Soccer—1973—US National Team." Society of American Soccer History (website). American Soccer History Archives. https://ussoccerhistory.org/ASHA/ASHA/year/1973.html.

Holt, Emily. *John Wycliffe, the First of the Reformers, and What He Did for England*. London: John F. Shaw & Co., Paternoster Row, 1884.

Holt, Richard. *Sport and the British: A Modern History*. Oxford: Clarendon Press, 1989.

Hopkins, Gary. *Star-Spangled Soccer: The Selling, Marketing and Management of Soccer in the USA*. New York: Palgrave Macmillan, 2010.

Hytner, Mike. "Edgy England on verge of World Cup last 16 after fortunate draw with USA." *The Guardian*. November 25, 2022. https://www.theguardian.com/football/2022/nov/25/england-usa-world-cup-group-b-match-report.

______."Lionel Messi says his Argentina career is over after Copa América final defeat." *The Guardian*. June 27, 2016. https://www.theguardian.com/football/2016/jun/27/lionel-messi-says-he-is-quitting-argentina-team-after-copa-america-final-defeat

Jose, Colin. *The American Soccer League: The Golden Years of American Soccer 1921–1931*. Lanham, MD: Scarecrow Press, 1998.

Kelly, Jim. "Rutgers Is Revolutionary . . . Even in Football." 1766 Alumni Magazine, Rutgers Alumni Association, Vol. 36, no. 1, Spring 2019.

Kilpatrick, David. "New York Soccer Pioneers." In *Soccer Frontiers: The Global Game in the United States, 1863-1913*, edited by Chris Bolsmann and George N. Kioussis, 65–89. Knoxville: University of Tennessee Press, 2021.

Kuper, Simon. *The Barcelona Complex: Lionel Messi and the Making—and Unmaking—of the World's Greatest Soccer Club*. New York: Penguin Books, 2022.

Lamb, Bill. "Charles A. Stoneham." Society for American Baseball Research (website). Spring 2017. https://sabr.org/bioproj/person/charles-a-stoneham/.

"Landon Donovan's Other Legacy: Challenging the stigma of mental health." National Network of Depression Centers. NNDC.com. November 24, 2014. https://nndc.org/landon-donovans-other-legacy-challenging-the-stigma-of-mental-health-the-word-2/.

Lange, Dave. *Soccer Made in St. Louis: A History of the Game in America's First Soccer Capital*. St. Louis: Reedy Press, 2011.

______. "St. Louis Soccer Club tour of Sweden, 1920." Society of American Soccer History (website). February 8, 2023. https://www.ussoccerhistory.org/st-louis-soccer-club-tour-of-sweden-1920/.

"The Last Days and Valiant Death of Nathan Hale." *American Heritage* magazine. American Heritage Inc. April 1964. Archived from the original on September 29, 2007 (vol. 15, issue 3). https://www.americanheritage.com/last-days-and-valiant-death-nathan-hale.

Leptich, John. "The Day America Shook the World Cup." *Chicago Tribune*. June 29, 1986. https://www.chicagotribune.com/1986/06/29/the-day-america-shook-the-world-cup.

Lichfield, John. "Jules Rimet: The man who kicked off the World Cup." *The Independent*. June 5, 2006. https://www.independent.co.uk/news/people/profiles/jules-rimet-the-man-who-kicked-off-the-world-cup-481145.html.

"Lionel Messi calls Argentina federation 'a disaster' after flight delay." ESPN.com. June 24, 2016. https://global.espn.com/football/story/_/id/37476788/lionel-messi-calls-argentina-federation-disaster-flight-delay.

Litterer, David. "American Soccer History Archives." Society of American Soccer History (website). https://soccerhistoryusa.org/asha.html.

Longman, Jere. "How a 'Band of No-Hopers' Forged U.S. Soccer's Finest Day." *New York Times*. December 9, 2009.

______. "Miracle Worker or Nutty Professor? U.S. Coach Has Yet to Decide." *New York Times*. May 30, 1994. https://www.nytimes.com/1994/05/30/sports/soccer-world-cup-94-miracle-worker-or-nutty-professor-us-coach-has-yet-to-decide.html#:~:text=Come%20on%20in%2C%20the%20culture's%20fine.&text=An%20investigation%20into%20C%2Dsections.

Magoun, Jr., F. P. "Football in Medieval England and in Middle-English Literature." *American Historical Review*, October 1929, Vol. 35, No. 1.

Markovits, Andrei S. and Steven L. Hellerman. *Offside: Soccer and American Exceptionalism*. Princeton, NJ: Princeton University Press, 2001.

Marston, Tallec and Mike Cronin. "The Origins of Football in the United States." In *Soccer Frontiers: The Global Game in the United States, 1863–1913*, edited by Chris Bolsmann and George N. Kioussis, 18–45. Knoxville: University of Tennessee Press, 2021.

McCabe, Tom. "Loose Threads." Society of American Soccer History (website). May 27, 2015. https://www.ussoccerhistory.org/loose-threads/.

______. "Tom 'Bullets' Cahill: A Reappraisal of a Founding Father of American Soccer." Society for American Soccer History (website). Video podcast, June 7, 2024. https://

www.ussoccerhistory.org/sash-session-friday-june-7-at-12-pm-et-tom-bullets-cahill-a-reappraisal-of-a-founding-father-of-american-soccer/.

Meacham, Scott. *Old Division Football: The Indigenous Mob Soccer of Dartmouth College*, 2006, http://www.dartmo.com/football.pdf.

Messinger, Elmer A. "Elmar A. Messinger Diary, 22 November 1862." Letters Home. University of Virginia. The Institute for Advanced Technology in the Humanities. https://community.village.virginia.edu/nauletters/node/10592.

"A Modified American Plan." *Sports Illustrated*. May 31, 1980. https://vault.si.com/vault/1980/03/31/a-modified-american-plan-americanization-three-north-americans-on-the-field-instead-of-two-is-the-new-buzzword-in-the-nasl-it-might-add-a-little-pizzazz-to-a-league-that-could-use-some.

"The Mystery of Robert Guérin, the man who founded FIFA." Scottish Sport History (website). September 9, 2022. https://www.scottishsporthistory.com/sports-history-news-and-blog/the-mystery-of-robert-guerin-the-man-who-founded-fifa.

Neal, Rome. "The Goal That Shocked the World." CBS News.com. July 2, 2003. https://www.cbsnews.com/news/the-goal-that-shocked-the-world/?utm_source=chatgpt.com.

Panja, Tariq and Kevin Draper. "U.S. Says FIFA Officials Were Bribed to Award World Cups to Russia and Qatar." *New York Times*. April 6, 2020. https://www.nytimes.com/2020/04/06/sports/soccer/qatar-and-russia-bribery-world-cup-fifa.html.

Patch, George H. "George H. Patch to George Patch and Mary Patch, 27 November 1862." Letters Home. University of Virginia. The Institute for Advanced Technology in the Humanities. https://community.village.virginia.edu/nauletters/node/16846.

Perrigo, Billy. "Why Do Americans Call It Soccer Instead of Football? Blame England." *Time* magazine, July 11, 2018. https://time.com/5335799/soccer-word-origin-england/.

Phillips, Hal. *Generation Zero: Founding Fathers, Hidden Histories & the Making of Soccer in America*. Dickinson-Moses Press, 2022.

Plenderleith, Ian. *Rock 'n' Roll Soccer: The Short Life and Fast Times of the North American Soccer League*. First U.S. edition. New York: Thomas Dunne Books / St. Martin's Press, 2015.

"Putin says World Cup has broken stereotypes about Russia." Reuters.com. July 6, 2018. https://www.reuters.com/article/sports/putin-says-world-cup-has-broken-stereotypes-about-russia-idUSKBN1JW1GB/.

Raskin, Alex. "The Miracle on Grass: US Soccer's 1950 upset of 70-1 favorite England." The Daily Mail.com. November 12, 2022. https://www.dailymail.co.uk/sport/football/article-11378907/US-Soccers-1950-upset-70-1-favorite-England-remains-greatest-World-Cup-triumph.html.

"Regret league action against three clubs." *Bethlehem Globe-Times*, September 25, 1928. https://bethlehemsteelsoccer.org/gl092528b.html.

"The Revolutionary War Spy Who Loved Soccer." Clubeleven (website). July 1, 2025. https://www.clubelevenmail.com/p/the-revolutionary-war-spy-who-loved-soccer.

Schaerlaeckens, Leander. "Chasing Gaetjens." ESPN.com. February 26, 2010. https://www.espn.com/world-cup/story/_/id/4937012/ce/us/real-story-1950-world-cup-hero.

Sharrett, Cody. "Q&A: MLS Commissioner Don Garber." ColumbusCrew.com. May 2, 2013. https://www.columbuscrew.com/news/qa-mls-commissioner-don-garber.

Silverman, Alex. "Mark Abbott: The O.G. of MLS." *Sports Business Journal*. December 19, 2022. https://archive.is/NhAR8#selection-1317.0-1317.28.

"Sir Hugh." British Folk Song Characterized as Blood Libel (collecting variants). https://en.wikisource.org/wiki/Sir_Hugh.

Sjödin, Connie. "Ransom note [full text] for the Jules Rimet Trophy, 1966." Of Lost Time (website). June 11, 2021. https://www.oflosttime.com/ransom-note-for-the-jules-rimet-trophy-1966/.

Smith, Melvin. "America and the 1863 Football Association Code." American Soccer History (website). October 6, 2015. https://www.ussoccerhistory.org/america-and-the-1863-football-association-code/.

"Soccer Goes Sexy South of Border." *New York Times*. June 27, 1971. https://www.nytimes.com/1971/06/27/archives/soccer-goes-sexy-south-of-border-womens-world-cup-aimed-at-the-2.html.

"Soccer shocker: Lionel Messi says he will join Miami's MLS team." NPR.org. June 7, 2023. https://www.npr.org/2023/06/07/1180822756/lionel-messi-inter-miami-mls-soccer.

Sons of Ben. Directed by Jeffrey C. Bell. Written by Jeffrey C. Bell. Produced by Debbie Axel, Jeffrey C. Bell, and Mike Dieffenbach. USA: Rothbury Road Productions, 2016. Documentary film.

Stubbes, Phillip (sometimes spelled Philip Stubbs). *The Anatomie of Abuses*. 1583. Reprint, London: N. Trubner & Co., Ludgate Hill, 1877.

"A Swing Along Athletic Row." *Bethlehem Globe-Times*. August 15, 1929. https://bethlehemsteelsoccer.org/gl081529.html.

"A Swing Along Athletic Row." *Bethlehem Globe-Times*. October 13, 1928. https://bethlehemsteelsoccer.org/gl101328.html.

Taylor, Matthew. "Transatlantic Football: Rethinking the Transfer of Football from Europe to the USA, c. 1880–c. 1930s." *Ethnologie française* 41, no. 4 (September 2011). https://doi.org/10.2307/41318945.

Tenorio, Paul. "Don Garber: 25 years of the MLS commissioner who became the most powerful man in American soccer." *The Athletic*. July 24, 2024. https://www.nytimes.com/athletic/5653462/2024/07/24/don-garber-mls-commissioner-25-years/.

______. "A new reality in MLS: Homegrown players will be as important as DPs in next phase of league's growth." *New York Times*. April 22, 2019. https://www.nytimes.com/athletic/938495/2019/04/22/a-new-reality-in-mls-homegrown-players-will-be-as-important-as-dps-in-next-phase-of-leagues-growth/.

Thring, J.C. *The Winter Game: The Rules of Football*. 2nd ed. London: Hamilton, Adams & Co., Paternoster Row, 1863.

Townsend, Jon. "How America's team of amateurs beat England at the 1950 World Cup in one of the greatest upsets." These Football Times.com. December 5, 2019. https://thesefootballtimes.co/2019/05/12/how-americas-team-of-amateurs-beat-england-at-the-1950-world-cup-in-one-of-the-greatest-upsets/.

Turner, David. *The Old Boys: The Decline and Rise of the Public School*. New Haven, CT: Yale University Press, 2015.

United States Census Bureau. *Facts by decade*. https://www.census.gov/about/history/historical-censuses-and-surveys/decade-facts.1790.html#list-tab-2036066290.

"Up in Arms: British Press Doesn't Think Highly of Loss to United States in Soccer." *Los Angeles Times*. June 11, 1993. https://www.latimes.com/archives/la-xpm-1993-06-11-sp-1992-story.html.

U.S. Soccer. "Alston & Bird's Report to the U.S. Soccer Federation." USSoccer.com. March 10, 2023. https://ussoccer.app.box.com/s/ycsf3xneaqbph329kilqy5upmk45sotb.

Vidmer, Richards. "Stark's Five Goals Help U.S. Beat Canada at Soccer, 6 to 1." *New York Times*. November 9, 1925. https://timesmachine.nytimes.com/timesmachine/1925/11/09/issue.html.

Wahl, Grant. *The Beckham Experiment: How the World's Most Famous Athlete Tried to Conquer America*. New York: Crown Publishers, 2009.

______. "USMNT Finally Turns to New York Area for Key World Cup Qualifying Match." *Sports Illustrated*. SI.com. August 29, 2017. https://www.si.com/soccer/2017/08/29/usmnt-new-york-world-cup-qualifier-sunil-gulati-us-soccer.

Walter, Dan and Matt Ford. "Fact check: How many people died for the Qatar World Cup?" Deutsche Welle. DW.com. November 16, 2022. https://www.dw.com/en/fact-check-how-many-people-have-died-for-the-qatar-world-cup/a-63763713.

Walvin, James. *The People's Game: The History of Football Revisited*. Edinburgh: Mainstream Publishing, 1994.

Wangerin, David. *Distant Corners: American Soccer's History of Missed Opportunities and Lost Causes*. Philadelphia: Temple University Press, 2011.

______. *Soccer in a Football World: The Story of America's Forgotten Game*. 2nd ed. Philadelphia: Temple University Press, 2008.

Wertmann, Patrick, et.al. "New evidence for ball games in Eurasia from ca. 3000-year-old Yanghai tombs in the Turfan depression of Northwest China." *Journal of Archaeological Science: Reports*. Volume 34, Part B, December 2020. https://www.sciencedirect.com/science/article/pii/S2352409X20303679?via%3Dihub#b0205.

West, Phil. *The United States of Soccer: MLS and the Rise of American Soccer Fandom*. New York: The Overlook Press, 2016.

"What Is 'Dos a Cero'? A History of the USA-Mexico Rivalry's Signature Scoreline." FoxSports.com. July 4, 2025. https://www.foxsports.com/stories/soccer/what-dos-cero-history-usa-mexico-rivalrys-signature-scoreline.

Whelan, Frank. "Charles M. Schwab: Steel Titan at Twilight." WFMZ.com, WFMZ-TV, September 18, 2023. https://www.wfmz.com/features/historys-headlines/historys-headlines-charles-m-schwab-steel-titan-at-twilight/article_34937f2e-5578-592f-991f-83b7fca713c6.html.

Williams, Jack. "Bert Patenaude, the Forgotten Hero Who Scored the First Ever World Cup Hat-Trick." *The Guardian*. July 19, 2015. https://www.theguardian.com/football/blog/2015/jul/19/bert-patenaude-first-world-cup-hat-trick-usa.

Wilner, Barry. "World Cup Has Produced Grass Under Glass." *Seattle Times*. January 19, 1994. https://archive.seattletimes.com/archive/19940116/1889888/world-cup-has-produced-grass-under-glass?utm.

Winner, David. *Brilliant Orange: The Neurotic Genius of Dutch Football*. London: Bloomsbury, 2000.

______. *Those Feet: A Sensual History of English Football*. New York: Overlook Press, 2013.

"Wolf chosen as 2018 FIFA World Cup Official Mascot and named Zabivaka." Inside FIFA (website). October 21, 2016. https://inside.fifa.com/tournaments/mens/worldcup/2018russia/media-releases/wolf-chosen-2018-fifa-world-cup-official-mascot-and-named-zabivaka-2845435.

"Women give Blatter short shrift." CNN.com. January 16, 2004. https://web.archive.org/web/20231104173153/https://edition.cnn.com/2004/SPORT/football/01/16/blatter.women.reut/.

Wood, William. *New England's Prospect*. Edited by Alden T. Vaughn. 1963. Reprint, Amherst: University of Massachusetts Press, 1977.

Zenou, Theo. "When the World Cup Trophy Was Stolen—and Found by a Dog Named Pickles." *Washington Post*. November 20, 2022. https://www.washingtonpost.com/history/2022/11/20/world-cup-trophy-heist-pickles/.

ACKNOWLEDGMENTS

This book wouldn't have been possible without the support of many people. To the architects, Richie Graham and Nooha Ahmed-Lee—thank you not only for giving me the greatest job in the world (teaching English to elite soccer student-athletes), but also for asking me to write a book about the history of elite men's American soccer for students and fans everywhere. To my interviewees—Tim Howard, the Sullivan clan, Ernst Tanner, Chris Albright, Jim Curtin, Will Kuntz, Cobi Jones, Ryan Richter, Sheldon Phillips, Jon Scheer, Marlon LeBlanc, Jared Micklos, Ryan Mooney, Alex Ramos, and Eddie Mensah, plus about a dozen other professionals—on and off the pitch—who will remain anonymous (as promised when the interviews were pitched): Thank you for your candor and insights into the contemporary aspects and potential future of the beautiful game on American soil.

To my teacher colleagues at YSC Academy—thank you for the constant encouragement and for helping to spread the word about this project to nearly every VIP who came through the School's doors. My apologies for how often I jammed the copy machine (or used up all the paper) in the name of this book. And to the student-athletes in all my classes—past, present, future—thank you for your hustle, your resilience, and for reminding me almost daily that perhaps only teaching itself rivals the thrill of writing a book.

Thanks also to my agent, Nick Mullendore of Vertical Ink Agency, and to the incredible team at BenBella Books, Inc., especially my editor, Rick

Chillot. Books are big undertakings, and my publishing team provided many vital assists.

Finally, above the rooftops of all these words flies a giant thank-you banner to my mom and dad—and to my wife, May Mon Post, and our son, River, who graciously allowed me, over the past two years, to spend part of my life away from them, tucked in a corner of the house, kicking nouns against verbs. Thank you for never blowing the whistle.

ABOUT THE AUTHOR

Mark C Franek is an American sportswriter, former attorney, and educator. He holds a J.D. from Temple, an Ed.D. from Penn, and a B.A. and M.A.T. from Duke. Over his career, Mark has published more than fifty opinion-editorials and articles in major American newspapers and magazines on a variety of sports and human-interest themes. He currently teaches English classes and a series of electives, including a history of U.S. soccer course, at YSC Academy, an independent school fully embedded within Major League Soccer's Philadelphia Union franchise. Franek also served as an English teacher and dean of students at the William Penn Charter (Quaker) School, one of the oldest independent schools in the nation.

Over nearly three decades, Franek has had the privilege of teaching more than a score of student-athletes who went on to play professional soccer in MLS and Europe. His former students include Olympic and World Cup players. Others, after hanging up their boots, went on to become coaches, technical directors, general managers, part-owners of professional teams—or professionals in fields unrelated to soccer. Their DNA and dreams are in this book.